PREMONITIONS

"AK Thompson's meditations on love and insurrection provide crucial tools for untangling the neuroses that pervade our culture of revolt. From critical theory to Craigslist, Odysseus to Occupy, *Premonitions* challenges us to confront the world around us without becoming reconciled to a reality that debases us all."
—Mark Bray, author of *Antifa*

"A pleasure. This incendiary little book is also a finely balanced one. It combines anarchism with Marxism, academia with the street, generosity to both friends and opponents with fierce critique, imagination with politics, lingering over defeat with searching for forward motion. It asks the defining questions of our hard moment and shows why the answers are uneasy ones. One part an elegiac history of recent freedom movements and their quandaries, one part a caution against any too-easy commitment to nonviolence, *Premonitions* teems with insights. Among much else it reclaims Marcuse for our moment, provokes mightily on the idea of solidarities between the living and the dead, continues Thompson's inquires into whiteness, class, and militancy, and makes me understand some of my kids' tattoos."
—David Roediger author of *Class, Race and Marxism*

"Thompson, a brilliant political theorist, works from the ground up and provides a great, inspiriting, and clarifying lexicon."
—Lauren Berlant, author of *Cruel Optimism*

"In *Premonitions* AK Thompson displays an impressive mastery over a wide range of subjects. From protest politics and violence to critical theory and aesthetics, there are few scholars who can tie together the disparate fragments of this world in as intellectually compelling a manner as Thompson does. He is extremely well-versed in his theory, but he uses it wisely: as a way to clarify phenomena rather than obfuscate reality to impress (or discourage) interlocutors. All told, *Premonitions* is a deep dive into a provocative, creative, and brilliant mind."
—Stephen Duncombe, Professor of Media and Culture, New York University, and Co-Director, Center for Artistic Activism

PREMONITIONS

Selected Essays on
the Culture of Revolt

AK Thompson

This book is dedicated to
Himani Bannerji,
who saw it before I did.

And to Ace Tasker,
who always knew
how to push.

Premonitions: Selected Essays on the Culture of Revolt
© 2018 AK Thompson
This edition © 2018 AK Press (Chico, Edinburgh)

ISBN: 9781849353380
E-ISBN: 9781849353397
Library of Congress Control Number: 2018932255

AK Press   AK Press
370 Ryan Ave. #100   33 Tower St.
Chico, CA 95973   Edinburgh EH6 7BN
United States   Scotland
www.akpress.org   www.akuk.com
akpress@akpress.org   ak@akedin.demon.co.uk

The above addresses would be delighted to provide you with the latest AK Press
distribution catalog, which features books, pamphlets, zines, and stylish apparel
published and/or distributed by AK Press. Alternatively, visit our websites for the
complete catalog, latest news, and secure ordering

Cover design by Josh MacPhee | Antumbra Design
Printed in the USA on acid-free, recycled paper

Image credits:

Page 84: Dalia Shevin's "Your Heart is a Muscle" image used by permission. And available at:
https://justseeds.org/product/keep-loving-keep-fighting-2/.

Pages 95, 97, 101, and 104: Eric Drooker used by permission.

Page 166: Jacques-Louis David, "The Tennis Court Oath": © RMN-Grand Palais / Art
Resource, NY

Page 166: Photo by Wasim Ahmad used by permission.

Page 201: Hugo Gellert, courtesy of Mary Ryan Gallery, New York.

Page 207: Hoover Dam, U.S. Department of the Interior - Bureau of Reclamation, used by
permission. Photographer: Alexander Stephens.

Page 213: Jean-Victor Schnetz "Funeral of a Young martyr in the Catacombs of Rome": ©
RMN-Grand Palais / Art Resource, NY

CONTENTS

"The revolutionary judges what exists in the
name of what does not yet exist, but
which he regards as more real."
—Maurice Merleau-Ponty

"What is needed is to hold oneself, like a sliver,
to the heart of the world."
—Frantz Fanon

"The cowardice of the living … must
ultimately become unbearable."
—Walter Benjamin

INTRODUCTION

"All memory is melancholy—
all premonition joyful."
—Novalis

In October of 2005, I found myself staring out a window from my spot on the couch in my therapist's office. Like a cramped warren on the main floor of a moldering university building, the practice where she worked was geared toward helping students reorient to the problems they confronted so that they might not lose sight of their schoolwork. It was a three-session stunt in cognitive therapy, and the whole scene would have made Frederick Taylor smile. Well, I thought, at least it was free—and that's how I ended up on the corduroy couch. To be sure, I had reservations about the model, and I made them clear upon intake. It must have been on a lark that they agreed to work with me, and that my therapist agreed to unlimited sessions. After ensuring that some red flags could be lowered (yes, I did check the box on the intake form that says I think about death; no, I'm not currently in danger of killing myself), I tried to make the best of it.

I wanted the sessions because I needed help coming to terms with the world's incommensurability. I hated that everything could seem fine, objectively, but that at the same time it could feel so terribly wrong. I hated the estrangement I felt from those closest to me—my friends, my colleagues, and even my comrades. And I hated that I didn't know how to win. Like the soaring chorus of some misguided emo anthem, the depth of my estrangement had become clear to me with the conclusion of an intimate relationship. But while I missed the connection I'd once shared with my lover, I realized that—even when things seemed good—the gulf separating each of us remained immeasurable.

My therapist kept asking me how this made me feel. She wanted me to emote, I think, because she found my verbal *description* of the feelings to be far too mediated, far too cerebral. True to my disposition (and wary of anything that smacked of Robert Bly), I questioned the premise that a feeling described in words was inevitably less acute than one allowed unmediated, guttural expression. Still, I liked the idea that there could be a perfect correspondence between feeling and action, Being and doing. I kept going back, but we'd reached an impasse. "I'm perplexed," she said. "From the standpoint of cognitive behavior, you seem perfectly well-adjusted." I cringed. "I think that's the problem."

It became clear to me that I didn't want to be at peace with or reconciled to a reality that debased us all. Either I had to be undone or the world did. So it was that, with little confidence in my capacity to force an accord between infinite desire and petrified Being, I opted for self-dissolution. I was therefore not surprised when, wanting badly to find that point without mediation (and feeling painfully bored by my therapist's limp probing), I finally snapped: "I don't think this is going to work unless you traumatize me!" She blanched, stared. Slowly, composing herself, she became an angel of compassion: "maybe we should develop a rapport first."

I didn't make it to my next appointment, though I didn't cancel it either. My therapist's words had become a sliver in my brain. Up until that point, my orientation to problems on the radical Left had been largely analytic. I imagined that reason alone could change the course of a debate, and that comrades—by definition—were those who would be compelled to abandon false premises as soon as they were pointed out. And though my experience in actual movement-based discussions should have led me to view this presupposition with skepticism, it was one to which I clung as though my life depended on it. Only slowly did it dawn on me: my therapist's insistence on "rapport" did not have to be antithetical to the trauma (to the encounter with shocking realization) for which I longed; instead, it was a pathway—a plausible strategic means of achieving it. Could the same be true in radical scenes as well?

◼

Over the decade that's elapsed since I left that corduroy couch to molder on its own, my engagement in radical politics has alerted me to a series of problems pertaining to what I've come to understand as "the culture of revolt." Through my engagement with radical coalitions, my participation in street actions, and especially through my editorial responsibilities at *Upping the Anti: A Journal of Theory and Action*,[1] I became unsettled by the regularity with which these problems found expression. But it was not solely their persistence that alarmed me. What, I wondered, was I to make of the fact that these problems tended not to register as such? Indeed, their apparent self-evidence seemed to suggest that they constituted what Raymond Williams would have called a "structure of feeling"—a tightly bound but barely conscious set of principles enlisted to make an obdurate world pliant.[2]

Since my general orientation to life and struggle during this period meant that my time on the barricades had become fleeting when compared to my time in the stacks (and since, as a result, I found my name on mastheads more frequently than I did on most-wanted lists), the problems I catalogued under the "culture of revolt" heading were confronted first and foremost as analytic fixations. Nevertheless, my commitment to movement growth and development obliged me to concede that—at its logical conclusion—the act of clarification needed to give way to the act of presentation, and that the climate-controlled library needed to spill out onto the hot, hot streets. In this way, a new obstacle presented itself: how could a critical assessment of the culture of revolt be conveyed to comrades who inhabited the radical scene's structure of feeling without misgiving? What, I wondered, would building a rapport mean in a case like that?

"Culture," Williams observed, was one of the most enigmatic words in the English language.[3] In its most primitive sense, the term normally denotes those crafted representations that embody and express our collective desires and misgivings, memories and premonitions. Taken together, such forms amount to what social scientists sometimes refer to as "big c" Culture. From Hollywood blockbusters to the radical posters that still mummify the lampposts of neighborhoods scheduled for social cleansing, this Culture provides documentary evidence of our struggle to resolve the tensions inherent in a life torn between intoxicating possibility and the bludgeon of finitude. Revolt has yielded a compelling assortment of such artifacts, and several of the essays in this book engage these cultural offerings directly.

Surrounding such productions and assuring their intelligibility, however, is a broader field of "little c" culture that must be conceived in a related but distinct sense. Here, we are confronted with the aspirations, predispositions, and habits that shape our struggles. When conceived in this encapsulating second sense, "culture" reveals its profound co-implication with the structure of feeling. At its best, it feels like home. Still, the resulting configuration is far from inevitable—and its desirability should forever remain an open question. This is so not least because the culture of revolt that currently prevails within the Anglo-American radical scene seems beset by what might euphemistically be called idiosyncratic mannerisms. More accurately (and strictly between us), we might concede that what we're dealing with are in fact neurotic tendencies.

According to Freud, neurosis was an inevitable outcome of our repression (equally inevitable, he thought) of libidinal drives.[4] Confronted with the world's incommensurability, we strive to resolve it as best we can. Since we can't get what we want, we develop a catalogue of compensatory proxies and substitute objects; deferral and displacement become commonplace. Still, the drive to reconcile desire and world is unrelenting. Slowly, our proxies lose their luster, and even the most staid demonstration provokes recollections of the martial force to which it was once precondition. Lacking the confidence or capacity to remake the world by following the proxy back to its more concrete but demanding referent, however, we opt instead to refurbish the substitute. Energy that could have been directed toward the resolution of reality's inadequacy thus falls victim to the unrelenting parasitic appetite of the proxy. In this way, succor becomes affliction. This is the tragedy of neurosis. At its threshold, it proves also to be a fundamental component of our culture of revolt.

I will be the first to concede that neurosis has a bad name. Indeed, even the spottiest recollection of our struggles against mainstream psychiatric regimes is enough to remind us of the harm such a diagnosis can cause, has caused. Still, an honest appraisal of the radical tradition simultaneously forces us to acknowledge the important ways that engagements with neurosis have contributed to critical intellectual and movement-based work. In these contexts, and in opposition to its standard deployment as stigmatizing pathology,[5] neurosis reveals itself to be the normal state of affairs. Brought on by the everyday repressions demanded by the war between what is and what's longed for, neurosis permeates our being and gives shape to the terrain of struggle.

It's difficult, for instance, to recount the exploits of the Situationist International (and thus, for some, even to imagine May '68) without first recalling Georg Simmel's formative analysis of the psychic transfigurations prompted by the early-twentieth century conjunction of "Metropolis and Mental Life."[6] Similarly, Frantz Fanon's messianic injunction that anti-colonial movements overcome historic particularity so that they might yield a "new man"[7] is unintelligible if we fail to recall the "nervous condition"[8] upon which his analysis is founded. More cautious in his pronouncements, even urban sociologist Ray Oldenburg captured the essential when he noted how "the relationship between the social system and the nervous system is a close one."[9] The implication is clear: when the "social system" is assimilated, so too are its irreconcilable demands. We try to resolve them, but we can't. Not yet. But while our neurotic agitation telegraphs the world's inadequacy (and, in this way, provides a compelling point from which to begin social analysis), it also amounts to a source of explosive energy that—*if harnessed*—might yet serve as a pathway to absolution.

As the observations of Simmel, Fanon, and others have made clear, developing an awareness of our common and inevitable neuroses might reveal the means by which Being has been shaped by incommensurability. Analytically, this awareness is important because it provides an embodied point from which to map the social field.[10] Politically, by underscoring the constitutive lack at the heart of all human experience, it also provides a basis for potentially universal claim making.[11] Finally, and strategically, the universal human struggle against incommensurability provides the most tangible and concrete grounds for solidarity. "If you have come to help me, you are wasting your time," said Lilla Watson. "But if you have come because your liberation is bound up with mine, then let us work together."[12]

Despite the promise inherent in this "neurotic turn" [13] in critical social theory, however, we must still confront the problem of rapport. Because—by definition—neuroses are difficult to look at, we cling to our substitute objects. We invest in the succor they afford but fail to calculate its price (and here it suffices to recall how even the unprecedented scale of the demonstrations that unfolded on the eve of America's shock and awe campaign in Iraq failed to yield a qualitative transformation to the basic protest script—nor did it prevent George W. Bush from citing these same mobilizations as an example of the very democracy he was hoping to deliver to Saddam Hussein's beleaguered stomping grounds). In the end, our will to renounce posited resolutions by pointing to their inadequacy is often bested by the still more powerful desire to cling to the devil we know.

Meanwhile, if—through coercion or some other means—the proxy *is* discarded at the outset, the implications of the desire that prompted the initial attachment are likely to evade scrutiny. We should therefore not be surprised to find that the discarded object is followed by another equally unrealized substitute (as when the disenchantment of my Catholic youth seemed inexorably to lead toward a morbid tryst with Trotskyist sectarianism). Under late capitalism, the logic of abstraction underlying fetishism has grown increasingly acute, and the fetish object now tends to be venerated not on account of its scandalous referent but rather for the erotic *frisson* yielded by its unending euphoric slide down the chain of signification. And though even the most resolute fetishist is likely to concede that the erotically charged proxy is still a stand-in, by following increasingly refracted "next level" resolutions through the unending mutations of *différance*, we all but ensure that the desire that prompted the initial identification remains concealed.

Given this dynamic (and despite its dissimulations), it seems preferable to provisionally *accept* the given object—along with our fumbling apperception of the desire that stimulated our identification with it—as the starting point of analysis. Only then (and slowly, and through rapport) shall it become possible to reveal how, just as objects in general tend to fall short of the concepts that animate them, so too will the object of identification never live up to the *implications of the desire* that compelled our initial attachment. Awareness of this kind cannot help but yield a powerful disassociation from the world-as-given. For Walter Benjamin, such a posture could be observed among historical materialists, for whom it was impossible to look upon society's "cultural treasures" with anything other than "cautious detachment."[14]

Despite its psychic costs, the payoff associated with such detachment can be measured through the clarifications it engenders with respect to the animating desire. Once made conscious, desire is freed to find a more concrete pathway toward its realization. This aim is achieved not through the selection of a new object but rather through the *completion* of existing ones and the subsequent creation of a new reality. For Max Horkheimer, this posture was vital enough to become axiomatic: "the critical acceptance of the categories which rule social life," he proposed, "contains simultaneously their condemnation."[15] So while, in mainstream therapeutic practice, the posited resolution to the war between desire and matter is normally sought through the management (ultimately, the diminishment) of expectations, this same incommensurability can also become—through its *analytic intensification*—a starting point from which to map the contours of an unresolved world that perpetually feigns its own resolution.[16]

Normally we don't get this far. Our compensations habituate us to irrationalism, and our initial aims fall from view. We move the goal posts. We devise desperate new visions of what "winning" might mean. In the short term, our neuroses smooth out contradictions— but there is always an associated cost. Among the most significant of these is the fact that the proxy's allure can't be maintained without actively working to suppress conflicting evidence. To be sure, directing this energy toward the resolution of the incommensurable would be more productive; however, because such an approach requires candid admission of the unbearable dimensions of our own life's *non*-resolution, it remains inaccessible to those unwilling to take a walk along the vertiginous edge. More pragmatic in his orientation, C.L.R. James must nevertheless have had the challenges associated with this ordeal in mind when he called his major contribution to the revitalization of American communism *Facing Reality*.[17]

As an occasional student of the autonomist tradition, I find James's text to be provocative and important. Still, because his effort was devoted primarily to providing a more-real account of the reality he confronted, much remains to be said about why we find reality to be so difficult to face in the first place. Because nothing adds up, we suture the fragments together as best we can so that our lives might amount to more than slapdash collage. The stories we tell to account for this composite become the substance of consciousness, the very foundation of our structure of feeling. Conceived in accordance with established narrative conventions, few would doubt that such stories are reassuring. Still, they can't help but to come into conflict with reality and all its contradictions (whether natural, cultural, or historic). Such contradictions can never be reconciled by purely—or, rather, merely—intellectual means. And when conflicts between "story" and "world" become inevitable, the desire to preserve the story becomes overwhelming. At this point, consciousness and neurosis become indistinguishable.

If this is true for people in general, it is doubly so for those of us who make transforming the world our vocation. We evaluate what is against our vision of what ought to be and forever find the former to be lacking. However, unlike our mainstream counterparts (and like agitated children who, from the comfort of their bedtime story nook, urge Hansel and Gretel to suppress feelings of longing and desolation so that they might steer clear of the gingerbread house), we hesitate before the cornucopia of substitute objects. Aware of the conflict between "is" and "ought," and aware of the snares laid by proxy resolutions, we disengage and become subcultural. Alternately, we engage but promise not to be seduced (Siddhartha may have moved in with the merchant, we reason, but still he refrained—at least for a chapter—from eating meat[18]). Mostly, we try to resolve matters through willpower. We become terribly sincere.

What is sincerity? Discredited folk wisdom alerts us to a time when something was "sincere" when it was found to be "without wax," a filler purportedly used by ancient merchants to make hollow objects appear solid. Over time, this "literal" meaning gave way to a more metaphorical one. Here, the word's synonymous bond with consistency (achieved, for instance, through the identity of inside and outside) finds accord with those etymologies that more reliably trace "sincerity" back to the Latin *sincerus*, which meant "pure" or "unmixed." Identity and consistency are important aspirations, and they're prized precisely because they are so difficult to achieve. Metaphysically, they mark the point of absolution, that zenith where things and desires become indistinguishable.[19]

As with Weber's Calvinists, who became transfixed by the frightening implications of predestination,[20] contemporary radicals struggle anxiously to provide evidence of our sincerity. Only too late do we discover that "keeping it real" in a simulacral world is about as plausible as making it onto some divine, secret guest list. At its threshold, the Calvinist anxiety prompted by possible exclusion from the ranks of the elect yielded a paradoxical kink, a kink that made instrumentality its own reward. By Weber's account, this outcome greatly helped the development of capitalism—a kink, we might say, that ultimately ended in bondage (it's not for nothing that *The Protestant Ethic* concludes with iron-cage confinement). Radicals have occasionally conceded that the performances we stage to substantiate our sincerity can become self-defeating.[21] But if we can't embrace the substitute object and can't give up on the desire for reconciliation, and if we are not yet able to resolve the contradictions inherent in the world's matter directly, then how else might we proceed?

An answer suggests itself by following the echoes of "sincerity" through another of its iterations—this time from Greek mythology, where we are tossed in among the men on Odysseus' ship. Knowing that they were about to sail past the island of the sirens, Odysseus instructs his crewmen to fill their ears with wax so that they might be guarded from the enchanting seductions luring them to peril. In anticipation of the encounter, he also asks that they tie him to the mast. A kink, to be sure, but a far healthier one than the perverse weirdness into which Weber's Protestants stumbled by mistake. Odysseus, after all, had the good sense to ask for what he wanted—and to choose it voluntarily.

This is the meaning of sincerity to which we must once again aspire. Unlike his crewmen, Odysseus confronted his situation "without wax." Aware of the siren song because unprotected from it, he nevertheless remained resolute. Moreover, because he did not deny his crewman the protection of wax, he was able to cultivate rapport. Despite his protestations that they release him, Odysseus' men remained steadfast and instead tightened his bonds. In this way, a collective subject (greater than the sum of its parts) was born. Though consciously acknowledging the sirens only to refuse them was agonizing, Odysseus accepted that the seductions of this world would only find fulfillment through the production of the world to which he aspired (a world of homecoming, of resolution, in which the outcast sovereign returns as usurper). The siren song promised to reveal the future; for Odysseus, the seduction was overcome by assuming the burden—along with his crewmen—of producing the future directly. This is how we too shall make our way home.

■

If my writing has been guided by a single consistent motive over the past decade, it has been to tie us collectively to the mast. "Facing reality," as James proposed, requires that we confront the world with sober senses. To get to this point, however, it is first necessary for us to build rapport with those who might aid us even though their confrontation with the world's incommensurability might be less acute. Only then can we begin to work through the allure of our proxies without losing sight of the desires that compelled us to identify with them in the first place. In devising this approach, I have been tremendously indebted to the work of Walter Benjamin. Indeed, Benjamin's methodology, his catalogue of resonant themes, and many of his most prized bibliographic staples are woven through—and provide an overarching coherence to—the essays in this volume.

As a writer, Benjamin preferred showing to telling, and many of his works never aspired to forms more monumental than the essay.[22] Consequently, readers intent on extracting clear methodological premises from his oeuvre are left to glean insights from an unwieldy array of material. According to Benjamin translator and biographer Pierre Missac, this is best done *en passant*: "One must run the risk of a certain arbitrariness, which will pay off if a hitherto-unnoticed detail reveals itself in a fleeting flash of light."[23] Here, Missac hews closely to Benjamin's own contention that the effective *organization* and *presentation* of artifacts was more important to their ultimate illumination than any narrative explanation might be.[24]

Such a procedure left much room for uncertainty. In Adorno's estimation, it amounted to nothing more vivid than a "wide-eyed presentation of mere facts."[25] For his part, even Benjamin acknowledged that the endeavor required that he proceed along shaky terrain. This was so much the case that, in his 1929 essay on surrealism, he went so far as to claim that his chosen approach amounted more to "a trick than a method."[26] For thinkers intent on operationalizing Benjamin, the attributes of this "trick" must be clarified.

In order to do so, it is useful to begin by revisiting Benjamin's longstanding interest in the question of reflection. In his doctoral thesis on *The Concept of Criticism in German Romanticism* written in 1920, Benjamin began exploring the means by which objects could be forced to reveal themselves as metonymic encapsulations of the social totality within which they were embedded. Summarizing the Romantic orientation to criticism, he highlighted reflection's significance as a means of achieving a kind of concrete universality:

> The Romantics' endeavors to reach purity and universality in the use of forms rests in the conviction that, by critically setting free the potential and many-sidedness of these forms (by absolutizing the reflection bound up in them), the critic will hit upon their connectedness as moments within the medium.[27]

Benjamin's early analysis of Romanticism proved fruitful to the subsequent development of his unique materialist method, which sought to illuminate those points of unexpected rupture or convergence that gave history its dynamism and made revolution possible. On this basis, his famous final essay on the concept of history urged the historical materialist to gravitate toward moments of cessation in order to "blast a specific era out of the homogenous course of history—blasting a specific life out of the era or a specific work out of the lifework. As a result of this method the lifework is preserved and at the same time cancelled … in the lifework, the era; and in the era, the entire course of history."[28]

But while the essay on the concept of history gave these ideas their most concrete, mature expression, the epistemological uses to which Benjamin put reflection remain essentially unchanged from their earlier elaboration in the Romanticism thesis. The continuity underlying Benjamin's thought becomes explicit when one considers how applications of this reflection "trick" can be detected even prior to the doctoral thesis and as early as 1915 when, in his essay on "The Life of Students," Benjamin declared his intention to zero in on those moments in which "history appears to be concentrated in a single focal point, like those that have traditionally been found in the utopian images of the philosophers."

The elements of the ultimate condition do not manifest themselves as formless progressive tendencies, but are deeply rooted in every present in the form of the most endangered, excoriated, and ridiculed ideas and products of the creative mind. The historical task is to disclose this immanent state of perfection and make it absolute, to make it visible and dominant in the present.[29]

It would be difficult to imagine a more fitting approach when considering the culture of revolt.

Although translation and circulation have made it ubiquitous, Benjamin's work only became widely available to English readers through the Schocken Books collections *Illuminations* and *Reflections*, which were respectively published in 1968 and 1978. For decades, these collections have been an invaluable resource to scholars and a source of bewildering pleasure to legions of readers seduced by Benjamin's insights and his mastery of the aphoristic form. Along with gathering the scattered fragments of his literary output and constellating them into dynamic assemblages, however, *Illuminations* and *Reflections* also served eponymously to foreground two of Benjamin's most cherished analytic premises.

To "illumination" and "reflection," I would like to add "premonition." An act of homage, to be sure—but also a fair description of the anxious epistemological posture unifying the works in this collection. Produced over the course of a decade and scattered like letters hellbent on tracing a course to their recipient, each of the essays in this volume attends to either a promise or a pitfall embedded in today's culture of revolt. Whether through exchanges with key interlocutors (Section I), engagements with mass- and movement-based cultural offerings (Section II), or meditations on our trembling before violence, history, and death (Section III), my aim has been to cultivate the sense of rapport that might allow us to admit that we don't yet know how to win—and that the costs of allowing current resolutions to stand are immense.

By definition, a premonition is an advance warning. It is an anticipation of the future extrapolated from the present. As such, its posture is foreboding—but it is also marked by joy, since (as Novalis proposed) it allows us to envision what must be done so that things might turn out otherwise. Recognizing the unbearable character of the present by confronting the future such a present is destined to yield urges us to consider the demands that befall us as we plot another course. "That things are 'status quo' *is* the catastrophe," said Benjamin.[30] He completed the thought when he noted that, from the standpoint of historical analysis, the definition of a catastrophe could only be: "to have missed the opportunity."[31] Alongside this account, Benjamin also proposed two other "definitions of basic historical concepts." These included: "critical moment—the status quo threatens to be preserved,"[32] and "progress—the first revolutionary measure taken."[33] I have adopted these basic historical concepts, along with their associated definitions, as thematic section headings for the material contained in this volume.

Unsettling though they may be, the premonitions heralded by our culture of revolt urge us to face reality. And unlike Cassandra, who was doomed to speak prophecies that no one would believe, we are blessed with opportunities to intervene directly. Such interventions arise naturally from our growing awareness of the limits inherent in the catastrophic status quo. At their best, premonitions alert us to the unresolved history contained within the smallest of fragments. The distress that such attentiveness yields makes sense; it corresponds to the developmental outcomes demanded by the neurotic course on which we're set. Such outcomes are not inevitable, however, and *Premonitions* may yet suggest another path.

I

CATASTROPHE

(TO HAVE MISSED THE OPPORTUNITY)

CHRIS HEDGES VS. CRIMETHINC.

Will We Get the Debate We Deserve?

The debate between Chris Hedges and the CrimethInc. Ex-Workers Collective scheduled to take place September 12 at the City University of New York Graduate Center is long overdue. Squaring off to determine what role—if any—violence is to have in movements like Occupy, the opponents will march into one of the Left's most treacherous minefields. And they want you to watch. If activity on Facebook is any indication, the hall at CUNY will be packed. Meanwhile, the showdown's promised livestreaming has prompted many activists to set up viewing events at infoshops, or at house parties with beer and popcorn. The terms of the debate are already well established; nevertheless, if ever there were such a thing as a diversity-of-tactics championship round, this would surely be it.

Up until now, Hedges has maintained that there's no point in engaging with black bloc advocates. In an interview posted on *Truthout* on

This essay first appeared on the website *Truthout* on the morning of September 12, 2012. It was written in anticipation of the debate between Chris Hedges and B. Traven of the CrimethInc. Ex-Workers Collective on the subject of violence in the Occupy movement. http://www.truth-out.org/opinion/item/11471-chris-hedges-vs-crimethinc-on-violence-will-we-get-the-debate-we-deserve.

February 9, 2012, he admitted to not having spoken with black bloc participants when coming to the conclusion that they were Occupy's "cancer."[1] In response, CrimethInc. declared that they would not enter into debate with figures like Hedges. In their introduction to a first-person black-bloc testimonial published on February 20, 2012, they wrote: "We do not accept the terms set by the mudslingers: Our intent is not to compete for ideological legitimacy on a battlefield of abstractions."[2] Now, seven months later, they've resolved to go toe to toe. Of course people want to watch. But will the event be a mere spectacle, or will we rise to the occasion to ensure that it becomes something more?

From the Battle of Blair Mountain to the eviction of Occupy, the story of American radicalism is inseparable from the question of violence. Sometimes embraced, often denounced, but even more often sidestepped, debates about violence have tended to return (like all repressed phenomena do) with a frequency that only underscores their importance. But while activists on both sides of the violence/nonviolence divide seem committed to their respective certainties, few would suggest that either position has brought us any closer to a collective understanding of what we must do to win.

Maybe this means that "we" will never be a unified force, that agreement on ends is not enough to see us through. Maybe it means that the violent opponents of constituted power are in fact enemies to the pacifists who trust that power can be shamed into doing the right thing. Then again, maybe it means that "we"—pacifists and advocates of a diversity of tactics alike—still haven't grasped what's essential.

In a context where the State continues to enjoy a monopoly on the legitimate use of force, it's hardly surprising that many of us go to great lengths to avoid describing our actions using the language of violence. Around the time that Chris Hedges denounced the black bloc as "the cancer of the Occupy movement,"[3] activist-journalist Rebecca Solnit proclaimed that social change arose not from violence but from "people power."[4] In her estimation, this power was evident during November's general strike in Oakland, where activists helped to shut down the ports in what she described as "a triumphant and mostly nonviolent day of mass actions."[5]

I will be the first to concede that "people power" sounds good. At very least, it doesn't have the bad name that violence does. Nevertheless, it's hard not to wonder what this "power" amounts to, or where it ultimately comes from. Given its broad appeal, it's not surprising that Solnit landed upon the general strike as a compelling example of people power. But if people's power is the antithesis of violence as Solnit proposes, and if the general strike gives that power a concrete form, then what are we to make of the fact that the general strike was a significant reference point for some of the twentieth century's most significant meditations on the question of political violence?

In his "Critique of Violence" first published in 1921, Walter Benjamin recounted how strikes called the state's monopoly on the legitimate use of force into question and how, in response, capitalist countries began incorporating the "right" to strike into their legal paradigms.[6] In this way, they began placing restrictions on what strikes might look like. Today, strikes have become highly ritualized procedures that bear little resemblance to their violent precursors. Nevertheless, as the recent Quebec student strike has made clear, they continuously threaten to erupt into moments of sovereign contestation. For this reason, and as Benjamin indicated, the strike remains essentially violent because its participants tend to "exercise a right in order to overthrow the legal system that has conferred it."[7]

In Benjamin's account, violence either works to preserve an existing legal framework or to establish a new one. Law-preserving violence commits people (police and bosses, to be sure, but also "innocent" bystanders) to custodial care for a crumbling world. In contrast, law-making violence arises between competing sovereignties, one ascendant and one in decline. In this formulation, the measure of violence ceases to be "harm" and becomes instead the degree to which the status quo is maintained or transformed. Law-preserving violence is generally sanctioned; law-making violence is not. The realm in which there is no violence at all becomes infinitesimally small. Even doctrinally nonviolent protesters don't escape, since their actions rely upon the violence that established the legal rights and legal power to which they appeal.

In a recent edition of Occupy's theoretical journal *Tidal*, Gayatri Chakravorty Spivak outlined the history of the general strike and elaborated the means by which it could be retooled for our new global situation.[8] Along with other figures, Spivak's history makes reference to the work of the now mostly-forgotten French theorist of the general strike, Georges Sorel. But while Sorel gets a nod, Spivak makes no mention of the fact that his considerations on the general strike are to be found in *Reflections on Violence*, a pro-violence tract of the first order.[9] This omission must surely have been deliberate, since she goes on to insist that the general strike is "by definition nonviolent."[10]

Strategically useful though it may have been, Spivak's assertion does not stand up to scrutiny. Following in the tradition of Sorel and Benjamin, even the provocative Black cultural nationalist Amiri Baraka gravitated toward the general strike as oppositional violence's most obvious political form. Contemplating the 1963 bombing of the 16th Street Baptist Church in Birmingham, Baraka (then LeRoi Jones) suggested that, in response, "The US Steel plant in that city should have been shut down by Negroes."

> Black workers should have walked out of every job they hold in the city. A general strike should have been called. An attempt should have been made to shut down completely the city's industrial resources. That city should have died, should have been killed by Negroes.[11]

Such urbicide, he avowed, was unquestionably an act of violence. However, as with Marx (who professed that the proletarian revolution would make the bourgeois individual "impossible" [12] without requiring that every shop owner be killed), Baraka envisioned the general strike as a form of violence that could transform social relations without ever requiring that physical harm be inflicted on people.

This past spring, the Occupy movement became enthralled by visions of a post-thaw resurgence that would culminate in a general strike starting on May Day. But despite these ambitions, which were endorsed by activists on both sides of the diversity-of-tactics debate, many movement participants ignored—or remained oblivious to—the violent character of their proposed plans. Had this violence been acknowledged, we may have discovered (tactical differences notwithstanding) that the movement's nonviolent wing had more in common with its putative "cancer" than we'd previously realized.

But rather than acknowledging the tendency toward violence underlying both the movement's most significant moment and its most significant aspirations, commentators on both sides of the violence/nonviolence divide have tended to allow the debate to slip back into a well-carved and circuitous groove. Like a broken record, the proponents of nonviolence have asserted the strategic and moral superiority of their position without ever acknowledging the State violence that underwrites it. Nevertheless, and as punk-rock klezmer icon Geoff Berner put it, "To live outside the law, you must be vicious / to live inside you must depend upon the viciousness of strangers."[13] Meanwhile, activists who have come to recognize violence's productive character have opted once again to convey their discovery in the coded, user-friendly language of a "diversity of tactics."

Does that mean that the scheduled debate brings us back to the "battlefield of abstractions" that CrimethInc. hoped to avoid? It might not be inevitable, but reading the comments on activist web sites makes me worry. Although it's an arbitrary sampling method, I can't shake the feeling that we've reached a point of intractability that makes learning new things impossible. We've already chosen sides. And what we want most is the fight.

How else are we to explain the dramatic recurrence of pugilistic metaphors on activist message boards? "Hedges is about to be so smacked down," wrote one message board contributor on August 16, 2012.[14] Pleased that the debate would be livestreamed, they concluded by promising a "viewing party at [their] apartment." "Mine too," wrote another, adding: "If ever there was a celeb death match to remember, this would be it." Extending the metaphor in a subsequent entry, another participant expressed hope that the CrimethInc. speaker would be "working up a sweat everyday … in preparation for this debate!!" The entry concludes in an explosion of fandom enthusiasm: "We love you and don't let us down!!"[15]

Others weighed in too. "This is going to be awesome," wrote one commenter. "I hope Hedges cries." "I hope Hedges bleeds," wrote another, perhaps concerned that crying was not sufficient for a contender guilty of taking pot shots at the black bloc. In the end, however, even bleeding was not enough: "I hope Hedges dies." Taking a more cautious tone, another participant wrote: "I got nothing but love for CrimethInc., just hope they really throw a good punch."[16]

Are we waiting for a boxing match? A case could be made that we're about to witness the activist equivalent of the Rumble in the Jungle. A clever journalist could claim that CrimethInc. can float like a butterfly and sting like a bee (it's not for nothing that one of the books that most defined them in the early years was called *Evasion*[17]). Meanwhile, Hedges—a former boxer himself—could be considered a miniature George Foreman.[18] Unrelenting and unapologetic, he may well be the heavyweight champion of moral journalism. As was true of Ali in 1974, CrimethInc. seems to be the underdog favorite going into the bout; and, like Ali before them, it seems like their strategy will be to stand firm, cast evasion aside, and draw Hedges out.

But a debate is not boxing, and activism is not a spectator sport. As we prepare for this important event, let's not lose sight of how inadequate our certainties have proven to be thus far. Neither doctrinal nonviolence nor respect for a diversity of tactics has allowed us to come to terms with violence's omnipresence and inescapability, or to develop a response that's equal to the challenges we confront. The debate is a tremendous opportunity, but only if we concede that we don't yet know how to win. If we don't start with this simple—brutal—fact, September 12 risks degenerating into one more spectacle to keep us mesmerized as the world burns.

DID SOMEONE SAY RIOT?

James M. Jasper, in Conversation
with AK Thompson

AK THOMPSON: Back in 2010, I published a book with AK Press called *Black Bloc, White Riot.*[1] Throughout its pages, I revisited the struggles against corporate globalization that marked the beginning of the twenty-first century to assess the role that violence plays in political change. My thesis was that, while the movement's limited experiments with violence were tactically inconclusive, they nevertheless signaled both a desire and a means for movement participants to reconnect with the political sphere in a moment marked by its general decline. This was especially significant, I argued, for the movement's white and middle class participants since their status as privileged subjects actually made their expulsion from the political sphere more acute. In the end, by broadening the scope of what it meant to be violent, I tried to raise the bar for what it meant to be political.

Although the book developed a small following among movement participants and a subset of radical intellectuals, it never generated the kind of engagement that my publisher had hoped it might. In part, this owed to the challenges of writing a crossover hit that could appeal to scholarly and movement-based audiences alike. Fearful that I'd

This interview first appeared in *Social Movement Studies*, Volume 15, No. 2 (2016). It is based on a dialogue that took place at a public event entitled "Did Someone Say Riot?" hosted by The Brecht Forum in New York on October 30, 2013.

gotten the balance wrong, I respectfully declined many invitations to speak at big-box bookstores. Gradually, I discovered that promoting the book filled me with dread. The fact that I had no difficulty standing by what I'd written did nothing to keep me from being terrified by its implications.

Meanwhile, I was discovering that my efforts were viewed as perplexing by many movement-based readers. Part of the problem was my scholarly training, which compelled me to write (as one reviewer observed) like a cross between Judith Butler and Hegel.[2] More fundamental, though, was the fact that—by 2010—the question of violence had been sequestered to a nebulous realm accessible solely by way of "respect for a diversity of tactics," a curious incantation indeed.

Although it put me at odds with my comrades, I objected to this mantra. For, while the call for "respect" exonerated certain violent acts, it made no strategic claims about the importance of any given tactic. And this problem pointed back to the more fundamental one concerning the relationship between violence and politics itself. Through the course of my research, I'd come to conclude that the terms were inseparable. Violence, I discovered, was neither an abhorrent refraction nor an exceptional supplement to politics; instead, it was its precondition.

Indeed, even the putatively non-violent demand-based demonstrations of modern social movements rest upon the history of violence that inaugurated representational politics at the end of the eighteenth century. Not only do such demonstrations presuppose a field—the so-called public sphere—that found its precondition in regicide, they also owe their effectiveness to the implicit threat of violence they continue to harbor. In both cases, violence underwrites representation as either its motive force or its condition of possibility. At the same time, however, the dynamics of representational politics make this violence as difficult to countenance as it is to perceive.

Since its publication in 2010, many of the questions raised by my book have returned—as I suppose all repressed phenomenon do—with an urgency that forces us to consider them once again. From the street fighting and torched police stations around Tahrir Square to the dramatic confrontations that made Occupy Oakland a constant YouTube hit, 2011 witnessed the global return and intensification of movement-based violence. At the same time, we saw the return of more populist rioting in places like London—and even in Vancouver when the home team's Stanley Cup dreams went up in flames.

Different though they may be, what remains most striking about the flare-ups in both London and Vancouver is what they reveal about the tension between political claim making (which remained ambiguous) and the political character of the actions themselves. Frightened by what they took to be unbridled opportunism, many social movement commentators failed to see their affinity with the looters, arsonists, and street fighters. It's hard to blame them. Still, closer consideration reveals that this failure to identify is best understood as a symptomatic expression of the challenges associated with operating in a political field constituted through the representational subsumption of its own condition of possibility. It is to such problems that my book was addressed, and it's in light of such events that my thesis might transcend the case study from which it arose.

JAMES M. JASPER: I think books like this are promising because they promise to solve what has been a serious problem in scholarship on protest and social movements.

Academic theories of protest have been notoriously bad at linking up with what protestors themselves actually know about what they do. Early in the twentieth century, crowd theorists and mass-society theorists portrayed protestors as barely human, and instead saw them as automatically following demagogues or bowing to the pressures of the crowd at any given moment. Marxists were the only ones in this era who recognized that protestors face dilemmas, produce strategies, make choices—in other words all the stuff that people actually do in social movements. But, of course, they were mostly excluded from the academy, at least in the US. They were practitioners.

In the late '60s and 1970s, Marxists bought their way into the academy, but at the price of turning into structuralists and forgetting all the strategic stuff that they knew from Lenin and from decades of Communist Party organizing. Marxist theory was never an easy read, but it became even more esoteric, like the rest of the university world, more removed from the day-to-day concerns of actual protestors and organizers. In the hands of someone like Louis Althusser, in the '60s, Marxist theory could be both impossible to read and at the same time a thuggish intervention to defend the official party line from the students who were discovering the young, humanist Marx on their own.

Another shift at the time were the new movements of the 1960s, especially Civil Rights. But you had fewer class based movements, which would naturally have been Marxists' specialty. The study of labor movements shrank and became its own specialty, without much connection to the rest of scholarship on social movements.

On the one hand, from the 1970s on, you had academic structuralists who talked about shifts in the structure of the state, which created political opportunities for protestors. In the meantime, protestors didn't have anything to do, apparently, but sit around and wait for a political opportunity to emerge. On the other hand, there were rational-choice theorists with basically microeconomic theories who talked about individual incentives, choices, and free riders. The rational-choice theorists caricatured what it is to be human, while the structuralists simply ignored it. It took a kind of culturalist reaction against the structuralists and the rationalists before you had a real effort to see the world from the point of view of the protestors themselves.

In the last 10 or 15 years there've appeared academic models in which we might actually recognize real human beings. Two things in particular make these descriptions humanly familiar: Protestors have emotions, a range of emotions, some positive, some negative; some helpful and some harmful to their causes; some fairly permanent like group loyalty, others fairly fleeting like anger or fear. Second, protestors make strategic choices, they face strategic tradeoffs and dilemmas, for which there is not always one right decision. They struggle with the fact that every option carries a long list of costs, of risks, of potential benefits, of impacts of all sorts. So even on those rare occasions when academics try to advise activists, we aren't especially good at it, since there's no one right answer, but lots of tradeoffs. The best that scholars can do is to point out those tradeoffs, and what risks to watch out for.

One of the big dilemmas protestors face is what I call "naughty or nice." Do you try to please those in authority, or do you defy them, try to disrupt things, break laws and norms? For many, intimidation and disruption work very well. For others, they bring on severe repression that might mean the end of the team. In order to work, aggressive techniques usually need very specific and immediate goals: you can intimidate a corporation into recognizing a union, you can scare a dictator into fleeing. But the cost is in broader public opinion, if you care about that, or in arousing a reaction from authorities. In other words, the short-run gain has to be important and relatively irreversible, because there is usually long-run damage to your reputation.

A lot of players have tried to work this dilemma by having a distinct radical flank that plays rough, so that the mainstream can distance itself from the extreme actions but perhaps still benefit from them. But of course this just opens up a whole *new* field of struggle: *can* you keep your distance, or does the whole team or coalition get branded as extremist? You have to work hard to manage public impressions. In a way, what a strategy of aggression and intimidation can do is split apart an opponents' coalition so that individuals or organizations defect because they're bearing too great a cost themselves. But the rest of the coalition will put a lot of pressure on them *not* to defect.

Take the anti-abortion movement, which has scared a lot of doctors away from doing abortions; the numbers who do have dropped steadily. The dangers, whether they are real or perceived, are just too high for a lot of doctors to face. Meanwhile, the pro-choice movement pressures them to keep practicing. For the anti-abortion movement, it's a strategy that has worked well: In almost 90% of the counties in this country, there are *no* abortion providers any more.

Related to naughty or nice is what I call the "dirty hands dilemma." You can only achieve certain goals by using means or by working with people you find morally repugnant. This isn't really a tradeoff between different means, it's more a tradeoff between means and ends.

Riots are a great example of the naughty option: They get attention, they sometimes frighten elites into concessions, but they risk bringing down enormous repression, and they tend not to make protestors more popular with the general public. Now, that is partly due to how the media frame riot; however, in today's world, it is a pretty standard, predictable effect.

It hasn't always been true. The media haven't always portrayed rioters as, basically, criminals, as a threat to basic values of property and justice. Historians like E.P. Thompson have shown that food riots actually followed an intuitive communal morality, asking for just prices for bread and cheese and other basics, and destroying grain mills primarily when they were refused or when the peaceful crowds were met with violence from the other side. A handful of social scientists like Frances Fox Piven have shown that disruptive strategies like riots are what lead elites to grant concessions to poor people.

Nonetheless, the standard story about the Civil Rights gains of the 1960s has come to focus more and more on the preachers in their blue suits and less and less on the riots that followed and may have actually led to greater gains. But riots have made a comeback in the last decade or so—as has the aggressive policing of crowds, which is often what sparks riots. All of which is a little background for AK Thompson's book, which argues that violence was, or perhaps should have been, central to the global justice movement.

Now I want to ask him a number of questions that I think get at what is fresh and radical about the book.

JMJ: I guess we should start by asking: what is violence? The usual distinction is between vandalism and sabotage against property and attacks on beings who can feel pain, although neither of these is especially popular in the US. What's the relationship of violence to aggression, to protest?

AKT: When discussing violence, it's necessary to bracket normative conceptions so that the problem can be investigated analytically. The distinction you highlighted, for instance, rests on a normative conception that associates violence with harm and harm with sentience. Now, there may be something valuable about such associations—and it's certainly not possible to ignore them, since they carry tremendous normative weight; however, given the stakes, it's necessary for them to be subjected to closer analytic scrutiny.

Failing to do so means that we presume the norm and then develop a strategy on that basis. From there, we might advance an analysis; however, rather than being the *basis* for the chosen strategy, this analysis becomes a justification for it. Following Marx from the 1844 *Manuscripts,* we can say that this procedure assumes "as a fact, in historical form, what needs to be explained."[3]

In the case of the normative claim you mentioned, closer consideration suggests that its payoff owes primarily to the fact that it allows activists to conceptually distinguish what they do from "violence." There may be moral reasons for adopting this position; however, its allure seems to owe primarily to the fact that it concedes (without ever acknowledging) the state's monopoly on the legitimate use of force. A virtue is thus made of necessity, and analysis is enlisted to provide cover for our strategic subordination to social norms that are presumed (rather than demonstrated) to be intractable.

How, then, might we approach the question from the standpoint of analysis? In my work, I propose that violence is best understood as a productive force. The human relation with nature, which—for Marx—was the starting point for the analysis of production, is one in which the world is transformed in accordance with human desires. For most of human history, the basic forms of this metabolic relationship (e.g. agriculture) were rarely considered violent. Recently, ecological consciousness has helped to reverse this trend by raising questions about the costs of our particular habits. But while this is a positive development, a number of points need to be made.

The first is that, despite the growing critique, the violence inherent in agriculture is still not widely recognized. The second is that broad insensitivity to this violence has not prevented people (and especially state agencies) from recognizing the violence at work in the destruction of GMO crops or in the release of animals from fur farms. When considered from the standpoint of "harm," the eco-activists engaged in these practices clearly have the moral high ground. Nevertheless, these same activists have become significant targets for America's "anti-terror" efforts. Why, we might ask, is the agricultural sequence—deforestation, breaking and degrading soil, domesticating plant species and forcing them to yield fruit at unsustainable rates—not commonly understood as violent while the interruption of these same processes is?

A satisfactory answer begins by noting that the initial violence is wholly commensurate with the forms of production that prevail in our society. Violence of this sort is omnipresent and inescapable; however, since it accords with the fundamental dynamics of our social organization, it tends to pass under the radar (what, in my book, I call the "threshold of recognizability").[4] Along with agriculture, other forms of unremarkable everyday violence that operate in this way include education and childrearing, which—as Freud pointed out—can never be successful without also being traumatic.[5] On the whole, the violence inherent in these practices is motivated not by sadism but by production itself.

But even though this kind of violence tends to operate below the threshold of recognizability, people struggling to create different social relationships have occasionally managed to make it visible. To evaluate the historic success of these efforts, it suffices to consider how there are now sanctions against hitting one's children that would have been inconceivable in the past. Strategy thus seems to recommend that we draw attention to violence so that we might call for it to stop.

I don't want to downplay the value of such campaigns; however, to the extent that they ever aimed at eradicating violence, they've clearly failed. Not only do they rely on the violence that inaugurated the public sphere to advance their demands, they fail to recognize that squashing an overt regime of violence within a constituted field tends to pave the way for a more nuanced and productive one. As Foucault's *Discipline and Punish* makes clear, violence didn't disappear in the interval between the medieval era's tortured body and the modern preoccupation with the soul.[6] Rather than signaling a humanizing shift away from violence, the object substitution at work in such instances is best understood as a change in violence's productive modality.

On this basis, one might observe that there is no better way to discipline workers than to make them owners within the capitalist production process. To be sure, such ownership makes the violence of production more bearable and lucrative for those directly affected by it; however, it does nothing to disrupt the fundamental violence of capitalist production itself. In a way, worker ownership comes to the same impasse that Freud confronted when he conceded that, in a society like ours, the best people could hope for was to *choose* their repression.[7] So long as we participate in relations we neither devise nor control, we remain complicit in this society's everyday, omnipresent violence.

For this reason, I think Weber's formulation, which defines the state in part through its monopoly on the legitimate use of force, needs to be extended slightly. Normally invoked to capture the police and the army, it seems that (when pushed to its logical conclusion) Weber's "monopoly" should apply to the violence of productive social relations more generally. Capitalism compels people to commit great acts of largely unrecognized violence in the course of their everyday lives; however, if these same people were to commit comparable acts in pursuit of their own ends and outside of the capitalist purview (and here we can think of squatters, but also of bank robbers and others that Hobsbawm might have called "primitive rebels"[8]), they would be doing so in direct violation of the production-force monopoly legitimated by the state. At this point, their acts tend to be declared violent and thus to get shut down.

What this line of reasoning makes clear is that, when it comes to violence, there's no way to remain innocent. And though it may be strategically useful to declare our innocence in light of the state's monopoly, honesty itself compels us to acknowledge that, while the relations we devise upon breaking the monopoly might be more humane, they will not be less violent. Once this is accepted, we discover that the important political question is not whether or not to engage in violence (since there is, in fact, no way *not* to). Instead, the question becomes: how do we break the monopoly so that we might gain control over—and thus assume responsibility for—the violence of our own productive activity? This question leads to a second one, which is the most important question of all: once it's up to us, what will we produce?

Since they are generally reactive in character, riots don't often develop to the stage where this question is posed directly. Nevertheless, because riots—like strikes, before they became legally neutralized—mark points where the monopoly gets called into question, they tend to foster shifts in our understanding of the political. In these moments (brief though they may be), people become far less concerned with being properly represented and far more concerned with securing and controlling territory. The basic framework of politics shifts. Representation—the crowning achievement of bourgeois politics—is supplanted by territorial war.

At their best, riots remind us that the basic unit of politics is not representation, as our bourgeois rulers have insisted, but regicide—as they themselves learned from historical experience! And though riots are far from being the ideal form for effective sovereign contestation (and though they tend to announce their doom from the outset), they remain felicitous in the short term on account of their availability.

JMJ: What role do the media play in the impact of violence and riots, and protest generally? In a lot of movements, the media pick up the issues in a sympathetic way even when they are quite unsympathetic to the protestors, portraying them as foolish, naïve, or dangerous. Protestors are often sacrificing their own public image to get the message across, especially with radical flanks that are extremely unpopular.

AKT: From their inception, modern social movements have been concerned with persuasion. As social formations arising from the bourgeois public sphere, movements became adept at framing demands to persuade political representatives to act more resolutely on their behalf. As Charles Tilly recounted, the basic means of achieving this goal was through displays of worthiness, unity, numbers, and commitment.[9] Given this legacy, social movements have correctly recognized the media as an important field of operations and, on occasion, as an important broker.

There is obviously a lot that can be achieved here. Since bourgeois rule gains legitimation through the myth of the consent of the governed, and since the bourgeoisie's idealistic proclamations of what *ought to be* vastly outstrip *what is* (the impoverished reality they've actually produced), movements have historically made significant gains by exploiting the tension between "is" and "ought." This was especially true of what you've described as "citizenship movements," where struggles for suffrage, abolition, and voter registration leveraged bourgeois claims about universal equality to improve the social standing of women and Black people.[10]

But alongside this important representational demand-based work, these struggles also contained a violent dimension. The story of the Civil Rights movement is incomplete without a nod to the Deacons of Defense. For their part, British suffragettes physically attacked politicians and even planted bombs in their homes. As every organizer knows, media can be fickle when it comes to representing movement demands. In contrast, street-level violence—despite the fact that it exists outside of and at odds with the representational paradigm—guarantees coverage.

A problem thus arises: even though the media can be counted on to report on riots, they have consistently proven incapable of recognizing that these events are political. As if on cue, reporters documenting the 2011 London riots chalked up the arson, looting, and street fighting to hooliganism. What sense are we to make of this love-hate relationship? An answer suggests itself if we foreground the schizophrenic dimension of contemporary mass media.

On the one hand, mainstream media outlets present themselves as lords of the Fourth Estate, venerable institutions entrusted with minding representational power while providing conduits for its practical realization. On the other hand, they are major commercial enterprises and purveyors of salacious little trinkets called "news." The riot is definitely news; however, it also marks an explicit break with the norms of representational politics. As such, it undermines the political framework that legitimates the commercial enterprise—and it's not surprising that, during many riots, media vehicles are targeted along with fast-food joints and corporate chain stores. The whole scene becomes vertiginous, and the media responds by adopting a position that mixes lurid scopophilia with puritanical denunciation.

What's interesting is that media representations of riots end up being extremely compelling even when they're larded with disapproval. As Lesley Wood pointed out in her recent book on diffusion, mainstream depictions of the besieged WTO did as much to popularize the anti-summit repertoire as Indymedia or the Ruckus Society did.[11] To be sure, the people activated by these images may not have understood exactly what they were seeing; details of protest planning and coordination could not have come through clearly in the footage. Still, the most significant things did, and glimpses of a new kind of politics began to push through the representational screen.

Around the same time, however, many activists became critical of the representations of riots that had begun to circulate in both mainstream and movement-based media. By focusing on fleeting moments of macho glory, activists alleged that such "riot porn" (as it came to be known) distracted from movement building. The representations were thus condemned for undermining the work of organizers while attracting irresponsible thrill seekers. Although I am sympathetic to these concerns, they say little about the *reasons* that riot porn was so compelling in the first place.

Why are such scenes of confrontation irresistible? If my analysis is correct, it becomes clear that what people are identifying with is not so much the promise of *jouissance* as it is the promise signaled by the breach in the representational field. This breach attests to the fact that another production is possible. It's a frightening proposition, since it puts a tremendous burden of responsibility on the viewer. However, when the problem is considered from the standpoint of a world bereft of opportunities for consequential action, it becomes clear that this same responsibility is a tremendous seduction too.

JMJ: And how did the events of 9/11 change images of crowds and of riots, among media audiences, among the forces of order, among protestors themselves?

AKT: In the immediate aftermath of 9/11, activists called off scheduled protests against the IMF and World Bank. Meanwhile, the meeting of the World Economic Forum was moved from Davos, Switzerland to New York City. In the midst of mourning and fear, constituted power saw an opportunity and seized it—some might say cynically—for all it was worth. For their part, protestors were put on the defensive and struggled to address the clampdown on civil rights at home and the violence of the "war on terror" abroad.

It's important to remember, however, that many of the police-state developments we associate with the post-9/11 period were already well underway before the chickens came home to roost. As author and legal activist Kris Hermes points out in a forthcoming book on the subject, the police response to the Philadelphia Republican National Convention (RNC) protests in 2000 probably marked the turning point.[12] In this view, by underscoring the need for new levels of surveillance, infiltration, inter-agency-coordination, and police-force militarization, the Seattle generation's short-lived successes furnished the emergent national security state with a compelling motivation.

Especially after 9/11, this anti-dissident groundwork helped to vastly increase the ease with which protest actions could be conflated with terrorism. The cynicism of this conflation cannot be overstated. Despite a report from its own people indicating that there was "no credible threat" of a terrorist attack against the 2010 G20 meeting in Toronto, the federal government exploited public anxieties it had deliberately inflamed to justify its bloated billion-dollar security budget.[13] In addition to bankrolling experiments in the suspension of the rule of law, this money was also used to gather information on activists through surveillance and mass arrest.

The conflation of activism and terrorism has also been used to target us directly by increasing the costs of opposition. In 2008, eight protestors were charged with "Conspiracy to Riot in Furtherance of Terrorism" for their role in demonstrations against the RNC in St. Paul. Later dropped, these charges echoed developments taking place in the radical environmental and animal liberation scenes, in which people had begun to get picked up on terrorism-related charges stemming from the Animal Enterprise Terrorism Act (AETA).

Within the context of escalating consequences, there's little wonder that activists became preoccupied with conceptually distinguishing themselves from terrorists. One of the principal means by which this was done was to associate terrorism with violence and activism with legally protected forms of speech. The logic is clear: since activists don't engage in violence, they can't be terrorists. But while this approach offered succor, it came at a tremendous price—and I don't think that price has always been recognized.

Not only does accepting the homology between terrorism and violence throw the movement's radical flank under the bus, it also disregards the historic difference between terrorist violence and the forms of violence occasionally marshaled by movements. With respect to the problem of the radical flank, movement efforts to cut losses in order to continue struggling may have seemed advisable; however, even a brief consideration of post-9/11 policing strategies reveals that movement denunciations of the radical flank have coincided with—and even helped to intensify—new restrictions on the terrain of legally protected expression. As I recount in my book, the logic of policing during the staid 2002 anti-G8 protests in Kananaskis insisted that, even though they weren't going to cause trouble, the "good" protestors needed to be kept in check to prevent them from inadvertently providing cover for evildoers.[14]

With respect to the difference between terrorist violence and movement-based violence, it's important to note that, from the standpoint of its political logic, terrorism is primarily representational in character. In contrast, movement-based violence tends to arise when movements push beyond the representational frame. Here, violence manifests itself as a practical expression of what Georges Sorel called the "ethics of the producers."[15]

When terrorists use violence, they do so in order to coerce power into acting more resolutely on their behalf and in accordance with their interests. Like modern social movements, modern terrorism emerged alongside the bourgeois public sphere. Although the tactics deployed by terrorists clearly intensify the meaning of "persuasion," the relationship to constituted power remains fundamentally unchanged. It's on this basis that we can understand how *activist* the anarcho-terrorist Auguste Vaillant sounded when—after throwing a bomb in the French National Assembly in 1893—he proclaimed: "the more they are deaf, the more your voice must thunder out so that they will understand you."[16]

In contrast to terrorist violence, which reiterates the representational presuppositions of bourgeois rule, movement-based violence tends to coincide with efforts to seize control of territory. This was especially evident during the movement of the squares, but it's also a common feature of urban riots and insurrections. As people begin to produce their reality directly, calls for greater representation are temporarily eclipsed. If followed to its logical conclusion, this observation forces us to conclude that the point of contact between activism and terrorism arises not from their common use of violence but rather from their common immersion in the demand-based world of representational politics. If activists want to conceptually distinguish themselves from terrorists, they are better served by denouncing representation than they are by denouncing violence.

Of course, this doesn't resolve the problem. At present, there's little we can do to keep the state from finding terrorists where it will. Nevertheless, it's important that we clarify the matter analytically, since failing to do so muddies strategy by forcing violence to remain unthinkable.

JMJ: When does violence work? What kinds of goals can it help attain, and what can it not? How do different audiences, different strategic players, respond? Did it make a difference in Seattle in 1999? How does this differ in different countries?

AKT: In the United States and Canada, we are currently living through a moment in which non-state actors are extremely limited in their capacity to win even short-term gains through political violence. This owes not to the inefficaciousness of violence per se (after all, these same actors remain complicit in the everyday violence required to maintain a society like this one), but to the effectiveness of the state's monopoly, on one hand, and to some combination of organizational disarray and risk-averseness on the other. Even strikes, which historically became a "right" through the use of violence (through implicit or explicit declarations of sovereign control over the means of production), have degenerated to the point where the form no longer corresponds to the historic threat.

But while our capacity for collective violence may be at a low point when compared to moments like the Battle of Blair Mountain or to the urban uprisings that marked the transition from Civil Rights to Black Power, and while the limited experiments with violence that occasionally punctuate contemporary demonstrations can often seem tactically inefficacious, it's important to note that these experiments remain pedagogically important.

Let me give an example. For most people, the demonstrations against the 2010 G20 in Toronto will forever be associated with images of cop cars burning in the financial district. Several prominent leftwing commentators, including Judy Rebick and Neil Smith, suggested that these fires originated in cynical police inaction and, as such, were orchestrated to legitimate the suspension of rights that would follow.[17] This may have been a useful strategic frame; however, the tacit assumption is that people would never feel compelled to breach police lines and to destroy cop cars of their own volition. As it happened, participants in the black bloc set those fires, and many people became enthralled. And though the police might have set one car out as bait, the fires that got set in the heart of the financial district clearly took them by surprise.[18]

Although she championed the "militant" protestors who tried in vain to reach the summit site, Judy Rebick decried the black bloc and claimed that it was responsible for the police violence that followed.[19] Nevertheless, and in contrast to the honorable militants rebuffed by police lines, the black bloc successfully entered the financial district and gained access to the restricted area surrounding the elite gathering. Seeing the opportunity, other demonstrators followed in their wake. Rebick's hope that militant protestors would be able to voice their opposition at the summit site was thus realized through the actions of the force she denounced.

What sense are we to make of such contortions? We might begin by observing that contemporary social democrats want the benefits of violence without ever having to incur the associated costs. Perverse as it seems, this posture can be explained historically by recalling the experience of the postwar compromise, which marked social-democratic forces indelibly. During this period, social democrats and labor leaders were granted a "seat at the table" on the basis of their constituency's demonstrated historical capacity for violence. This threat, which could potentially be avoided by granting concessions, was enough to secure the framework of negotiated settlement.

Through the course of their development and further legal entrenchment, social democracy and the labor movement became disconnected from—and even began to repudiate—the social force that won them the seat at the table in the first place. This produced a situation where, even though neo-liberalism called an end to the compromise (which had only ever applied to a small segment of the population), labor leaders and social democrats continued acting as though they could negotiate. The abstract force of ethics supplanted the concrete force of violence, and cries of "bad faith bargaining" rang out across the land. Meanwhile, the metaphoric "table" had disappeared along with the labor leaders' cherished "seat," and the capacity for violence that had allowed them initially to gain their spot had either atrophied through neglect or been suppressed through legal constraints.

Under such conditions, the violence that occasionally erupts at demonstrations is pedagogically significant, since it helps to illuminate the mythological thinking that holds both labor leaders and much of their membership in thrall. We must ask: what will it take to collectively break from the certainty that negotiated settlement can continue in a period when the ruling class has unilaterally suspended the postwar compromise? And how might we rekindle the capacity for violence that historically made such compromise conceivable at a time when violence itself is everywhere repudiated?

To begin, we must insist that acts of political violence be evaluated less on the basis of their immediate tactical effects than on the basis of what they reveal about politics itself. When labor leaders, social democrats, and their members complain—as they did in the immediate aftermath of black bloc actions during the G20—that such acts "ruin it for us," it's necessary to point out that the "it" that's supposedly being ruined (the negotiated settlement of representational politics) in fact no longer exists. Moreover, to the extent that it ever did, "it" came into being precisely by virtue of the violence inherent in—and historically manifested by—the "us" for whom things are supposedly now being "ruined." Conceived in this way, it becomes evident that the only thing being ruined is the self-defeating mythological certainty that there can be politics without violence. To be sure, the forms and points of application for that violence remain open questions; however, these are questions that are impossible to contemplate without having first faced the simple, brutal fact.

Approaching the problem in this way is tremendously liberating, since it points beyond the paternalistic horizon of bourgeois representational politics. At the same time, however, the proposition is terrifying, since it means ceding the cover of legal recognition and rights.

But given the extent to which such recognition and rights are already widely under attack, our options are limited. In the end, we are called upon to question the wisdom of clinging to a sinking ship.

JMJ: You point out that there's a kind of cult of the local, of the community, as the main source of authentic experience. This whole cult of the community began with the Romantics—and therefore, after 1789, was briefly a radical leftist trope before it became a standard banner on the Right. In both cases, it was opposed to markets and to capitalism. On the Right, it reached its apotheosis with fascism, in which the Nation became the community (thus revealing the dangers of assuming that all people share a vision and that anyone who does not needs to be eliminated). Afterward, the concept of community was discredited for a generation. When it was revived in the '60s, it was by people on the Left who still used it as a counterweight to rampant capitalism. Like all collective identities, it seems to have both benefits and risks. Could you talk about those?

AKT: In my book, I recount how the question of race played out in the anti-globalization movement through discussions about the importance of "local organizing" and, eventually, through an identification with "the community" as both a means and a field of struggle. What struck me about these deliberations was that, although "the local" suggests both a scale and an analytic orientation in which anyone— by virtue of their very embodiment—might participate, many white activists had difficulty perceiving it as a category that applied to them. As such, they found themselves in the unusual position of having to go *search* for "the local." In the end, they found it in "the community," which—for the most part—meant the oppressed community.

Movement participants and commentators called for the turn to local and community-based organizing as early as 2000. And, as the movement degenerated after 9/11, such organizing became a useful framework for amassing and redirecting scattered energies. Nevertheless, the turn away from mass confrontations deprived us of an important field of operations, and I don't think the cost of our reorientation was always fully understood.

With respect to "community," it seems clear that movement participants were motivated on the whole by sincerely anti-racist impulses;

however, as was the case during the New Left, these impulses were difficult to separate from a concurrent Romanticism that produced both strategic and analytic distortions. And here, it's useful to recall how—in *Black Power*—Stokely Carmichael described the white radicals attracted to groups like SNCC who, "like some sort of Pepsi generation, have wanted to 'come alive' through black communities… They have wanted to be where the action is—and the action has been in those places. They have sought refuge among blacks from a sterile, meaningless, irrelevant life in middle-class America."[20] The Seattle generation's turn to community-based organizing played out in a similar way; however, this time around, there were few people like Carmichael to insist that white radicals set up freedom schools in white suburbs—and fewer still who would concede that white radicals might need "refuge" from anything.

In addition to allowing the concrete dimensions of white experience to remain unspecified (a problem that dovetails with the racist tradition that holds whiteness to be an abstract universal), the movement's Romantic orientation to community also frequently prevented radicals from acknowledging the term's significant social ambivalence. Nevertheless, as David Harvey has noted, capitalism makes use of community primarily as a means of organizing consumption.[21] Similarly, Miranda Joseph has presented community as a hegemonic strategy for the management of explosive social contradictions.[22] Meanwhile, in the Canadian context, Himani Bannerji has pointed out that community is a managerial category inextricably bound to the project of official multiculturalism.[23]

To the extent that the movement's identification with community was about base building, I think it marked an important development. To the extent that it played the role of affective compensation, however, both the term and the orientation should be held up to further scrutiny.

JMJ: I have a couple other questions about collective identities. You talk about the "middle class," or more specifically about the white middle class, as though that were an unproblematic entity. For that to work, analytically, do members have to think of themselves as middle class? In other words, do they have to identify with their class, or is this a category that you are imposing on them, making sociological claims about their origins, habitus, and so on?

AKT: Regardless of its precise demographic composition, the movement against corporate globalization in Canada and the US was regularly *critiqued* on the grounds of its white and middle-class composition and character. Such critiques were normally aimed at either pushing the movement to become more inclusive (by changing its culture and, potentially, its action repertoire too) or at rendering it politically inadmissible.

As a result, people who wanted to defend the movement tended to do so either by saying that it was *not* actually white and middle class (for example, by pointing to the involvement of people of color) or by insisting that—even if the movement was primarily white and middle class in its composition—it was nevertheless following the lead of activists in the global south and, as such, could not be conceived as being white and middle class in its *orientation*. Movement participant and scholar Amory Starr was among those most committed to defending the movement on these various grounds.[24]

What both of these responses have in common is that they concede from the outset that the movement's white and middle class character was a problem to be solved rather than a thing to be understood. What I try to show in my book is that, not only does such a position lead to profoundly inadequate strategic conclusions (conclusions which fly in the face of anti-racist insights from *Black Power* onward), it also dodges the challenge of trying to explain a phenomenon before trying to "fix" it. Instead of setting out to disprove unflattering allegations, I opted instead to conduct an immanent critique. Consequently, I asked: assuming that what movement critics say is true, how can we develop an understanding of the phenomenon that might help to channel its tremendous energies toward something more transformative?

Almost immediately, what come into view are the many reasons that white and middle class people have for struggling (or, as I put it in my book, for reconnecting with the political sphere).[25] And here we might think of C. Wright Mills' brilliant socio-psychological profile of the white collar worker forever frozen in social inaction,[26] or of Georges Sorel's portrayal of a middle class deluded by its own incessant but meaningless chatter.[27]

Historically, people like this have played the role of social ballast. When they renounce the narcotizing comforts of inaction (comforts granted for being Leviathan's ideal subject), they have tended as often to move rightward as they have to the Left. In retrospect, the rise of the Tea Party in the wake of the anti-globalization movement's decline should have been predictable. I can understand why many radicals may feel annoyed by the need to pay close attention to what appear to be white and middle class movements. At the same time, however, the political stakes are far too high to do otherwise.

JMJ: Finally, I want to raise the issue of representation. This has been a popular word lately—especially with respect to critiques of representation. The word seems to have at least two meanings, but they're related. One has to do with images, with the society of the spectacle replacing real social life somehow. The other has to do with political representation: Is it possible for one person to represent others, to speak on their behalf? They claim to do this either because they were asked—elected—to do it, or because there is a collective identity so strong, so homogeneous, that one person can somehow know the will of her fellow group members. This idea came under a lot of attack during the global justice movement, and the related idea of collective identities did too—as if they were necessarily a distortion of individual needs and visions. Could you talk about this a bit?

AKT: The thing that unites the two forms of "representation" you describe is the fact that, by the end of the twentieth century, they seemed to constitute the entirety of what people understood as "the political." Through the nineteenth century and the early part of the twentieth century, social movements fought to extend political representation to those who had previously been excluded from its purview. With the rise of new social movements, this form of representational struggle was joined—and, on occasion, supplanted—by struggles to determine how the social groups to which we belonged would be perceived by others.

To the extent that the struggle for political representation is connected to the more fundamental struggle for recognition, the character of the demand for recognition seemed to shift at this point. Initially, social movements sought recognition from the state. With the rise of new social movements, this recognition was sought increasingly from more "superstructural" fields and actors—corporations, the media, and "culture" writ large. In the final instance, the demand for recognition fell upon the activist community itself. To the extent that it has allowed us to learn a great deal about each other and to support one another better, this has been useful; however, it has also amounted to a significant diminishment of the scope of the political.

The revitalization of direct action that began in Seattle breaks from both of these forms of representation and forces us to begin thinking about politics in terms of production once again. It's important to note, however, that committing to proceed in a post-representational way is not enough to break representation's grip. The ease with which riots can become spectacle attests to the fact that the representational subsumption of political production will continue right up until representation itself is buried along with its bourgeois architects. For this reason, it's necessary to consider how the representational field might best be strategically exploited even as we work to undermine it. This is one of the questions to which my research currently attends.

MAKING FRIENDS
WITH FAILURE

Some Observations Regarding Richard Day's *Gramsci is Dead: Anarchist Currents in the Newest Social Movements*

It's nice to have a victory every once in a while. As someone who lived through the rise and fall of militant action on this continent during the last dozen years, I should know. These days, there's something demoralizing and vaguely absurd about our habits. We issue urgent call-outs for demonstrations against even more brazen acts of injustice. We look around. We feel our hearts sink a little. But we are reminded over the demonstration PA that today is "only a beginning." A glimmer of hope, you might say. But the tacit acknowledgment is that there's no way for it to get any worse. Welcome to rock bottom. And though there might be some cold comfort in this certainty, when witnessed from the standpoint of a broken heart, it's hard to imagine how the freedom of having nothing might ever be transformed into a program for a better world.

This essay first appeared in *Upping the Anti: A Journal of Theory and Action*, Number Three, November 2006.

We adjust. We become a subculture of compulsive beginners. After all, the energy of the beginning is almost always more satisfying than the dead reckoning required by that moment in which we recognize that we can never go back. Only a beginning—we're not building, we're *prefiguring*. It's as if, all of a sudden or once again, activism means being bound by a ritualized therapeutic injunction to perpetually return to the site of trauma. Cynics might even announce that, since we have shown ourselves to be incapable of winning the list of demands under which we've mobilized, the true act of courage is admitting that we can't win. Not like this, anyway.

The secret is out. "Activism" and its contentious repertoires have become ritualized. In 2003, CrimethInc. proclaimed it with usual gusto in their *Inside Front: International Journal of Hardcore Punk and Anarchist Action*: "We have worked hard to improve activism—now it must be destroyed!"[1] And again, "We activists have tried to develop a code of behavior and language that is free of domination, an alienation free protocol—but protocol itself is alienating, unless one is among those actively developing it."[2] We lament the fact that the movement doesn't grow. We steel our resolve. We try to become more open, more inclusive. And even though it might not lead to active engagement from broad sectors of society, our ritual—admit it—has become comforting.

For those who live them, the dynamics of contention follow the rhythms of the seasons or of the religious calendar. They reintroduce the cyclic time of a world that capitalism left behind. The coalitions we plant today produce neither roots nor fruits but only momentary flowers before dying of chill or neglect.[3] It is painful, pitiful. But there is no other remedy than the repetition of the act. Lather, rinse, repeat: the act becomes everything. It is therefore not surprising that some of us sew patches onto our clothes so that we can make our profession of faith to the world: "Even if the world was going to end tomorrow, I would still plant a tree today" [Fig. 1]. Somehow, this religious notion (often attributed apocryphally to Martin Luther) has become the pinnacle of activist non-compliance with the means-ends tyranny of capitalism's incessant productive rationality. Our actions don't have to be rational. They don't even have to accomplish anything. They just have to be good. Good in and of themselves.

But it can't go on forever. There's a point when the memory of victory kicks in and taunts us, though we might try to ignore it. Images of

Fig. 1.

the Paris Commune infect our dreams. N30 becomes fuel firing cylinders in the engine of a powerful myth. And so a problem arises: what do you do if you need a victory but can't win? If you're one of the activists that Richard Day champions in his well-received book *Gramsci Is Dead: Anarchist Currents in the Newest Social Movements*,[4] you change the rules of the game. Better yet, you turn your radical act of refusal into an ethical principle of the first order and remind everyone around you that you wouldn't waste your time playing according to those rules anyway.

I've got to admit it's a pretty seductive argument. Moreover, it seems to capture perfectly the spirit of defeat that hangs over these trying times. Released in 2006, the text is in many ways a eulogy for the anti-globalization movement. And it feels like seditious reading—the kind of thing that gives you a front row seat to a fistfight between delusion and the reality principle. From this vantage, it's easy to believe that the bravest act of all is admitting that the thing we all loved is now gone. Time to move on.

It's on account of Day's ability to combine crisp writing with unrepentant iconoclasm that we can understand the remarkable resonance the book has had among activists beleaguered by the humiliations of failure. Day's is a New Testament. Gone are the days of hegemonic combat where we trade eyes for eyes. The days of war, whether carried out in the spirit of the lion or the fox, are over. In their place, we're offered a vision of affinity based on "groundless solidarity and infinite responsibility."[5] Love thy neighbor. Turn the other cheek. Build the New Jerusalem right here in the lapses and gaps of neoliberalism's totalizing vision.

The anti-globalization movement, which was never able to pull itself out from under the rubble of the World Trade Center, is dead. In the opening passages of *Gramsci*, Day admits that his personal confidence in that movement faded at the demonstration against the WTO mini-ministerial meeting in Montreal during the hot summer of 2003. Having been in the streets on that day, I can understand his dismay. What a disaster. There's something grotesque about being outnumbered and outmaneuvered by riot cops, chased this way and that through back alleys and parking lots and then calling the whole thing "resistance." Whatever bravado had steeled our spines at the perfunctory spokescouncil the night before evaporated as we watched our comrades get arrested *en masse* outside the *Librairie Anarchiste* on Rue St. Laurent.

For Day, however, the experience was one of liberating proportions. Notepad and pencil in hand, he stares down a riot cop blocking his exit. The cop hits baton against shield. Day hits pencil against paper. Visions of mighty pens and meager swords light the scene with euphoric incandescence. And so, while "the response to 9/11, coupled with the ongoing wars in Iraq and Afghanistan, has dealt what looks like a death blow to the most visible expressions of resistance to neoliberalism in the global north," things can't possibly be as bad as they seem. "This could mean that a time of mourning is at hand," says Day soberly; however, "many do not lament the demise of this phase of struggle."[6] This was because the logic underlying the convergences in Seattle, Quebec City, and Genoa had limited value. Specifically, while Day saw these moments as an opportunity to illuminate the barbarity of the neoliberal project, the protests could not undo the logic of a system organized to perpetually reproduce itself. Worse, the protests—in those instances in which they revealed a will to hegemony—may even have managed to reinforce that logic.

The big question posed in *Gramsci is Dead*, then, is "now that the cops of the G8 countries are no longer surprised by direct action tactics, now that their political masters are willing to broadly adopt the repressive tactics of what are hypocritically called 'Third World dictatorships,' how will the struggle against globalizing capital—and the many systems of domination and exploitation with which it is inextricably linked—continue?"[7] For Day, the answer to this question can be found in an assessment of the "deeper, broader and longer-running currents"[8] guiding the struggles of Indigenous peoples and the people of the global south. This orientation, to which Day attributes a mythic longevity ensuring that it will "continue as it always has, for hundreds of years, taking a multiplicity of forms,"[9] is characterized by its emphasis on affinity.

Starting in Ancient Greece and moving sure-footedly toward Deleuze and Guattari's *Thousand Plateaus*, Day devotes considerable effort to producing a genealogical account of how currents of affinity and hegemony have evolved over time and within different political traditions. However, while the genealogies Day provides allow us to understand the manner in which *ideas* about polity and struggle have come to take the forms they sometimes have, they do not in and of themselves explain why contemporary political actors engage in the *manner* that they do. After all, a genealogy cannot in itself explain how an idea becomes a material force, or how it comes to saturate the air at a given moment.

This problem becomes especially evident when one considers that most of the activists in Day's "newest social movements" are neither likely to possess his archival facility nor to be familiar with his chosen citations. Since this is the case, the orientation to struggle championed by Day—one that yields "semi-permanent autonomous zones"[10] even as it eradicates (or dismisses as unimportant or dangerous) the capacity to produce mediated means-ends correspondences—requires another explanation. This explanation is not to be found in the *logic* of either hegemony or affinity but rather in the ongoing defeats of anti-capitalist hegemonic struggle and, correspondingly, in the ongoing hegemony of bourgeois norms.

But rather than investigate the concrete problems that led to such a profound demobilization of what had during the short years between Seattle and Genoa become a kind of nascent world historical force; rather than provide a critical account of our failures so that they might serve as the basis for reassessment and rebuilding, Day chooses instead to disengage from the activities of those who have failed (because they are bound by their still incomplete break from the logic of hegemony to always do so) and to point, triumphantly, to those few who have managed to win some small piece of freedom right here in the present—the crusty punks, the Food Not Bombs kids, the sleep-and-sun deprived nocturnal creatures that make indymedia.org an object of wonder. If this sounds too harsh, it suffices to jump past the book's 200 odd pages of dusty genealogical suasion to get to the heart of the matter:

> Revolution and reform have failed to produce the goods, it is true, and neither the masses nor the mass have any political potential. However, what it seems cannot *ever* be done *for anyone at all* using hegemonic methods can perhaps be done *by* some of us, *here and now.*[11]

Day is willing to admit that this argument has an elitist ring to it. However, he is unwilling to let that get in the way. Since the premise of the argument is that the logic of affinity draws its inspiration from the struggles of those in the global south, activists in the North engaged in acts of prefiguration are in fact showing respect and solidarity toward those who have paved the way. And while all this may be fine in principle, the argument—as presented—relies upon and is made possible by unscrupulous distortions and glaring acts of omission.[12] And so it is that, historical details, messy though they are, need to be addressed. However, instead of history, what Day offers is an erudite but unconvincing theorization of the shortcomings of revolutionary hegemonic politics based on their identity—at the level of *desire*—with the politics of the system of control.

> Because they share ... the desire for emancipation by extra-individual, extra-community structures of coercive power, (neo)liberalism and (post)marxism can be said to participate in an *ethics of desire*, a set of principles and outlooks that perpetuate a self-imposed failure and provide a cover for the abdication of the difficult tasks associated with autonomous individual and communal self-determination.[13]

Revolutionaries are just like those who maintain order in the present because both are bound by a desire to have power over others. This desire, when expressed by those who aim to change the world in the name of autonomous individual and communal self-determination, becomes a cipher through which the inevitable self-imposed failure passes and becomes invisible. In order to get out of this cycle, Day points to the example provided by movements of the global south and the North American anarchists who have dutifully followed their lead. It is a celebratory and self-valorizing move.

Admittedly, Day is not the first to make it. Perhaps most memorable amongst the numerous prior instances was the post-A16 edition of CBC's Counterspin, during which an overenthusiastic Avi Lewis barely contained his glee as guest Vandana Shiva proposed that the organizational paradigm for the DC action had "a third world flavor." Whatever one might choose to understand by such a peculiar phrase, such flavor proved insufficient to entice DC's vast Black population to participate. Irene Tung, who was interviewed for a *ColorLines* article dealing with precisely this problem, provided the following striking summation:

> There was definitely an insider's culture at A16, especially at the convergence spaces. There was a vocabulary and behavior,

an assumed cultural commonality, that was somewhat eerie. It seems that the ideals of absence of leadership and 'facilitated chaos'—as they say—function best in a homogenous group.[14]

Although they were supposed to be inclusive and sensitive to experiences of oppression, many activists pointed out how the movement's sensibilities did not resonate with most of the city's poor and Black residents. Despite being concerned with issues that directly affected those communities, DC's Black residents seemed not to recognize either the viability of the tactical paradigm or the possibility that the rain-soaked kids were somehow "allies." In order for this recognition to emerge, it would first have been necessary to produce a situation that would have allowed people to envision a common project in which all might feel a pressing implication. In short, it would have required a hegemonic orientation and a willing-ness to forge a collective "we" out of disparate, scattered, and often contradictory experiences.

As John Sanbonmatsu has suggested, politics requires assertion. Rather than starting from the standpoint of an imperfectable ethic of inclusion, the task of political actors is to demonstrate—through their actions—that another option exists. It is only by creating conditions whereby others can see the common thread connecting seemingly dis-crete moments that politics moves beyond the processual equivalent of good table manners. Sanbonmatsu explains: "Radical pedagogy as such functions to reveal or bring to light what would otherwise remain unseen—the hidden structures of meaning and power that shape our lives—and this can only happen by revealing the whole."[15] This project takes the form of a general necessity, a procedure without which politics itself would be impossible.

Every so-called critical social movement seeks to reveal the background itself—that is, to make the background, as it were, become figure. For only once the background becomes figure does the perceiver comprehend that what she or he first took to be an "isolated datum"—e.g., a rape, a layoff of workers, a cleared rainforest—is in fact nothing of the kind, but rather a "moment" in a larger structure of meaning that can be known, analyzed, and potentially defeated.[16]

Such a capacity is not currently in evidence in North America, where a vast gulf continues to separate the dying fragments of a white middle class movement from the rest of the population. Prefigurative experiments, despite the pedagogical opportunities that they could in principle furnish, cannot in and of themselves do the hard work of analysis—nor can they uncover the points at which multiple grievances intertwine to form the fabric of solidarity.

In *Pacifism as Pathology*, Ward Churchill advances a damning critique of prefigurative politics and the decoupling of means and ends that often accompanies their expression. In his account, middle-class North American pacifists are indicted for leaving the difficult and potentially costly aspects of struggle to those who are objectively least able to carry these burdens but who nevertheless do the lion's share of the fighting in the global struggle for justice. And while North American pacifists, in Churchill's estimation, are willing to support the armed struggles of Third World revolutionary movements, they are far less willing to engage in acts that might lead them to confront the force of their opponent directly.

In order to resolve this contradiction, Churchill argues that these activists advance either moral or tactical arguments against the use of violence. Now on this high horse, it becomes possible to prefigure the kind of society that people ought to live in once the revolution arrives. "What we are left with is a husk of opposition," says Churchill, "a kind of ritual form capable of affording a sentimentalistic ... satisfaction to its subscribers at a psychic level but utterly useless in terms of transforming the power relations perpetuating systematic global violence."

> Such a defect, however, can readily be sublimated within the aggregate comfort zone produced by the continuation of North American business as usual; those who remain within the parameters of nondisruptive dissent allowed by the state, their symbolic duty to the victims of U.S. policy done (and with the bases of state power wholly unchallenged), can devote themselves to the prefiguration of the revolutionary future society with which they proclaim they will replace the present social order (having, no doubt, persuaded the state to overthrow itself through the moral force of their arguments).[17]

Among the activities that Churchill includes in his list of prefigurative practices favored by elite North American activists are sexual experimentation, refinement of musical or artistic tastes, going vegetarian or vegan, unleashing the id through meditation or drug use, overthrowing the gender hierarchy by redistributing household chores, and (his personal sore spot) engaging in campaigns to prohibit cigarette smoking. "Small wonder," says Churchill, "that North America's ghetto, barrio, and reservation populations, along with the bulk of the white working class … tend to either stand aside in bemused incomprehension of such politics or react with outright hostility."[18]

There's a bit of an industry of critique established for dealing with arguments such as this one. And Churchill sometimes makes an easy target of himself. Surely there is something to be gained, at the level of gender equity, in the redistribution of household chores. And while such gestures do not in and of themselves amount to a dismantling of the gender hierarchy, they do enable people to build trust and respect and they can on occasion allow women to participate more directly in political decision-making and task sharing. Nevertheless, the bemusement and hostility Churchill points to can hardly be disputed.

Although the prefigurative acts it cites are somewhat different from the ones highlighted by Churchill, *Gramsci is Dead* sets out to describe the varied practices by which contemporary activists try to carve out spaces of humanizing autonomy: independent media centers, critical mass bike rides, and squats are all given due consideration. However, among this list of "non-branded" tactics (each of which holds a place of prominence in the North American repertoire of action), Day inserts some unlikely contenders—like the *piqueteros*, Argentina's unemployed workers movement. According to Day, such an inclusion is justified by the fact that the *piqueteros*, like the anarchists of the newest social movements, organize according to the premises of autonomy.

RTS [Reclaim the Streets], IMC [Independent Media Center], neighborhood assembly, Social Centre, Food Not Bombs, land and factory occupation—all of these tactics consciously defy the logic of reform/revolution by refusing to work through the state, party, or corporate forms. Instead, they are driven by an orientation to meeting individual/group/community needs by direct action. Not only do they refuse to deploy traditional tactics that seek to alter/replace existing nodes of power/significa-cation, their own organizational structures are designed so as to avoid situations where one individual or group is placed 'above' others in a hierarchical relationship.[19]

Given this assessment, it is hard to imagine how the *piqueteros* could be collapsed into Day's vision of affinity. Indeed, the actions of the *piqueteros* are not ends in themselves. The point of unemployed workers blocking major roads is not to have a party or engage in an act of reclamation pure and simple. Rather, it is an instrumental use of coercive power exerted to accomplish political ends that, in the first instance, are not immediately achievable by the actors themselves. They act so that others might act as they would like them to. It is a negotiation with power based on emergent capacities, an instance of the "politics of demand" that Day derides.[20]

Here, Day argues that the manner in which social movements make demands on the state often ends up perpetuating state power by expecting that it will respond. Loosely following Žižek and Lacan, Day proposes that what is needed to break out of the loop created by the politics of demand is a politics of *the act*. This politics, which for Day demands a one-to-one correspondence between means and ends, involves "inventing responses that preclude the necessity of the demand and thereby break out of the loop."[21]

But while the possibility that State control might increase as a result of the inadvertent recognition extended by those advancing political demands makes some sense as an abstract model, it begins to fall apart when considered in light of examples like the *piqueteros*. When approached as an historical rather than a theoretical problem, the politics of demand reveal themselves to be crucial in the move from disparate "of itself" formations to conscious "for itself" ones. Moreover, the suggestion that those advancing demands are simply recognizing the sovereign authority of the state denies that such demands might be advanced strategically and without illusions. In order to get a sense of how such a strategic orientation plays out in practice, it suffices to recall a number of *piquetero* actions staged in August and September of 2004 and described by journalist Marcela Valente.

Over the past few weeks, the demonstrators have occupied ticket booths in the Constitución train station in Buenos Aires, securing a promise from the private concessionaire running that railway line to reinstate nine employees who were laid off and create 52 new jobs. "Our goal is not to interrupt transit or make problems for the passengers of trains, but to pressure the companies to create jobs, by hurting them economically," said the activist. In this case they are doing that by occupying ticket booths, a form of protest that enables passengers to ride the trains for free, thus gaining the protesters support that they were not earning with the roadblocks.[22]

Moreover, it can hardly be said that the *piqueteros* refuse to work through the state since many of their community endeavors are made possible by limited funds provided by Argentina's welfare rolls. In short, what the *piqueteros* have produced is a practical model of struggle that bears little resemblance to the vision of autonomy fostered by the theorists of the global north who celebrate them. It is hard to imagine how Day would reconcile his vision of groundless solidarity and infinite responsibility with the fact that *piqueteros* who fail to show up for their regular community work details are cut off from needed funds. Far from being an expression of affinity as Day describes it, the *piquetero* struggle is predicated on a collective agreement amongst participants to abide by the disciplinary pull of coercive power. It's a simple method. And it is one that is very effective.

And so while Day is able to draw parallels based on a superficial similarity in sensibility, he cannot address the problem of formulating goals or determining how we will move from here to there. Since, by definition, such goals are instrumental and imply a degree of coercion, they are not on the agenda for Day's politics of affinity. It makes for strange reading. For instance, while Day acknowledges that none of the practices catalogued in the opening section of his book are *purely* based on affinity, he nevertheless ignores the obvious point that it is precisely on the basis of the *piqueteros*' attempt to make *hegemonic* assertions—by creating a "we," advancing demands, and organizing to assert oppositional power—that they have been as effective as they have.

Instead, by pointing to a superficial similarity, Day makes it possible for the desperate-hopeful reader who has lived through the tragic demise of the North American movement to believe that their Food Not Bombs group is as consequential as a several-thousand strong national movement that has managed through its actions to shut down a country's entire transportation infrastructure. In order to see the folly of such an approach, it suffices to contrast, without comment, Day's own account of the successes of the *Piqueteros* to the description of Food Not Bombs provided by that organization on its website.

Argentina's *Movimento de Tra-bajadores Desocupados* ... have been extremely successful in using the tactic of highway blockades to express frustration with existing institutions. In August 2001, for example, a nation-wide mobilization of federated local groups managed to close more than 300 highways, thereby severely limiting the ability of the capitalist economy to maintain the flow of goods upon which it depends.[23]

Food Not Bombs is an all-volunteer organization dedicated to nonviolent social change. Food Not Bombs has no formal leaders and strives to include everyone in its decision making process. Each group recovers food that would otherwise be thrown out and makes fresh hot vegetarian meals that are served outside in public spaces to anyone without restriction. Each independent group also serves free vegetarian meals at protests and other events. The San Francisco chapter has been arrested over 1,000 times in government's effort to silence its protest against the city's anti-homeless policies.[24]

The tragedy of Day's argument lies in the fact that all of this has happened before. It's been played out, and the results are in. Politics without force of assertion is unworthy of the name. Force of assertion implies conflict between antagonists. And whatever wisdom can be salvaged from the idea that we ought to try to build a better world in the cracks of neoliberalism's totalizing reach crumbles in our hands when we assert that these prefigurations, these semi-permanent autonomous zones, ought to be *consequential*. The second they're consequential is the second they'll be noticed. At that point, it becomes impossible to break the cycle of antagonism by will alone. They will come after us. They have before.

In 1649, a group of peasants in Surrey, England created a semi-permanent autonomous zone. Outraged at enclosure and motivated by a peculiar reading of Christian scriptures, the Diggers—like many of the sects that came into being during the Protestant Reformation—believed that their vision of a better world could be lived in the present. And so they set out to occupy wastelands, denounce landlords, and make the Earth "a common treasury." Under the guidance of Gerrard Winstanley, they staked their claim on St. George's Hill. In many respects, the logic that guided them is indistinguishable from the one underlying Day's thesis.

In his prophetic writings, Winstanley divides the England of the world, which he associates with the lingering traces of Norman rule and the hypocrisy of clerical law (hegemony), from the England-Israel that seeks to make liberty manifest through its acts (affinity). According to Winstanley, "not one word was spoken in the beginning, That one branch of mankind should rule over another." His reasoning had to do with reason itself: "And the reason is this, Every single man, Male and Female, is a perfect Creature of Himself; and the same Spirit that made the Globe, dwels in man to govern the Globe."[25]

Having established this principle, the Diggers were able to act with conviction and in an ethically consistent manner. Their plan was to heal the divisions of the world by living *as if* it was a common treasury. They argued that people should take over the wastelands so that they might be sown. In the process, they would do more than free themselves from hunger; they would expel those who abided by the letter but not the spirit of the law, those that "made the Earth stinck every where, by oppressing others, under pretense of worshipping the Spirit rightly, by the Types and Sacrifices of Moses Law."[26] Since men of this kind were still among them, they felt a moral and political obligation to rid themselves of their presence so that the Earth could once again be made whole—could once again reflect the light shining from the New Jerusalem.

That such direct action was intended to bring the New Jerusalem into being is beyond doubt. When recounting the words that God had spoken to the Diggers, Winstanley makes clear that theirs was the struggle to set Israel free. In this moment, he also outlines the program for the Digger rebellion, detailing the strategy, the manner by which it would be implemented, and the means by which it could be generalized. For instance, Winstanley enjoins workers not to sell their labor to others or to pay rent, since doing so meant submitting to the will of another and disrupting the equality at the heart of Creation.

"But they that are resolved to work and eat together, making the Earth a Common Treasury, doth joyn hands with Christ, to lift up the Creation from Bondage, and restore all things from the Curse."[27]

One can see in this vision the same spark that catches Day's eye when he recounts Gustav Landauer's claim that new forms of social cohesion needed to be created "alongside, rather than inside, existing forms of social organization."[28] Like Landauer, Day's argument rests on the premise that the social revolution "should be carried out here and now, for its own sake, by and for those who wished to establish new relationships not mediated by state and corporate forms."[29] But the desire to live in an unmediated state is not all that is required to create it, or to ensure that the forces of repression do not intervene. And while Day assures us that the totalizing reach of the neoliberal project will always crack under the weight of its own logic and leave unguarded spaces in which activists can live free of constraint, he neglects to consider how liberated ground might be defended in those instances when—as a result of our initial successes—movement participants begin spilling out from the safety of the cracks.

As is well known, the Diggers did not prevail. And their failure can only be understood if it is examined from the standpoint of the course they plotted between means and ends. Winstanley's account reveals that the Diggers had both a clear vision of the political problem and a clear basis on which they thought it could be opposed. However, the means chosen to enact that opposition did not take into full consideration the conditions of the struggle itself. Attempting to oppose the dominant order of their day by creating an approximation of the future order alongside it (a strategy that Day, following Landauer, endorses), Winstanley and his followers turned their attention away from the landlords' power. And while there may be no swords in God's kingdom, it might have been useful for the Diggers to have had access to some on St. George's Hill.

The posited identity between means and ends demanded by the politics of affinity will no doubt be satisfying to those for whom it is a possibility. For the rest of us, there is struggle. War, sometimes open, sometimes hidden, has never stopped being a political reality. For his part, Day acknowledges that revolutionary political orientations can't be discounted in all cases, and that models based on affinity can't be applied across the board (since to do so would be to render them hegemonic). However, he does assert that these models need to be investigated more fully than they have been to date.[30] Only then, Day claims, will it become possible to recognize the limited prospects of the revolutionary orientation.

I would like to propose an alternate conclusion. It takes the form of a passage from *The Eighteenth Brumaire*, in which Marx recounts the orientation to failure adopted by the revolutionary movements of the proletariat. These movements, Marx thought,

> criticize themselves constantly, interrupt themselves continually in their own course, come back to the apparently accomplished in order to begin it afresh, deride with unmerciful thoroughness the inadequacies, weaknesses and paltriness of their first attempts, seem to throw down their adversary only in order that he may draw new strength from the earth and rise again, more gigantic, before them, recoil ever and anon from the indefinite prodigiousness of their own aims, until a situation has been created which makes all the turning back impossible, and the conditions themselves cry out: *Hic Rhodus, hic salta!* Here is the rose, here dance![31]

Failure is endemic to any project whose goal is as lofty as human emancipation. It cannot be ignored or appeased. It cannot be buried under good intentions or changed into its opposite by holding it up to the mirror of wishful thinking. What failure calls for most of all is honesty. And the truth should hurt. What Day offers up is salve for the wounded. But the price of that salve is the forfeiture of the "indefinite prodigiousness" of our own aims. In the end, this is the greatest failure of all.

"DAILY LIFE" NOT A "MOMENT" LIKE THE REST

Notes On David Harvey's "Organizing for the Anti-Capitalist Transition"

I

There's something sobering about taking stock. Coming to terms with the enormity of a problem, cataloguing the resources at our disposal, daring to dream, and plotting a course out of the storm by fixing our sights on that sun rising in the sky of history: these *should* be the habits of highly effective radicals. However, as David Harvey points out in his "Organizing for the Anti-Capitalist Transition," we are currently living through a moment when exactly opposite habits seem to prevail. And so, while the current capitalist crisis *should* be pushing "the future of capitalism itself" to "the forefront of ... debate," the sad truth is that there's "little appetite for such discussion, even among the left."[1]

This essay first appeared in *Interface: A Journal For and About Social Movements* (Volume 2, Issue 1, May 2010) in a special section entitled "Debating David Harvey." Along with this piece, contributors including Willie Baptist and Laurence Cox were invited to respond to Harvey's "Organizing for the Anti-capitalist Transition," an article based on his comments at the 2010 World Social Forum in Porto Alegre, Brazil. http://www.interfacejournal.net/2010/05/interface-21-crises-social-movements-and-revolutionary-transformations/.

I know the truth should hurt. But even as I wrote that paragraph, I thought about deleting it.

It ruffled my feathers, and the rebuke flew from my mouth before the words hit the page: surely Harvey is overstating the problem. True, the crisis of capitalist legitimacy that threatened to overwhelm the system in 2008 may be on the wane for the countless millions who rely on *Fox* for their news of the world. But can the same really be said for "the left?" For those of us who have devoted our lives to infusing that category with substance, the current crisis (and the possibilities it's opened up!) can often seem like the *only* thing we talk about. And more: though they remain pitifully small, we shouldn't ignore the many new forms of anti-capitalist analysis and action that have come into being as a result of the meltdown.

In Toronto, where I currently live, a newly formed workers' assembly has brought together diverse forces from the social movement and trade union Left. It's stated objective has been to forge a fighting collective capable of exerting a power greater than that of its constituent parts. Along with its diligent assessment of opportunities for mobilization, the assembly has also committed itself to developing popular anti-capitalist educational resources for use in workplaces and community spaces. As outlined on their website, their goals are:

> To bring together activists within the broad working class movement, … [t]o share our understanding of the problems created by capitalism and the current economic crisis and the need to develop alternative visions … [and] … to identify and develop concrete strategies and organizational forms of struggle which defend working-class people's immediate needs and lay the groundwork for an equitable and democratic alternative to our present economic and political system.[2]

On the other side of the planet (and well outside the bounds of the familiar activist scene), mainstream Japanese book publishers have begun cashing in on the renewed popularity of works by Karl Marx. According to EastPress representative Yusuke Maruo, "people are looking to Marx for answers to the problems with the capitalist society. … Obviously, the recent global crisis suggests that the system isn't working properly." In 2008, EastPress issued a comic book version of *Capital.* It quickly became a hot commodity. According to

Maruo, the publisher thought that the book would strike a chord with thirty-something office workers. It turns out they were right.[3] A lover of both communist kitsch and sequential art, I'm eagerly awaiting the North American edition.

II

Depending on how broadly we set our criteria (and depending on how optimistic we might be feeling after a good demo or a few drinks), the number of possible entries to a catalogue like the one I just began assembling can seem inexhaustible. So why did I allow Harvey's assessment, recounted in the first paragraph, to stand?

The sad truth is that, despite their promise, current anti-capitalist experiments remain insignificant when measured against the monumental challenges we face. And though the dynamics of crisis may call taken-for-granted assumptions into question, there's no guarantee that these assumptions will be replaced with anything resembling a coherent program for change. Indeed, radical responses to crisis often tend to oscillate between an unstrategic immediatism and a fetishistic devotion to the challenging work of a "first instance" that, in fact, never ends.

To get a sense of these oscillations, it suffices to consider how, in response to the looming ecological catastrophe, forest defense activist Jeff Free Luers has advanced antithetical propositions as though the crisis itself reconciled them. Sentenced to 23 years for setting three SUVs ablaze in Oregon, Luers writes that the ecological crisis requires that we "smash it, break it, block it, lock down to it." In fact, Luers proclaims, "I don't care what you do or how you do it. Just stop it. Get out there and stop it."[4] However, a few pages later, Luers calls this very same bravado into question. "Building community is the first phase of building effective revolutionary movement (it also takes a really long time…)."[5] Considered independently, both pronouncements appear coherent and wise. Taken together, however, it's difficult to ignore how profoundly unresolved they remain from the standpoint of strategy.

There's no doubt that crisis stimulates action. However, there's no guarantee that this action will be strategically coherent or consistent. We must therefore concede that, despite the enormity of the obstacles we face, the only thing worse than *doing nothing* is *doing anything*.[6] It's therefore important that we contemplate (as Harvey does) Lenin's perennial question: what is to be done?

III

But while I find Harvey's account of the current capitalist crisis to be for the most part correct, and while I think his typology of forces capable of partaking in the struggle to transform the world is for the most part accurate,[7] I have some concerns with his presentation of the "co-revolutionary" theory of political transformation. According to Harvey, "social change arises through the dialectical unfolding of relations between seven moments within the body politic of capitalism." In order for this process to add up to a revolutionary transformation, it's crucial that the "political movement" move from "one moment to another in mutually reinforcing ways."[8]

All of this sounds fine. Things get complicated, however, upon consideration of the divisions that Harvey draws between the seven "moments." According to Harvey, the co-revolutionary process must operate within and between 1) "technological and organizational forms of production, exchange and consumption," 2) "relations to nature," 3) "social relations between people," 4) "mental conceptions of the world," 5) "labor processes," 6) "institutional, legal, and governmental arrangements," and, finally, what he calls 7) "the conduct of daily life that underpins social reproduction."[9] Harvey notes that each of these moments is dependent on and evolves with the others. Consequently (although he does not say so explicitly), the distinction between them is best understood as a formal-conceptual one rather than one grounded in social ontology.

I will concede the value that such an approach may have when trying to schematically convey the multiple intersecting aspects of this world. However, as a conceptualization of the *terrain of struggle*, I fear that such schematism is doomed to be inadequate. This is so not only because consideration of actual social relations reveals the extent to which the distinctions drawn between Harvey's different "moments" is arbitrary; it is also because—from the standpoint of social ontology—the conceptual categories that make up Harvey's schema are in no sense isomorphic. More specifically, I fear that Harvey's formalization of the seven moments misses the fact that what he calls "daily life" should, in fact, be granted analytic and strategic primacy.

In making this case, I'm aware that Harvey will likely dismiss me along with other social theorists that view one "moment" as the "'silver bullet' that causes all change."[10] However, such a response must still contend with the fact that "daily life" is not a "moment" like the rest. Despite being cast as one term among others in Harvey's formal typology, "daily life" both predates and permeates all the others. It is their social base and their condition of possibility. And it's on this basis that it must be given both analytic and strategic primacy. This does not mean that the other moments are unimportant; however, it does mean that—if we are to understand them correctly—it's necessary to avoid describing (or engaging with) them solely from within the framework of their own conceptual relevancies.[11]

IV

In what follows, I highlight what I view to be the analytic centrality of daily life in Marxist thought. However, my objective is not simply to refurbish orthodoxy in the face of its inevitable decline. Instead, I raise the question of daily life's analytic importance in the hope of clarifying what I view to be its strategic significance for contemporary radicals. Significantly, the connection between daily-life-as-analysis and daily-life-as-strategy finds expression in Harvey's own contribution in his consideration of contemporary "anarchist, autonomist, and grass roots organizations." Despite their small size and political limitations, these formations are significant for their tendency to emphasize the importance of "daily situations" and for their "experiments with anti-capitalist politics." As such, I argue that they must be at the forefront of our strategic considerations when determining how to constitute a new anti-capitalist "we" in the global north.

But while the anarchist and autonomist formations mentioned by Harvey are unique in making daily life the basis of their anti-capitalism, it's not my intention to claim that these forces are in and of themselves sufficient. Nor do I believe that, when a broad anti-capitalist "we" is finally constituted, it will resemble these formations in any obvious sense. However, given the Left's limited energies and the enormity of the challenges we confront, I believe that it's necessary for us to consider both what can be learned from these formations and how their insights might be extended and clarified in the process of constituting a broader anti-capitalist "we" capable of initiating a revolutionary transformation.

By infusing their consideration of the dynamics of everyday life with a deeply felt anti-capitalism, today's autonomists distinguish themselves from the other forces on Harvey's list. It's therefore not surprising that, when considered alongside "NGOs," "traditional labor organizations and left political parties," and "contemporary emancipatory movements focused on questions of identity,"[12] these formations show exceptional vitality. Whereas the other forces listed by Harvey have all (to varying degrees) been absorbed into the representational paradigm of liberal democracy, autonomists have been resolute in their disavowal of what some theorist's have called the politics of demand. As Harvey himself notes, they are marked by "a common antipathy to negotiation with state power and an emphasis upon civil society as the sphere where change can be accomplished."[13]

What these groups lack in terms of coordination, scale, and discipline is offset by their robust—if primarily affective—conception of the promise and possibility of building, living, and loving in another world. Alongside those movements that Harvey identifies as resisting "displacement and dispossession,"[14] contemporary autonomists have made the everyday a site of analysis and strategic engagement. However, unlike movements against displacement and dispossession, the anarchist and autonomist engagement with the everyday has not been "pragmatic."[15] Instead, it has been informed by what Harvey calls a "particular political philosophy."[16] And so, despite the possible emergence of "organic intellectuals" within the struggle against dispossession,[17] it's only amongst autonomists that the material apperception of everyday reality is currently linked directly to an explicit theory of revolutionary change.

Whenever these movements have escaped the bounds of their own natural enclaves, the results have been striking. It's therefore not surprising that, when considering the past few years, anarchist or autonomist inflections have marked many of the most intense and inspiring mobilizations against capitalism. In their actions, these movements have managed to concoct an intoxicating mix of what Herbert Marcuse called a "biological hatred" of capitalism with a disavowal of political claim-making in order to foster a (sometimes naïve) conception of unmediated actualization.[18]

V

The uprising in Greece at the end of 2008 and the ongoing wave of student occupations in the United States (to cite but two recent and prominent examples) are best understood in these terms. At the outset of the uprising in Greece, Valia Kaimaki reported in *Le Monde Diplomatique* that the revolt was being led by "the very young." This was because "daily life for most young Greeks is dominated by intensive schooling aimed at securing a university place. ... But once the lucky ones get there, they soon discover the reality of life after university: at best, a job at €700 ($1,000) a month."[19] In this account, the connection drawn between daily life and analysis is explicit. But the emphasis on daily life permeated the movement's strategic considerations too.

As Kaimaki reports, everyday people in the riot zones intervened on behalf of those with whom they shared social bonds: "they have often tried to chase off the riot police. Small shopkeepers shout at them to get lost; passers-by wade in to try and rescue students they've arrested. Having understood they cannot keep their children at home, parents and grandparents join them on the streets in order to look after them."[20]

In the US, students involved in the occupation of the UC system have issued startling pronouncements that (despite their undeniably Romantic inflection) have elaborated both an analysis and a radical refusal of the capitalist catastrophe from the standpoint of their own situated experience. Here, for instance, is an account from *After the Fall*, a collection of communiqués from "Occupied California."

> Before the Fall we felt it briefly, in each hour and a half interval: the ten minute grace period between classes, waiting for a lecture to begin, assigning ourselves one uncomfortable chair amongst 130 other uncomfortable chairs. ... We are kept alive, vaccinated, some even plump, yes, but we feel our surplus status. Excess. Excessive. This excessiveness animates our underlying dissatisfaction. ... And yet in the Fall something broke. Students and staff made a different claim on the university.[21]

Historically speaking, the actions in Greece and the occupations in California find their most obvious antecedent in the uprisings of May '68. International in scope but expressed most vividly on the streets of Paris, these uprisings were notable for their politicization of daily life. Situtationist agitator Raoul Vaneigem produced what remains one of the most provocative accounts of this emphasis: "People who talk about revolution and class struggle without referring explicitly to everyday life, without understanding what is subversive about love and what is positive in the refusal of constraints—such people have a corpse in their mouth."[22]

The obvious connection between today's politicization of daily life and the events of May '68 signals both promise and danger. As in 1968, the emphasis on the everyday reveals how analysis can be materialized so as to constitute a "we" on the grounds of an increasingly concrete universality. However, as a political category, "the everyday" has always traced a hazardous course between concrete reckoning and self-valorizing subjectivism. Indeed, '68 shows just how easily the energetic outbursts of a movement focused on daily life might be reabsorbed by the shrewd maneuvers of constituted power and the seemingly infinite flexibility of capitalism.[23] Given these hazards, it's necessary to develop a clear analysis of (and clear strategic orientation to) the limitations of current movement conceptions of the everyday.

As should by now be clear, by emphasizing the analytic and strategic primacy of daily life, my intention is not simply to celebrate those groups that are, at present, most preoccupied with this question. Indeed, the way that "daily life" gets taken up in contemporary radical scenes often tends toward the self-valorizing subjectivism mentioned above. As I've argued elsewhere,[24] this impulse finds its roots not in revolutionary politics but rather in early-nineteenth century Romanticism. Despite being a radical expression of the antithetical pole of bourgeois consciousness, the Romantic orientation to daily life remains at odds with the demands of class war.

At best, movement Romanticism provides a catalogue of wish images that can remind people of the *reasons* they're struggling. At worst, it encourages forms of self-valorization wholly commensurate with the logic of the market. As many now recognize, the tragic outcome of the partial revolution of May '68 was that it ended primarily by revolutionizing capital. For this reason, it's necessary to clarify (both analytically and strategically) what we mean by "daily life." Practically speaking, this means supporting the movement impulse to emphasize daily life while quarreling with its particular conceptions whenever these appear to be at odds with those demanded by the material conditions of struggle.

Despite their shortcomings, today's anarchist and autonomist formations are unique in simultaneously emphasizing daily life and anti-capitalism (it's a telling sign of the times that such an orientation has all but disappeared from today's trade unions, another force considered by Harvey).[25] As such, it's necessary to take them very seriously. To be sure, it's likely that these formations will not be the dominant force in the new anti-capitalist "we." Nevertheless, as was the case in 1968, they remain the force most likely to ignite widespread opposition to capitalism's convenient—but ultimately untenable—answers.

VI

Since I'm not an economist, I've avoided commenting on Harvey's numeric descriptions of the current implosion. Nevertheless, as a radical who came of age during the triumphant and catastrophic ascent of neo-liberalism, I found his phenomenal description of this period to be spot on. At its highpoint, neo-liberalism managed to embody the contradictory logic of capitalism with a perfect and ferocious intensity. It was simultaneously more weightless and more brutally material than the remaining vestiges of the New Deal to which I clung without conviction. In response to the shake up, students of my generation began mobilizing against the wholesale transformation of the university. A few years later, I found this same cohort on the streets of Seattle and Quebec City.

Situated in the global north and shaped by the sallow habits of a middle class in decline, the activists with whom I organized had what can only be understood as a particular experience of what was going on. As with Camille de Toledo (who captured the dynamics of these years with great acuity in *Coming of Age at the End of History*), I felt that "the initial motivation behind the new spirit of revolt" wasn't so much economic as it was "respiratory."[26] Growing up in the neo-liberal heartland, the dynamics of late capitalism became real to me first and foremost through their symptomatic expression as claustrophobia. As was the case with so many others, respiratory distress was enough. I threw myself into struggle knowing that my life depended on it.

Still, many in my cohort harbored anxieties that their Zapatismo was fraudulent. After all, when compared to the plight of those locked in sweatshops or starving on the streets of glistening cosmopolitan wonderlands, our claustrophobia seemed like a poor little rich girl story. What was the connection between the pain in our chests and the far less sublime injuries endured by those who were unconditionally identified as enemies by neo-liberalism? We didn't know. As was sometimes the case for New Left activists a generation earlier, many of us ended up in the contradictory position of denouncing poverty while seeking to emulate the poor.[27] Rarely did we consider that our own experience of neo-liberalism was both a sufficient cause for revolt and a sufficient point from which to devise a coherent analysis of the problem.

According to Harvey, the experience of neo-liberalism "varied considerably … depending upon what part of the world one inhabited, the class relations prevailing there, the political and cultural traditions and how the political balance of political-economic power was shifting."[28] From this account, we can see how—even though an overarching material process was reorganizing capitalist social relations all over the globe—people's *understanding* of that process arose first and foremost through their partial, situated, and phenomenal experience of it. The challenge for radicals, then, is to determine how situated experience (the stuff of "daily life," the only thing to which we have access in the first instance) might become the basis not only for developing a comprehensive understanding of the overarching process but also for forging a "we" from different but converging experiences of a common enemy.

Although he does not state it directly, Harvey's assessment of the opportunities opened up by the current crisis suggests that he recognizes that the discrete spheres of subject and object begin to coincide when people perceive a problem. It's on this basis that he can claim (perhaps a little too optimistically) that, "at times of crisis, the irrationality of capitalism becomes plain for all to see."[29] On face value, this statement hardly seems contentious. What remains to be determined, however, is *how* people will come to recognize that the crisis is, in fact, a crisis. Indeed, this problem leads back to the paradox at the heart of Harvey's analysis: why *are* objective conditions in and of themselves insufficient for constituting a "resolute and sufficiently unified anti-capitalist movement?"[30]

VII

As it turns out, recognizing the crisis is more challenging than it sounds. Whether it takes the form of the "fetishistic disavowal" described by Slavoj Žižek[31] or the "passive nihilism" bemoaned by Simon Critchley,[32] people's capacity to live through a crisis without confronting it directly appears to be an enduring feature of experience in the capitalist present. And this should not surprise us. It suffices to recall that capitalism has, from its inception, been marked by dramatic bouts of self-destruction and reorganization. In other words, from the standpoint of capitalist social relations, "crisis" is not a crisis at all.[33] And though the current crisis has intensified the system's contradictions and made its irrationality increasingly visible, Harvey's assertion that the quantitative accumulation of tension will—at its threshold—produce a qualitative transformation needs to be qualified in one important respect. Specifically, we need to recognize that the "quality" of this qualitative transformation rests (in the final instance) on the success of our efforts to make the thought of reconciliation with the present unbearable.

When left to its own devices, capitalism's "qualitative" transformations have always ended by being rehearsals of the eternal return. As Bertolt Brecht rightly observed, these "transformations" usually involved the Old parading around dressed up as the New.[34] In this way, capitalism developed the means of enacting a seemingly endless substitution and deferral. This process has infused the system with longevity. However, as Walter Benjamin noted, "that things are 'status quo' *is* the catastrophe."[35] The trick for radicals, then, is to analytically seize upon the unbearable stuff of everyday life and illuminate it so as to strategically constitute a "we" on the most universal grounds imaginable.

Although those who have been most affected by the current crisis may seem like obvious candidates to place at the forefront of struggle, the qualitative transformation hinted at by Harvey can only arise from the recognition that—even in its moments of relative stability—capitalism is not good for anyone. This recognition played a key role in the May '68 uprising and in its rapid diffusion to all parts of society. From the demand that struggle focus not on acquiring more for alienated labor but rather on abolishing alienated labor itself to the universalist impulse underlying the insistence that "*nous sommes tous indésirables*,"[36] the movement's recognition of social co-implication via the politicization of daily life was the precondition to all that followed. It enabled the struggle to quickly overcome sectoral divisions and take on the dynamics of a general insurrection.

In light of this emphasis on politicizing daily life, and since Harvey's text stops just short of citing Lenin directly, it's useful to make the reference explicit. Here, then, is Lenin's account of how revolutionary consciousness must seize upon every moment of disquiet, regardless of where it emerges or who is affected: "Working-class consciousness cannot be genuine political consciousness unless the workers are trained to respond to *all* cases of tyranny, oppression, violence, and abuse, no matter *what class* is affected…"

> The consciousness of the working masses cannot be genuine class-consciousness, unless the workers learn … to observe *every* other social class in *all* the manifestations of its intellectual, ethical, and political life; unless they learn to apply in practice the materialist analysis and the materialist estimate of *all* aspects of the life and activity of *all* classes, strata, and groups of the population.[37]

VIII

Applying Lenin's insight to the challenge raised by Harvey's analysis, our task becomes one of determining how people's situated experiences of complex trans-local social relations like neo-liberalism (or the current crisis) can provide a starting point from which to analytically materialize those relations in order to make them "plain for all to see." As already mentioned, Harvey perceives "daily life" to be one of the seven key "moments" that constitute capitalist social relations. However, once this "moment" is considered alongside the others, it becomes clear that the distinction between them is formal-conceptual and not socio-ontological. Nevertheless, as a schematic account of capitalist social relations, Harvey's formal distinction remains useful since it highlights how people's finite and situated experiences are often organized in such a way as to call attention to one aspect of the puzzle at a time.

But as soon as this is recognized, it becomes clear that "daily life"—since it's the ground upon which these situated experiences transpire—does not and cannot bear any isomorphic relation to a category like "institutional, legal, and governmental arrangements." Indeed, the latter finds its precondition in the former. By transposing lived experience into a lexical frame enabling trans-local social coordination and regulation, the "institutional, legal, and governmental" is best understood as an example of what feminist sociologist Dorothy Smith has described as textually mediated relations of ruling.[38]

Smith's approach allows us to recognize how relations of ruling are put together through concrete practices in local settings and how—despite their trans-local conceits and effects—these practices can be investigated from starting points within these settings. This is significant since it suggests that social actors located at different points can find a material basis for convergence through a common process of mapping and analyzing the trans-local social relations that affect them. Although these processes are only partially observable from any given point and in the first instance, Smith's method proposes a concrete means of making them knowable. And so, while it has rarely been an explicit consideration in her work, Smith's institutional ethnography seems especially suited to the challenges of finding a stable ground for the development of meaningful coalitions.

Applied to our current investigation, Smith's method makes clear that "daily life" is both the analytic starting point for understanding "institutional, legal, and governmental arrangements" and the strategic basis upon which we can forge a broad-based anti-capitalist "we" capable of challenging them. This may not seem contentious. However, as a manner of proceeding, it stands in sharp contrast to Harvey's strategy of constituting a "we" by advancing normative ideals to which he feels people might gravitate. To be clear, I think the "respect for nature, radical egalitarianism in social relations, institutional arrangements based in some sense of common interests and common property, democratic administrative procedures," and "labor processes organized by the direct producers" called for by Harvey all sound like good things.[39] However, normative ideals will never constitute stable ground for anti-capitalist convergence. Moreover, when considered alongside the concrete universality that can be derived from people's analytic reckoning with their experience of daily life, such ideals become superfluous.

IX

Although I've only provided its most general outlines, Smith's feminist sociology provides a useful starting point for considering how daily life can be engaged analytically and strategically as a terrain of struggle. Applying her method to our current problem, it becomes clear that the everyday is an important point of engagement for radicals interested in constituting a "we" capable of changing the world. Like Harvey, Smith acknowledges her debt to Marx. How, then, are we to make sense of their significantly different understandings of daily life? In order to answer this question, it's useful to revisit some of Marx's own comments on the importance of the everyday.

Outlining his materialist conception of history in *The German Ideology*, Marx highlights how analysis must begin with "men, not in any fantastic isolation or rigidity, but in their actual, empirically perceptible process of development under definite conditions." He goes on to note how, "as soon as this active life process is described, history ceases to be a collection of dead facts as it is with the empiricists (themselves still abstract), or an imagined activity of imagined subjects, as with the idealists."[40] According to this perspective, understanding the world requires that we start with actual relations (and the people that animate them) rather than with conceptual abstractions.

Marx's emphasis on the "active life process" unfolding under "definite conditions" should not be confused with the idea that recounting experience is the whole of the investigation or that it somehow conveys "the truth" of the matter. Indeed, throughout his work, Marx highlights the distance between the immediate experience of social relations and their actual organization. For instance, in his account of "Rate and Mass of Surplus Value" in *Capital,* he notes how, "if we consider the process of production from the point of view of the simple labour-process, the labourers stand in relation to the means of production, not in their quality as capital, but as the mere means of and material of his own intelligent productive activity. In tanning, *e.g.*, he deals with the skins as his simple object of labour. It is not the capitalist's skin he tans."[41]

Quipping aside, Marx's point is that understanding trans-local relations of domination and exploitation requires more than describing immediate experience. This is not because the situated account is wrong but rather because, in and of itself, it remains incomplete. Marx's challenge, then, is to devise a method by which (in this case) the means of production to which the worker relates through the labor process might become visible in their quality as capital. Doing this does not involve supplanting lived experience with correct concepts. Instead, it involves mobilizing concepts not to "explain" the world but rather to provoke and organize investigations of those aspects of the world that aren't immediately perceptible.

This way of thinking about everyday experience is at odds with contemporary radical orthodoxies (where the emphasis is often placed on valorizing truths derived from immediate engagement). But these orthodoxies need to be contested—not least because, by limiting our consideration to the immediacy of the everyday, we dissolve its revolutionary potential into subjective particularism. In contrast, when everyday experience is taken as the starting point for social research, it becomes possible to map trans-local social relations from different but converging points. In the final instance, this process yields a concrete universality in which everyone can see the expression of their own situated experience.

For the time being, however, the social relations that make up neo-liberalism and the current crisis tend to be perceived as being outside of and prior to our experience of them. Consequently, our experience of these relations can often appear impressionistic and contingent upon our location or our normative ideals. Amidst this fragmentation, the Left has found it difficult to constitute a "we" capable of fighting for communism. For this reason, it's important to consider how what unites (or *could* unite) every one of us is the ultimate incommensurability of our experience under capitalism.

X

Although I have great respect for his Marxism (and was, like many students of my generation, deeply moved by *The Condition of Postmodernity*[42]), it's hard to ignore the fact that, in trying to assess our current situation, Harvey's account oscillates between the two epistemological habits critiqued by Marx in *The German Ideology*.[43] In his analysis, one can detect traces of the abstract empiricism of bourgeois economics (an explicative category that, as Marx noted, itself needs explaining) and the equally abstract idealism of professed revolutionary norms. In order to get off this seesaw, it's necessary to begin instead from an analysis of the relationship between part and whole, between daily life and the trans-local processes that organize it.

As I've noted already, conceiving of the world in this way has been a central attribute of Marxist thinking. But despite Marx's insistence that research be conducted in this fashion, and despite the compelling extension of his insights throughout the course of the twentieth century, "actually existing Marxism" (whether in the academy or in the various micro-party sects that Harvey rightly dismisses[44]) has often been characterized by economist distortions. These distortions undermine our ability to see how people—in our actual, empirically perceptible process of development under definite conditions—might take history itself as the object of our labor.

It's useful to recall that, in *Capital*, Marx's analysis begins not with an overview of bourgeois economic theory and its inevitable blind spots (although he does get around to talking about these) but rather with a phenomenal description of the twofold character of the commodity. In other words, the ordinary experience of encountering something on the market becomes the starting point for an analysis that ends up extending to cover not only the whole stretch of the globe but also the whole of human history. The analysis of the economic logic of capital is thus extracted from an experience that, despite being quotidian, nevertheless encapsulates the whole in metonymic form.

Paradoxical though it may seem, this mode of proceeding has not always been recognized as being properly "Marxist." For his part, Louis Althusser went so far as to propose that *Capital* ought to begin not with the phenomenal encounter with the commodity (As Marx's own Table of Contents proposes) but rather with the schematic conceptual elaboration of "The General Formula for Capital" outlined at the beginning of Part II.[45] But despite the pervasiveness of such distortions, the problem of the everyday cannot be ignored. It resurfaces with the intensity and resoluteness of a repressed phenomenon whenever a conceptual abstraction is probed to uncover its historical specificity.

In his *Critique of Everyday Life*, Henri Lefebvre provides what remains one of the most beautiful expressions of this premise. According to Lefebvre, "the simplest event—a woman buying a pound of sugar, for example—must be analyzed."

> To understand this simple event, it is not enough to merely describe it; research will disclose a tangle of reasons and causes, of essences and 'spheres': the woman's life, her biography, her job, her family, her class, her budget, her eating habits, how she uses money, her opinions and her ideas, the state of the markets, etc. Finally I will have grasped the sum total of capitalist society, the nation and its history. And although what I grasp becomes more and more profound, it is contained from the start in the original little event. So now I see the humble events of everyday life as having two sides: a little, individual, chance event—and at the same time an infinitely complex social event, richer than the many 'essences' it contains within itself. The

social phenomenon may be defined as the unity of the two sides. It remains for us to explain why the infinite complexity of these events is hidden, and discover why—and this too is a part of their reality—they appear to be so humble.[46]

To this assessment, I need only add that our objective in the present must not only be to analyze but also to strategize. Strategy, however, should not be viewed as a discrete function; it arises from and is made possible by the interconnections forged and made visible through analysis. Considered together, these two processes allow us to begin imagining how we might constitute a "we," not on the basis of abstract ideals, but rather on the solid foundation of lived experience.

Today, the political forces closest to actualizing this method are gathered amidst those that Harvey identifies as anarchists and autonomists. Although their conception of the political significance of daily life can sometimes appear to be dramatically at odds with what has been outlined above, they remain the most likely among actually existing Left forces to be moved by these arguments. As such, it's necessary for us to open up dialogues about the political importance of daily life in the context of the contemporary capitalist crisis within anarchist and autonomist spaces. The emphasis in these discussions should be placed primarily on the underlying continuity of experience under capitalism. Once this is established analytically, the discussion must be directed toward considering how it can be leveraged strategically in the process of constituting a "we" broader than our presently pitiful numbers.

II

THE CRITICAL
MOMENT

(THE STATUS QUO THREATENS
TO BE PRESERVED)

WAGING WAR ON VALENTINES DAY

I

Type "why is Valentine's Day" into Google, and the three top search suggestions come up as follows: "why is Valentines Day celebrated," "why is Valentines Day important" and "why is Valentines Day bad." Follow any of these threads for any length of time and it becomes clear that our collective answers have thus far been inconclusive. But while St. Valentine's shoddy martyrology and the dismal February snow may cast doubts on the holiday's provenance and advisability, it's hard to deny that the celebration of love resonates strongly with many of us—even if the festival's precise dimensions prompt feelings of anxiety, frustration, and rage.

In radical scenes, Valentine's Day is typically repudiated for being a gross and cynical corporate exercise. Nevertheless, the mass attention devoted to love on this day should be approached as a political opportunity. At the very least, it should prompt us to consider what we might want the term to mean as we struggle collectively to change the world.

It's no longer surprising to recount how capitalism abducts our desires to imprison them in commodities. But when the desire is love,

This essay first appeared on the website *Truthout* on February 14, 2014. http://www.truth-out.org/opinion/item/21795-waging-war-on-valentines-day.

and the commodities are grotesque cardboard abominations, it's hard not to conclude (*pace* Adorno) that writing poetry after Valentine's Day is barbaric. Be this as it may, people *en masse* continue to be seduced by the Valentine's Day industry. Along with the Romantics (whom Marx held to be their "legitimate antithesis"[1]), capitalists themselves have acknowledged that love is serious business. According to one recent report, Valentine's Day was estimated to have contributed more than $18 billion to the US economy in 2013. That sum, accumulated in the span of a single week's excess, is comparable to the annual contribution of Wisconsin's food and beverage industry to the Gross Domestic Product.

Little wonder, then, that many of us flee the marketplace to find a less-cardboard version of love in the horizontal embrace of community. But while such impulses are commendable, they can't match the juggernaut that turned Valentine's Day into an impenetrable storm of swirling pink confection. Capitalists may not have a monopoly on love, but they've certainly managed to shape our habits. Even outside the market, the nature of love has become fundamentally acquisitive.

Craigslist may not be a catalogue of our best moments, but it certainly provides a telling snapshot of our most honest ones. Throughout its posts, it's impossible not to be struck by both the enormity of our collective desire for love and the absolute inadequacy of the available means for its realization. A recent survey of "Missed Connections" was enough to confirm my worst fears. Alongside the lovesick M gushing malapropism to assure the bookworm on the Astoria-bound Q train that she was "unimaginatively beautiful," I found the following guy buying drinks for the ladies at the Charleston: "If I ever buy someone a drink, they always keep talking to me," he insisted. Nevertheless, "you kept giving me side-glances, but that was all. My guess? You're VERY shy and need someone to be persistent." Tormented by the looming holiday, and in response to the whole bleak scene, one brave W issued the following urgent appeal: "write me love letters."

> so its february and that most annoying of days is around the corner. except what if it wasn't annoying? what if it were thoughtful and careful and wonderful and a chance to tell someone, a stranger even, a beautiful and romantic sentiment.

Even when acknowledging the dread particular to this "most annoying of days" (even when confronted with the grotesque dimensions of our imperfect efforts), we still search out pathways for beauty, romance, and sentiment. Sooner or later, we admit that we're reluctant to renounce them despite all that's been done in their name. One of our greatest challenges, then, is to save the desire for loving connection—a desire as big as Wisconsin—from the inadequacy of the candy coating in which it's encased.

Prying the desire from the object is like splitting the atom; it has the power to release a tremendous energy that can be channeled into social transformation—but only if we recognize our common cause with the rose-wielding sucker armed with a box of chocolates.

II

In their recent issue devoted to the theme of love, the feminist stalwarts at *Shameless* magazine contended that it was "the most radical topic" they could write about.[2] Nevertheless, as editor Sheila Sampath confessed in her introductory remarks, the obviousness of love's importance to radical struggles did nothing to change the fact that it remained "by far" the hardest topic to address.[3]

In light of this difficulty, radicals have often preferred to sidestep analysis in order to embrace slogans and images that conduct a hasty marriage between love and our longing for social justice. How else are we to explain the profusion of heart motifs that exploded in the activist visual lexicon at the beginning of the twenty-first century? Why did the heart seem to become our movement's ascendant sign, and how did this icon that previous generations had surrendered to Hallmark (or ensnared in the cruel grip of a thousand barbed-wire tattoos) become as important as the star had been to previous insurgencies?

I will be the first to concede that Sapon-Shevin's Seattle-era block print was inspiring [Fig. 1]. Still, it begs the question: What *is* the connection between loving and fighting?

For anarchist feminist author and punk icon Wendy-O Matik, "radical love" is best understood as a spiritual pursuit. In her words, such love is "an opportunity to save the planet, heal Mother Earth, connect with the cosmos, and work towards … creating a sustainable community." For this reason, the concept has "a sacred global interconnection" at its core.[4] A polyamory advocate and regular workshop

Fig. 1: Like many riffs on the heart motif, Dalia Sapon-Shevin's block print produced around the time of the 1999 anti-WTO actions in Seattle has become a familiar visual reference point in the North American activist scene.

facilitator catering to "intimate revolutionaries & relationship anarchists," Matik recently concluded a radio interview by noting that one of her main objectives was to help people become "more enchanted with the world."

In the face of the disenchantment that overtook the globe with the rise of dark satanic mills, these sentiments are both noble and explicitly anti-capitalist. But sentiments are not strategy, and honesty compels us to acknowledge the ease with which re-enchantment has historically been enlisted to buttress a soulless status quo. This does not mean that the workshops are unimportant. After all, committing to honest communication while breaking the possessiveness straitjacket is likely to greatly improve people's intimate relationships. Nevertheless, while these skills may help us to become better people (and while they may even help us to be better fighters in the struggle against injustice), they are not the means by which that struggle can be conducted.

But if radical love of this sort leaves our revolutionary aspirations unfulfilled, where else might we turn to discover the connection between loving and fighting? A quick glance at the archive reveals that revolutionary thinkers have often felt compelled to address this question in the very midst of tumult. In his important 1965 dispatch from Algiers, Che Guevara famously (and "at the risk of seeming ridiculous") declared that "the true revolutionary is guided by great feelings of love."[5] Even today, the letter remains beautiful and insightful. And, though he probably hadn't intended it, something important about the libidinal source of the revolutionary's "great feelings" might be gleaned from its innuendo-laden account of Castro's relation to the people.

> At the great public mass meetings, one can observe something like the dialogue of two tuning forks whose vibrations interact, producing new sounds. Fidel and the mass begin to vibrate together in a dialogue of growing intensity until they reach the climax in an abrupt conclusion crowned by our cry of struggle and victory.[6]

Far from home and probably a little lonesome, it's easy to forgive Che's literary indulgence. What's less forgivable, however, is the regularity with which his "love" maxim gets cited without acknowledgment of the specific meaning he assigned to the term. "Perhaps it is one of the great dramas of the leader that he or she must combine a passionate spirit with a cold intelligence and make painful decisions without flinching," he writes. "They cannot descend, with small doses of daily affection, to the level where ordinary people put their love into practice."

This doesn't mean that such "daily affection" is irrelevant. On the contrary, it is the practical expression of people's desire for greater connection. For this reason, the revolutionary does not repudiate these desires; instead, she works to complete them by devising more perfect object resolutions. And though the revolutionary's own "great feelings" do not wallow in the Valentine's Day trenches where "ordinary people put their love into practice," both passionate spirit and cold intelligence alert us to the fact that we must nevertheless take these trenches as our field of operations.

III

In 1964, Martin Luther King went to Oslo to receive the Nobel Peace Prize. Accepting the award "on behalf of a civil rights movement which is moving with determination and a majestic scorn for risk and danger to establish a reign of freedom and a rule of justice," King underscored his refusal to "accept the cynical notion that nation after nation must spiral down a militaristic stairway into the hell of thermonuclear destruction."[7] His optimism was unrelenting: "I believe that unarmed truth and unconditional love will have the final word in reality. ... I believe that even amid today's mortar bursts and whining bullets, there is still hope for a brighter tomorrow."[8]

Fifty years later, "unconditional love" has itself become the target of "mortar burst and whining bullets." In December 2013, an American drone ostensibly aimed at taking out insurgents struck a wedding party in Yemen, killing 17 people.[9] Met with stern condemnation by the international community, the action was but the latest in a long series of US attacks against civilians celebrating love. In the four short months between July and November 2008, both Wech Baghtu[10] and Haska Meyna[11] become mass graves as dozens of Afghans were slaughtered by US bombardment while attending weddings.

If these events force us to call King's optimism into question, they also demand that we take a hard look at the intimate connection between love and war. What are we to make of the fact that imperial power can't tell the difference between a wedding and an insurgent deployment? The tendency to underscore the innocence of the slaughtered is overwhelming. But what might we learn if we viewed these airstrikes not as one of imperial power's regrettable "mistakes"[12] but rather as one of its most inadvertent but powerful insights? Can we imagine how even a wedding, if emancipated from its current social form and pushed to its logical conclusion, might constitute a threat?

As far as intellectual exercises go, I will concede that this one is taxing. The coalitions forged in marriage tend to be conservative, to wed their participants to the reproduction of a perpetually impoverished reality. Historically, the state has been so certain that marriage cemented the status quo that, in his infamous 1965 Report, even a brass-tacks bureaucrat like Daniel Patrick Moynihan felt confident endorsing the fiction that Black marriage might miraculously curb the spread of poverty—and, subsequently, insurrection—in America's ghettos.[13]

But while marriage has tied love to the social pacification project, it's equally true that relationships formalized through solemn commitment (regardless of the number of people involved) can be the cornerstone of anti-imperialist struggles as well. It's therefore not surprising that, even though his ultimate objectives were antithetical to Moynihan's, Malcolm X shared his adversary's commitment to strong social ties.

As I noted in the introduction to these comments, St. Valentine's martyrology is riddled with inconsistencies. Be this as it may, it's significant that—in some versions—he faced persecution for marrying second-century Romans against the wishes of the emperor, who maintained that such bonds detracted from the state's martial focus. The lesson is clear: Bonds of love forged on the horizontal plane pull people away from the empire and its demands. To be sure, such bonds are forever imperiled by the seductions of privacy and self-preservation. However, if the desire that compelled the bond can be kept from settling into the constraints of an imperfect resolution, love itself can become a violent, transformative force.

In the midst of El Salvador's armed struggle, liberation theologian Oscar Romero described how "the violence we preach is ... the violence of love."[14] The formulation remains shocking in its incongruity right up until the moment it's properly understood. For his part, Paulo

Freire noted how "the act of rebellion by the oppressed (an act which is always, or nearly always, as violent as the initial violence of the oppressors) can initiate love" by restoring the humanity of the oppressor.[15]

"Tremble to the cadence of my legacy," Sappho booms in Rita Mae Brown's second-wave classic *The Hand That Cradles The Rock*. "An army of lovers shall not fail."[16] Sappho is addressing the Sacred Band of Thebes, an elite core of 300 soldiers whose *esprit de corps* was matched only by the depth of their erotic love for one another. Instinctively, radicals recognize the importance of building such an army. What remains less clear, however, are the means by which to rescue the tremendous outpouring of "everyday affection" on Valentine's Day from the inadequacy of its cardboard resolution. How might we "combine a passionate spirit with a cold intelligence" to ensure that, when our collective heart bursts, the explosion is bigger than Wisconsin? When it comes to radical love, there is no greater question than this.

THE RESONANCE OF ROMANTICISM
Activist Art & the Bourgeois Horizon

I

For those who lived through them, the years of struggle against corporate globalization between 1999 and 2003 are memorable for having been marked by an extreme creative audacity. Along with that movement's tactical innovations—which included the elaboration of forms of horizontal organizing and the intensification of the capacity for violent confrontations—came a profusion of aesthetic interventions. Combining do-it-yourself ethics with a newfound sense of the pleasures to be had from lowbrow cultural hijinks, activists during this period began in earnest to retrofit the world. After a pabulum generation of post-New Left campaigns that could not help but leave the impression that social change meant fighting for bread and more bread (please), the movements against corporate globalization declared in no uncertain terms that both bread and roses were on the agenda once again.

It is within this context that we can situate that movement's profound interest in the work of Eric Drooker and Banksy. Although

---

This essay first appeared in Begum O. Firat and Aylin Kuryel (eds.), *Cultural Activism: Practices, Dilemmas, and Potentialities*. (New York: Brill, 2011).

working in different idioms, these two artists are notable for having become prominent visual reference points within movement culture and for having both captured and given form to the new spirit of resistance. The comments that follow are, in part, an account of this resonance. However, while their interventions were sometimes inspiring (and while they continue to speak to many of us), it's important—when considering their contributions from the standpoint of an analysis of *the movement*—to ask precisely what it was that their expressive outbursts expressed.

More specifically, we can ask: What can the content of the movement's resonant images tell us about the movement itself? And even more specifically: Can Drooker and Banksy's resonance serve as an index of the movement's historical and political possibilities? Why did a movement that professed with resolute sincerity that "another world is possible" gravitate toward works that seemed to draw upon (and thus helped to reiterate) major themes from the nineteenth-century Romantic tradition, an archive that—from the standpoint of the generalized dissimulations of late capitalism—has by now been largely forgotten?

II

For readers familiar with his work, this line of questioning will undoubtedly bring to mind the writings of Walter Benjamin who, in "Paris, Capital of the Nineteenth Century" and elsewhere, proposed that resonant images enabled people to anticipate the future by recalling traces of a mythical past whose promise had yet to be fulfilled. Because of this tendency, Benjamin contended that actors in the present always end up "quoting primeval history."[1] The purpose of these citations was to recall those unrealized elements in the hope that their iteration in the present might allow them to come to fruition. For this reason, Benjamin contended that "each epoch not only dreams the next, but also, in dreaming, strives toward the moment of waking."[2]

> In the dream in which, before the eyes of each epoch, that which is to follow appears in images, that latter appears wedded to elements from prehistory, that is, of a classless society. Intimations of this, deposited in the unconscious of the collective, mingle with the new to produce the utopia that has left its

traces in thousands of configurations of life, from permanent buildings to fleeting fashions.[3]

The present dreams the future by way of a detour through the mythic past. However, such dreams do not say anything about *the means* by which this future will be realized. But while they provide no blueprints for revolution, wish images signal the possibility that the human energies captured by capitalism might finally spill over and bring with them a moment of transformative intoxication. Although Benjamin never advanced a systematic program for the use of wish images, his insights allow us to consider why an assemblage as full of exuberance as the anti-globalization movement seemed unconsciously to reach back into the archive of the Romantic past (an archive that was itself composed of mythic citations) in order to augment its imaginative élan.

III

According to Isaiah Berlin, "the literature on Romanticism is larger than Romanticism itself."[4] To this provocative but undoubtedly true claim, we might add that many of the canonical contributions to this literature advance observations that are in contradiction with other equally canonical pronouncements. For this reason, it is difficult to provide a definitive account of the Romantic tradition. Despite this ambiguity, however, I would like to highlight a number of features that help to clarify Romanticism's enduring political significance. This account is based less on the attributes of the Romantic object than on the relationship that Romanticism posits between object and world, object and audience, and object and creator.[5]

First, Romanticism arose from the antithetical pole of the constitutive contradiction at the heart of bourgeois experience. It was a reaction to calculative rationality, the ascendant term of the bourgeois world. Arising from the Enlightenment, this rationality transposed the world into measurable units. These units enabled the standardization of both processes of production and habits of thought. However, while calculative rationality became the operational premise of capitalism and its modern institutions, the contradiction at the heart of bourgeois consciousness demanded that the incalculable remainder, those experiences that eluded capture, be addressed. Romanticism was one response to this need.

Second, although this remainder afforded spiritual seductions that seemed to be at odds with the bourgeois world, these seductions were nowhere truly outside of this world. Indeed, Romanticism could not have arisen had it not been for calculative rationality and the social conditions it enabled. Meanwhile, calculative rationality incorporated Romanticism into its own operations by turning it into an engine to stimulate the production of new needs. Indeed, as Carl Schmitt noted, "the Romantic hated the philistine. But it turned out that the philistine loved the Romantic, and in such a relationship it was obvious that the philistine had the dominant position."[6]

Third, the nineteenth-century tension between calculative rationality and its antithesis has yet to be resolved. And though the dynamics of this war have evolved over time, they could be discerned from the very first act of the bourgeois drama. Already they were present in the French Revolution, where they found perfect expression in the guillotine. On the one hand, the guillotine stood as emblem of calculative rationality's impulse to serialize death and free it from the drama of suffering and redemption. Where once the executioner had been God's proxy, overseer of the punitive liturgy, the guillotine turned him into a functionary (literally, an executive officer) of the nascent state. On the other hand, however, the guillotine revitalized forms of religious sacrifice that—for an anthropologist like René Girard—could only signal the constitution of community through collective responsibility for a founding murder.[7] These two premises (antithetical, and yet expressed simultaneously through an object that has come to stand in for the revolution itself) reflect the antinomies of bourgeois thought.

By jumping headlong into the fratricidal war between calculative rationality and spirit, Romanticism pushed itself past judiciousness and moderation in a bid to topple the sentinels guarding the knot at the heart of bourgeois experience. Finally, it stepped forward as a guiding star for rebels everywhere. All of this happened in the nineteenth century, and it continues to happen today. Why?

In order to understand Romanticism's recursive character, it suffices to recall that identification with the antithetical term of a contradiction is not a sufficient means of overcoming the contradiction itself. Burdened by this impasse, the bourgeoisie has occasionally endeavored to resolve its constitutive contradiction philosophically; however, the conditions required for such a resolution are nowhere to be found within the bourgeois horizon. According to Georg Lukács, for instance, the subjective rationalism inaugurated by Kant found its limit in the always-partial character of the rational system. Indeed, "in such systems the 'ultimate' problem of human existence persists in an irrationality incommensurable with human understanding." What's more, "the closer the system comes to these 'ultimate' questions the more strikingly its partial, auxiliary nature and its inability to grasp the 'essential' are revealed."[8]

Lukács' observation makes clear that the partitioning of object and subject, science and art, "is" and "ought" in the bourgeois imagination cannot be resolved philosophically, since bourgeois philosophy can go no further than what Marx once described as an incomplete subjective idealism or an incomplete objective empiricism. However, within these constraints, only the subjective-idealist pole developed by the Romantic worldview holds the promise of resolving the tension through a valorizing identification with *what ought to be*. In the contest between rationalism and its other, the rebel trapped within the bourgeois horizon has only one choice. For Lukács, this other is signaled by the "irrational" and the "essential." It is no mistake that these same terms are among the defining features of Romanticism.

Despite making positive claims about the intangible, Romanticism remains a refusal of the dominant—scientific and empirical—terms of bourgeois experience.[9] It is therefore not surprising that, since the contradiction underlying bourgeois experience has yet to be resolved or surpassed (since bourgeois politics continues to be marked by the irreconcilable tension between heart and mind, art and science, "ought" and "is"), political movements opposed to this order have disclosed a predictable tendency to find consolation in—and to align themselves with—the Romantic injunction to undo calculative rationality, the dominant mode of bourgeois experience.

IV

Eric Drooker began making art for the political scene in New York's Lower East Side during the 1980s. Home to successive waves of low-paid immigrant workers and socialist rebels during the late nineteenth and early twentieth centuries, the Lower East Side had by the 1980s become a site of intensive gentrification and a new kind of class struggle. Amid the tumult, Drooker developed an aesthetic deeply influenced by the radical culture of the protest scene and the visual archive of his neighborhood's past. Drawing inspiration from both the street and his formal training at Cooper Union, he began producing scratchboard images in the high contrast style of late nineteenth- and early twentieth-century expressionist woodcuts.

Since the late 1980s, Drooker has released a number of books, some of which have now gone into second editions.[10] Drooker images have also appeared on the covers of several activist publications, including *LiP* and *Punk Planet* (now, sadly, both defunct), as well as the more mainstream *New Yorker*. Throughout, he has developed a visual lexicon with remarkable symbolic and stylistic coherence. With the rise of the North American movement against corporate globalization, Drooker began producing works that pertained directly to the new cycle of struggle. It is in this context that we can situate the work that would come to serve as the cover image for the edited collection *The Battle of Seattle* [Fig. 1].[11]

Mixing Drooker's usual scratchboard and wash style with visual motifs arising directly from movement events, the image depicts a line of baton wielding riot cops trying to hold back a line of protestors. Behind the line of cops stands a chain link fence like the one that protected delegates to the Quebec City Summit of the Americas meeting in the spring of 2001. On top of Drooker's fence dances a protestor playing a trumpet. While most of the image is executed in a kind of comic book realism, the trumpet player stands out on account of a hyper-stylization reminiscent of nineteenth-century naïve art. It is an iconic intervention that—because of the visual uncertainty brought about by its lack of scale, proportion, and symbolic indexicality— seems to simultaneously push the image into the extreme depths of the single point perspective while (at the same time) flattening the surface so that all objects appear on the same plane. Perspectival realism is summoned and canceled in a single stroke. It evokes the feeling of being in a dream.

Drawing on the situational iconography of the Battle of Seattle and Quebec City, the image is a strange mix of the popular-familiar and the miraculous. Trumpet in hand, the figure dancing along the top of the fence appears to be totally free. The laws of gravity do not apply to him. He has even found a means of being *behind* the line of riot cops. Given his angelic demeanor, it is tempting to conclude that he levitated over them.

Fig. 1: Eric Drooker. *Direct Action* (2001)

But what is most significant about this trumpet player is how he allows the anti-summit protest to become an epic of biblical proportions. Drawing on the Old Testament account of Joshua's attack on Jericho, where horns make walls crumble so that the chosen can take possession of the city, Drooker turns the trumpet player into an allegory for radical political struggle. It's a representational strategy that pervades his work. People holding drums and guitars confront cops with guns and batons. From an objective perspective, these street conflicts demand heavy casualties. Nevertheless, the images remain ennobling and redemptive. Impossible to escape, the massacre is simultaneously asserted and averted by intangible means.

In these images, victory—as wish—is immanent even though its actualization is deferred to an indeterminate future or buried in an indeterminate past. From this perspective, to resist is already to win. Indeed, resistance itself becomes the sign of victory. The production recedes; the representation ascends. Convictions founded on such grounds are self-satisfying; they are also incredibly stimulating. As a strategy for solidifying identification with what ought to be, the mythical proclamation of victory helps to marshal the energy needed to enact an inversion of the world. The objective-empirical "what you see is what you get" is supplanted by the more radical subjective-idealist "what you get is what you see." Through his elaboration of visual motifs consistent with these premises, Drooker made important contributions to a movement in which activists began considering what it might mean to confront seemingly insurmountable odds.

In Drooker's images, one can witness the precise means by which history becomes mythically connected to redemption. Consider the image used by Washington DC's Direct Action Network for demonstrations against the IMF and World Bank in April 2000 [Fig. 2]. In an obvious citation of Goya's depiction of the massacre of *The Third of May* (1814) [Fig. 3], Drooker shows a group of activists on the left side of the composition facing down a line of riot cops on the right. The cops hold guns like those used in Seattle to launch tear gas canisters, beanbags, and rubber bullets. The activists hold musical instruments. Behind the cops is a row of buildings trembling with the reverberations of the activists' tremulous noise. And so, despite Drooker's invocation of the slaughter of innocents by the Napoleonic army, it is clear that (*this time*) the chosen people will win—as they

Fig. 2 (top): Eric Drooker. *Music Vs. Police* (2000)
Fig. 3 (bottom): Francisco Goya. *The Shootings of May Third 1808* (1814)

did in Jericho—because of their faith, and because of their belief in the possibility of another world.

By collapsing the historical and the mystical into a single representational register, Drooker's work suggests a means by which activists might enact a transposition from the ideal to the concrete and back again. Significantly, this ability coincides with the reappearance of religious iconography and forms of religious thought. And though rendered in the secularized idiom of late capitalism (an idiom that countenances no pretense to hermeneutic depth), Drooker's biblical allusions are unmistakable. They resonated with a movement in which people sought to realize the promise of all that remained incomplete, a movement that triumphed in the assertion of the possibility of another world. More than this: the allusions pushed them on, compelling them to expand the field of action and embrace risks beyond measure. Drooker's mythic past—a place where the massacre of Spaniards in 1808 is synchronous with Joshua's assault on Jericho, both coincided with and helped to amplify the strange form of intoxication that pervaded the movement.

V

In his 1992 masterpiece *Flood!* (re-released in 2002 for the anti-globalization crowd), Drooker depicts the descent of a working stiff into a spiral of despair after losing his job, his apartment, and his grip on reality. The second chapter of the three-chapter work finds the protagonist in the sub-basements of human cognition. Here, the rules of logic are swept away by the torrential movement of the rising stream of consciousness. Drooker locates this alter-world, this collective repository of wish images, in the deepest tunnels of the New York subway system.

Passing through despair, the protagonist comes into direct contact with the contents of the image archive. Fertility goddesses share space with Egyptian hieroglyphs that give way to cave paintings and tribal dance circles. Emerging from the archive and returning to the present, he is confronted in Chapter 3 with the catastrophic dimensions of the everyday. In one dreamlike scene, Drooker portrays a gust of wind carrying the protagonist into the sky by his umbrella. Hovering above the world, he is left to contemplate the devastating transformations brought on by industrialism and its aftermath.

Drooker uses this dream state as an analytic device. Imaginative detachment produces the critical distance necessary to perceive the world directly. Through efforts to arrest the flow of immediate perception and make strange the taken-for-granted, Drooker's city becomes a zone of architectonic exploration in which the underlying girders of capitalist social relations are laid bare. The brothel, the bar, the carnival, the dancehall: like Benjamin, Drooker descends on each of these sites and transforms them into the raw material for experiments in profane illumination. But while this dream state contains analytic potential, there is no guarantee that visiting it will prompt a naked reckoning with the world. As Susan Buck-Morss has noted in her consideration of Benjamin's assessment of the wish image, "the real possibility of a classless society in the 'epoch to follow' the present one revitalizes past images as expressions of the ancient wish for a social utopia in dream form. But a dream image is not yet a dialectical image, and desire is not yet knowledge."[12]

Drooker's work flirts with the dream state. It intoxicates. And though it affords moments of profane illumination, it seems in the end to remain bound by its allegiances to the nineteenth-century Romantic archive. How so? In order to answer this question, it's useful to begin by considering the approach to describing Drooker's work adopted by his contemporaries. In his introduction to the second edition of *Flood!*, Luc Sante—social historian of New York's mean streets and author of *Low Life*—proclaimed that *Flood!* was "a prophetic book" like "the Book of Amos."

> Maybe the events it depicts have already come to pass, maybe many times over, or maybe they never will, but either way the warning stands—and the promise, too, destruction and renewal being inseparably tied together. Drooker's mastery of the pure stark elemental expressionist line not only suggests volumes in every stroke, but also places the images it depicts in an eternal, un-nameable tense that is not quite the present but remains poised somewhere between past and future.[13]

In this account, Drooker's recourse to myth, temporal folding, the religious archive, and Romanticism are all presented in an obvious and unselfconscious way. It's a testament to their pervasiveness within the turn-of-the-century *zeitgeist* that Sante could draw upon them as commonsense reference points. Though waxing poetic, he expresses what he expects the reader will already understand. Significant, then, that he points toward the indeterminacy of historical time (a time that is at once mythic and objective) and the recursive character of the resonant artifact as wish image. By connecting the event with both the warning *and* the promise, and by locating it "poised somewhere between the past and the future," Sante effectively highlights both the seduction and the ambivalence of Drooker's work.

For Sante, Drooker's images become charged with critical potential precisely at the point where the everyday is transposed into the temporal register of the dream world—the world in which the wish image becomes a concrete index of yet-to-be-realized desires. This time out of time and this artifact out of place (this nostalgia for an elsewhere desired primarily on account of its status as counterpoint to the unbearable present) are hallmarks of Romanticism. It is therefore not surprising to find Drooker frequently borrowing—not only in form but also in content—from figures like Goya, Millet, and Blake [see Figures 4 and 5].

Drooker's populist citations confirm that Romanticism is more than a sensibility. It is also a historical archive to be exploited—a repository of wish images lying in wait for the moment at which they will be called upon to herald the future. His work induces a historical doubling over; the anxieties that attended to mid-nineteenth century industrialization reappear on the historical stage (it is the return of the repressed) precisely at the point of industrialism's anxious unraveling in the most intensive zones of twenty-first century capital accumulation.

Writing for *The Rocket*, Patrick Barber noted how "Drooker has an unsure obsession with New York City that reaches for its deepest mass humanity while being quashed by consumerism and the sheer bulk and impossibility of urban madness and impending death." Here, the spiritual pole of bourgeois experience (our "deepest mass humanity") is directly counterposed to an "impending death" brought about by consumerism. Meanwhile, consumerism—the sign under which the market appears—becomes aligned with calculative rationality in its war against spirit. In Drooker, Barber perceives a contest between the old and the new played out on a terrain divided according to the split in bourgeois consciousness. Because Drooker sides with our deepest mass humanity, it follows that Barber describes his work in terms appropriate to Romanticism. Indeed, for Barber, *Flood!* is a work of "apocalyptic mysticism, manic and complete."[14]

Fig. 4 (top): Eric Drooker. *The Grim Sower* (1999)
Fig. 5 (bottom): Jean-François Millet. *The Sower* (1850)

Writing in the *Graphic Novel Review*, Hubert Vigilla describes how some of this apocalyptic mysticism gets played out in "L," *Flood's* second chapter: "'L' is brimming with archetypes and primal imagery including wide-hipped fertility figures and ancient hieroglyphs," he recounts. "Several life-affirming images splash and rejoice across the pages of this chapter; a fire-lit cave erupts with rhythmic dancing, a crane soars into a glimmering night sky, and bodies entwine in a garden teeming with life." However, though these images offer a vision of emancipation in dream form, they remain insufficient to the task of transforming the objective world. Consequently, "'L' closes in downtrodden fashion as the ancient, fundamental joy of life gives way to cracked, mundane concrete and cold rain."[15]

Writing for the *San Mateo Times*, Rick Eymer suggests that, while Drooker's novel may seem depressing, "it ends with the transfer from oblivion to hope and love. Yes there are sharp images of decay and tragedy, but there is also a dream that things can change. We just need to wash away the filth."[16] In this account, we see how hope and love—by standing in opposition to decay and tragedy—are given the task of redeeming the world. Drooker concludes his story with a historical-mythical doubling over; New York drowns while Noah carries his timeless cargo to presumed safety. In this way, the artist offers an imaginative resolution to present-day contradictions. New York City (the zone in which the calculative rationality underlying intensive capital accumulation has succeeded most fully in harnessing the energy of dreams) is destroyed while the dream it once channeled is allowed to persist unencumbered. However, the fact that this conclusion leaves Eymer wanting to "wash away the filth" should alert us to the ambivalence of such wish images when considered from the standpoint of politics.[17]

VI

By popularizing the aesthetic repertoire of Romanticism and endowing his protagonists with a "more than" spiritual dimension, Drooker puts his work in a visual time fold. Sometimes, this doubling over becomes the explicit content of the images themselves. Jungles grow up to overtake a city populated by both elephants and commuter buses; Noah builds his ark atop a tenement building. As with Benjamin, who proclaimed that our lives amounted to "a muscle strong enough to contract the whole of historical time,"[18] Drooker's protagonists collapse the stages of history into a single moment of reckoning. However, unlike Benjamin, Drooker's reckoning tends to take the form, not of anti-capitalist struggle, but of personal (mystical) redemption.

This claim may at first seem odd. After all, Benjamin's work is often considered mystical and far from the realities of political struggle. In contrast, Drooker fills his images with rioting and social unrest. Nevertheless, in Benjamin, the reader passes through myth to arrive in the final instance at concrete reckoning. The profane struggle and its demands become clear all at once in a cessation of happening. At this point, the wish image becomes dialectical. According to Benjamin, such images had the power to transform history from prefabricated narrative (a sequence of events that could be contemplated in succession like the beads of a rosary) into a moment of reckoning. In contrast, Drooker leads his readers in the opposite direction; passing through riots and confrontations with police, we discover too late that we've been deposited before the divine.

Like Moses falling on the threshold of the Promised Land, Drooker's *Flood!* and *Blood Song* describe redemption as a two-stage process involving a kind of spiritual projection—an identification with a proxy that remains untouched by the constraints of this world. Moses struggled to cross the desert, but the mystical force of his efforts owes entirely to Joshua's later success. In *Flood!*, our drowned protagonist is survived (and thus redeemed) by his cat who makes it to the Ark and finds his double, the posited resolution to his lack. In *Blood Song*, though he is incarcerated for political activity, the heroine's partner lives on through their child who cries out with the same fiery voice as its father. Joshua's political significance is confirmed by the frequent allegorical mobilization of the assault on Jericho in Drooker's work. In the following image, simply entitled "Jericho," he makes the reference explicit [Fig. 6].

VII

At first glance, the only thing that Banksy seems to have in common with Drooker is that he too was loved by people who were more likely to throw a brick through a window at Starbucks than to order a cup of coffee there. Working in stencil, site-specific installation, and guerrilla intervention, Banksy's work tends to reiterate the content

Fig. 6: Eric Drooker. *Jericho* (1996)

and formal gestures of the early twentieth-century avant-garde. On the surface, these sources of inspiration seem to denote a break from the resolutely nineteenth-century references pervading Drooker's work. However, by submitting Banksy's oeuvre to a more thorough investigation, it becomes clear that he too owes an important debt to the Romantic tradition. And so, while art history tells the story of the avant-garde's decisive break from its nineteenth-century counterpoint, the resonant images of the struggles against corporate globalization tell a different tale.

Pointing toward the field of consumption, the social organization of mass society, and the contradictions arising from late capitalism's attempts to smooth over the rough edges of urban experience, Banksy owes much to the situationist interventions of the 1960s and to the avant-garde use of montage. Instances of these practices include his notices informing people visiting famous tourist landmarks that "this is not a photo opportunity,"[19] his sign stenciled in Trafalgar Square in advance of an anti-war demonstration urging people to respect the "designated riot area,"[20] the figure of the rat reappearing throughout his work to remind people of the need to look beneath the polished surface of the city, and collages like the one of Pham Thi Kim Phuc— the Vietnamese girl captured on film fleeing with arms outstretched

Fig. 7: Banksy. *Napalm* (2004)

from a napalm attack on her village in 1972—holding hands with Mickey Mouse and Ronald McDonald [Fig. 7].

Working in stencil, and using photos circulated over the Internet to extend the work's impact, Banksy images are by definition highly mobile and reproducible. By using capitalist seriality against itself, these images become novel interventions that throw into relief the environments into which they get placed. Mobilizing found images and pop culture citations, Banksy revitalizes the early twentieth-century practice of montage. Through this process, the social is rematerialized through the forced correspondence of its phenomenally discrete attributes. Skeptical of montage's political potential, Georg Lukács nevertheless conceded that it was "capable of striking effects, and on occasion can even become a powerful political weapon. Such effects arise from its technique of juxtaposing heterogeneous, unrelated pieces of reality torn from their context. A good photomontage has the same sort of effect as a good joke."[21] Although Lukács goes on to critique the limits of this representational strategy, we find in his initial description all of the important aspects of Banksy's work.

However, it is important to point out that, in the case of Banksy, the social environment into which the work is inserted *becomes one of the juxtaposed heterogeneous elements*. Since this is the case, the political power that Lukács attributes to the joke takes on its full significance. According to Freud, humor was one means by which elements repressed in the unconscious slipped past the censors. The alarming apparition of that which was always there but never acknowledged produces a shock that can only be released through laughter. At its best, humor demands that the narrative fiction rehearsed through conscious enunciation give way to a more vital truth. More often than not, however, laughter becomes the means by which the vitality of this truth is defused and diffused. By passing through laughter, jokes become catharsis. With Banksy, however, the joke cannot serve to defuse the tension and the interjection cannot be diffused; it remains visible until it is painted over. In this way, and at least potentially, laughter inaugurates analysis and Banksy enters a Brechtian territory in which interruption presages the shock of recognition.

Alongside this commitment to montage, Banksy's work seems to occupy an intriguing but indeterminate zone between the mass propaganda poster and the decorative arts. Like the May '68 rebels who rejected mass-printing technologies and chose instead to hand press their propagandistic interventions—like those *enragés* who called alienating seriality into question by forcing anachronistic means into a field commonly thought no longer to support them[22]—Banksy turns naïve folksiness into a strategy of aesthetic disruption.

In other words, Banksy couples citations of twentieth-century montage with representational strategies recovered from still-deeper chambers in the aesthetic archive. Both the cast of characters and the ethics of production that characterized Romanticism are conjoined to the avant-garde's idiom of serial repetition. Nineteenth-century motifs parade around in twentieth-century form. Moreover, though it betrays the commonsense of radical aesthetic theory, it appears that Banksy's work gains in critical force *not through its form* (which—it will become evident—falls victim to a sort of deliberate auto-cannibalization) but through its cited content. Because of this, it seems that Banksy is closer to the Romantic tradition than appearances first suggest.

How do such images play in the present? Consider how—in Banksy's work—the formal gestures of the early twentieth-century avant-garde (now domesticated by a bourgeois art world that could swallow even Duchamp's *Urinal*, and which today are more likely to be used by advertisers than by dissidents) seem to be cited *as* content.

Critical practice as *method* gives way to a *style* denoting "critical practice." Giorgio Agamben noted a similar transition when considering the shift that took place during the interval between Duchamp and Warhol. While Duchamp rematerialized social relations by inserting everyday objects into the aesthetic field, Warhol reversed the process by devising means through which the everyday itself could be aestheticized.[23] And while Banksy's *politics* seem avowedly closer to Duchamp's than they do to Warhol's, this observation brings us no closer to understanding the context in which these interventions now take place.

Although Duchamp and Warhol's gesture was superficially identical, the *pedagogical* premise of the readymade is obliterated in the transition to pop art. With Duchamp, the critical space opened up by alienating everyday objects at least potentially enabled people to contemplate the thingness of things so that they might become aware of the conditions that organized their presence and emergence. In the case of Warhol, the aestheticization of everyday objects becomes a pedagogical induction into a new mode of depthless, immediate contemplation. Through this process, every "thing"—and, in time, the whole of the social world—is reduced to the pleasure of its surface. History is supplanted by style.

But despite the domestication of the gestures upon which it relies, Banksy's work still *feels* like disruption. Just as Marcel Duchamp was able—for a time—to metonymically illuminate capitalist social relations through his anti-aesthetic readymade interventions, Banksy's use of captions and incongruous pairings show signs of enabling productive disorientation and shock. However, unlike the "shock of the new"[24] fostered by the readymade in its original context, the shock arising from an encounter with Banksy seems to be of a different kind.

Specifically, while the content of Banksy's interventions is ostensibly geared toward social criticism, the encounter with the work often ends up feeling like a Romantic re-enchantment of the world. Traces of this tension can be found in the snippets of dialogue published as captions to the images included in *Wall and Piece*, a book that has become Banksy's canonical testament. In one such caption, a Palestinian man comments on murals painted on the Apartheid Wall near Bethlehem. Recognizing the ambivalence of his position, Banksy highlights both his tendency toward, and his understanding of the limits of, enchantment:

Old man: You paint the wall. You make it look beautiful.
Me: Thanks
Old man: We don't want it to be beautiful, we hate this wall,
go home.[25]

VIII

Whether or not he intended it, Banksy's power to enchant by now seems to be his greatest gift to others. And artists working in his idiom (artists who have developed a similar repertoire but who have, on occasion, been more willing to elaborate the ethic underlying their productions) have often been explicit about their commitment to this goal. New York-based artist Swoon is an excellent case in point. Working primarily in paste up, her pieces share obvious aesthetic bonds with Banksy's creations. Anonymous and known only by pseudonym, Swoon brings elements of incongruity into the urban landscape in order to make work that's "engaging" with people's "daily lives" and "more involved in the daily activities of the city."[26]

The principle of montage so evident in Banksy makes a striking reappearance in Swoon's introduction of unlikely characters into even more unlikely surroundings. "I love adding that much texture, and maybe even a little bit of chaos," she says.[27] Read in a sympathetic light, it's difficult to ignore the similarities between Swoon's disruptions and those staged by Brecht, where the action of the protagonists with whom the audience has identified is broken by the introduction of an unlikely figure. At the moment of interruption, the viewer is forced to abandon passive contemplation. Once rendered alien, the depicted situation is thrown under a harsh analytic light. According to Benjamin, Brecht's interruption "arrests the action in its course, and thereby compels the listener to adopt an attitude vis-à-vis the process, the actor vis-à-vis his role."[28]

But despite the analytic potential of such disruptions, Swoon seems to position her work closer to Romanticism than she does to Brecht's scientific experiments. Sounding optimistic, she told *The New York Times* that her objective was to create "something that captured street life" and that enabled people to feel "a human presence in the city."[29] Initially benign, these sentiments disclose a disturbing subtext when considered in light of the fact that—but for the pervasive dissimulations of the commodity form—the city would be *nothing but* "human presence." However, instead of addressing the logic of the commodity directly (as did Duchamp with his ready-made), Swoon's practice seems aimed instead at reintroducing a feeling of wonder as a kind of compensation for the lack engendered by capitalist social relations.

In Swoon's work, the effort to re-enchant the world makes use of perceptual strategies wholly at odds with the aesthetics of the historic avant-garde to which the work superficially refers. Rather than using the jarring placement of objects in the aesthetic field as a means of illuminating the social world from which they derive (a process meant to yield both a socio-material history of the object *and* a means of dislodging the energy trapped in it by capitalism's cannibalization of need), Swoon seems instead to transpose the entirety of the everyday world into the domain of aesthetic contemplation. Instead of demanding (and providing the basis for) focused analysis, her work offers a general education for the aestheticizing gaze. And though this strategy may enable people to deal with the boredom and alienation of the late capitalist city (the boredom and alienation of endless seriality and repetition), it fails in the end to provide a means of transforming that reality. Instead, it offers a course in perceptually enchanting it.

It would be a mistake to draw too great a parallel between Swoon and Banksy. For one thing, Swoon's content has not to date been as explicitly "political" as Banksy's. Furthermore, while Swoon is admired by a small group of activists and cultural producers on the New York art scene, she has—unlike Banksy—yet to receive the kind of exposure that can turn an image into a material force. But despite these differences, one thing remains unmistakable: whether or not Banksy himself ascribes to the aesthetic remodeling of the everyday, it has nevertheless seemed self-evident for artists intervening in the dead and transitory spaces of late capitalism using similar means to pursue this goal explicitly.

IX

In Banksy, the analytic shock of twentieth-century montage is put to the service of resonant images from the nineteenth century. By suggesting (for instance) that "this is not a photo opportunity,"[30] Banksy enjoins the tourist to become the one who *lives* experience rather than simply documenting it (there is, of course, an inevitable tension here: the aesthetic intervention itself becomes the basis for a photo opportunity; it even redeems the act by presenting it as though it arose in response to a different object. In fact, only the perception of the object has changed; however, despite these problems, which are—at their heart—pedagogical, it is impossible to ignore the sentimental kernel underlying Banksy's intervention). Although compelled by means that bear no formal resemblance to the aesthetic principles of nineteenth-century Romanticism, Banksy's repudiation of the photo opportunity nevertheless reiterates its most cherished premise.

Likewise, in his more representational works, Banksy draws on the cast of characters that populated the sentimental art of the late nineteenth and early twentieth centuries. The coke fiend, the drug dealer with face concealed by shadow, the vagrant sitting on the street corner like a fallen angel (bottle of booze in hand), the rioter tossing flowers instead of a Molotov cocktail, the torture victim, the child pulled upward to freedom by the balloons clutched in her palm: each stands as testament to those who are not immediately visible but who are nevertheless presumed to share in a greater apportionment of the human spirit. They are characters mythically endowed with the ability to *really* feel, *really* live.

These images resonated strongly with activists engaged in the struggles against corporate globalization at the beginning of the twenty-first century. Nevertheless, neither the cast of characters nor their political limits are new. In fact, they are notable for their remarkable similarity to the bohemian riff raff paraded before us in Max Raphael's 1933 critique of Picasso's pre-cubist works.

According to Raphael, the history of art from 1789 onward can be read as a story of the tension between "a mythology-oriented group, and another group whose orientation is non-mythological." By observing their interrelation, Raphael imagined that the Marxist sociologist of art could "lay bare the immanent dialectics between a borrowed idealism and an approximate materialism."[31] Situated at the intersection of these two tendencies lay Romanticism, a mode of acknowledging the world-that-ought-to-be in the hope of redeeming the world-that-is. According to Raphael, Picasso's pre-cubist "sentimental" phase (1901–1906) was marked by this same disposition. Its references were "drawn from the fringes of nature and society: blind men, paralytics, dwarves, morons; poor people, beggars; Harlequins and Pierrots; prostitutes, tightrope dancers, acrobats, fortune tellers, strolling players; clowns and jugglers." This same cast of characters makes frequent appearances in both Banksy and Drooker's work. However, according to Raphael, despite the critical potential these figures might suggest, "one must not see anything resembling social criticism, any sort of accusation against the bourgeois order."

> Very much like Rilke, Picasso looks upon poverty as a heroic thing and raises it to the power of myth—the myth of "great inner splendour." Far from regarding it as a social phenomenon which it is up to those afflicted to abolish, he makes of it a Franciscan virtue heralding the approach of God. This virtue becomes sentimentality in his hands, because his purely emotional religiosity stands in opposition to the severity of the created world.[32]

I will be the first to admit that Banksy is not Picasso. Although their cast of characters may be drawn from the same regions of human experience, Banksy's novel use of montage (nowhere in evidence in Picasso's sentimental work) allows him to place his drug fiend directly into *the streets* of the late capitalist metropolis. For this reason, his interjections cannot be reduced to mere sentimentality. Potentially, they could prompt active investigation of real locations defined by real contradictions. This stands in sharp contrast to Picasso's canvas, where the "reality" of the real—especially when confronted from the standpoint of the present—seems to have been effectively aestheticized.[33] Even in the context of montage, however, the archival figures cited by Banksy cannot escape the weight of the narrative conventions with which they've been saddled. The representation moves away from the thing; finally, it becomes the thing itself.

Moreover, by *promising* to point the viewer toward the concealed within the late-capitalist city (that real thing that somehow withstood the transmutations of a world that changes everything into the image of itself), Banksy's Romanticism contributes—even if only inadvertently—to the capitalist project of re-infusing its dead spaces, destroyed by expert administration and calculative rationality, with a kind of life-affirming depth. In *Wall and Piece*, Banksy confronts this problem directly (although he does not resolve it) by presenting comments sent to him online: "I don't know who you are or how many of you there are but I am writing to ask you to stop painting your things where we live…"

My brother and me were born here and have lived here all our lives but these days so many yuppies and students are moving here that neither of us can afford to buy a house where we grew up anymore. Your grafitties are undoubtedly part of what makes these wankers think our area is cool.[34]

As is typical of Romanticism, the outpouring of sentiment made possible by Banksy images provokes feelings of resistance by conceptually negating calculative rationality. What these feelings fail to disclose is the extent to which identification with the antithetical term does not place the viewer outside of capitalism. Far from it: the bourgeois ability to identify with its own dark side, with its unanswerable questions and irrational propositions, has been a great strength since the nineteenth century.

When considered from within the epistemological constraints of the bourgeois horizon, resistance (a production) becomes *the image* of resistance. And though it may yield cathartic respite, the image of resistance cannot escape the expansionist logic of the commodity form. The distance between being enchanted by Banksy and changing the world could not be greater. It is the distance between the rebel and the revolutionary, between negation and "the negation of the negation," between Romanticism and a world in which the bourgeoisie have become impossible.

X

Activists engaged in the struggle against corporate globalization rarely articulated their longing to fill the lack endemic to late capitalism in the language of Romanticism. Nevertheless, the movement's slogans disclose the extent to which Romantic themes shaped its sensibilities. To get a sense of the importance that activists placed on Romanticism's indeterminate outside, one could do no better than to refer to the popular demonstration banner that enjoined people to "abolish capitalism and replace it with something nicer." By not asserting a positive content, the non-specificity of the injunction encouraged people to draw upon their catalogue of secret desires and to think in ways that were not bound by the logic of calculation. By filling their vision of that which was "nicer" with a positive content derived from a secret archive of wish images, activists seem to have uncovered a means of unleashing tremendous repressed energies. A similar effect could be noted each time an activist asserted that the movement was a composite of one no and many yeses.

Recognition of the repressed energies lying in wait beyond the bounds of calculative rationality alerted activists to the productive myth of "another world." As the activist love affair with Drooker and Banksy makes clear, the positive content of this imagined world was drawn from Romanticism's archive of wish images. However, while their identification with this realm seemed to mark a decisive break from all that had come before (another world is possible!), history tells a different story. Indeed, it is impossible to ignore the remarkable connection between the anti-globalization struggles that marked the beginning of the twenty-first century and the uprising of May '68.

When the students of the *Quartier Latin* went Lenin one better and demanded "all power to the imagination," they were reiterating the premise of dual power with an important difference. For Lenin, since the soviets were outside the *Duma*, they afforded the possibility of constituting a power in opposition to Russia's nascent bourgeoisie. By proclaiming that all power should reside in the soviets, Lenin sought to heighten the antagonism so that politics could escape the bourgeois delusion of negotiated truth and openly become class war. Realized as for-itself entities, two opponents could thus come into battle. And with the victory of one over the other, the univocality of truth would be established. However, for the *enragés* of 1968, politics was envisioned as more than a contest between enemy antagonists; it was also a contest between two principles operating within *a single individual*.

In opposition to the calculative rationality and heightened technicity of late capitalism, the rioters demanded that—precisely because it was calculative rationality's incalculable remainder—imagination itself needed to be advanced to the position of productive principle. In this way, Lenin's gesture (a gesture that arose from the need to come to terms with an extrinsic enemy) was superficially appropriated and applied to an internal division. And though the slogan was advanced in the name—and under the sign—of a radical past, the political contest between the proletariat and the bourgeoisie was ultimately displaced by a contest between two principles intrinsic to bourgeois experience. By heralding a future in which the fragmented world would once again be made whole, the movement's emphasis on imagination led directly toward a culture of *anticipation*—the characteristic posture of those who wait for God.

When considered alongside the Romantic rebellion of the nineteenth century, the insurgency of 1999-2003 reveals itself to have been another dramatic rehearsal of the yet-to-be resolved contradiction at the heart of bourgeois experience. At its best, it was an inspired attempt to free radical imagination from the grasp of calculative rationality. In the movement, mythical assertions of *the possibility* of another world arose in conjunction with efforts to displace neo-liberalism's economic presumptions along with its epistemic premises. In opposition to calculative rationality, the movement sought to fill everyday experience with consolidating meaning, proclaiming that there were important regions of human existence that could not be subordinated to quantification.[35] Neo-liberalism's clarion call—"There is no alternative"—would find its perfect negation in the movement declaration that "Another world is possible."

However, while Romanticism's contemporary resonance speaks to its enduring political relevance, it also stands as testament to the non-resolution of the historic contradiction from which it arose. From this perspective, the activist identification with Romanticism signals a kind of neurotic repetition compulsion, a return to the site of trauma carried out under the mistaken belief that the resolution might be found there. Though it is a shining star, Romanticism merely marks the outer limits of the bourgeois horizon. Moreover, because the enormous energies unleashed by Romanticism at semi-regular intervals since the nineteenth century have demonstrated themselves to be insufficient to the task of surpassing this horizon, we must acknowledge that its doubtful that these energies will ever—in and of themselves—be sufficient.

Resolution of the bourgeois world's contradictions will be found not in negation but sublation. The epistemological divide between calculative rationality and spirit—between the bourgeoisie's borrowed idealism and its approximate materialism—is reconciled by historical materialism alone. The image of resistance must cease being a form of wish fulfillment so that it might become the first step in a labor process aimed at transforming the world. Like conscious curators in the archive of dreams, Drooker and Banksy point us in this direction. But they also make clear how far we still have to go before our dreams can become real.

AVATAR AND THE THING ITSELF

> "Our motto must be: reform of consciousness not
> through dogmas, but by analyzing the mystical
> consciousness that is unintelligible to itself. ... It
> will then become evident that the world has long
> dreamed of possessing something of which it has
> only to be conscious in order to possess it in reality.
> ... It is not a question of drawing a great mental
> dividing line between past and future, but of
> *realizing* the thoughts of the past."
> —Karl Marx

I

The mainstream is polluted. It's clogged with the rot of a society that never stops cannibalizing itself. Nothing can live here anymore. Even protest anthems have become advertising jingles. And activists are no longer shocked to see our enemies appropriate the things we once found resonant. For many radicals who grew up—as I did—at the end of history, the decisive moment came when Bob Dylan's "The Times They Are a-Changin'" became the score to a 1996 Bank of Montreal ad.

We alternated between outrage and bewilderment when we noticed that the decisive line "your sons and your daughters are beyond your command" had been redacted from the version used by the bank. On first blush, the gesture was straight up censorship, an attempt to deny

---

This essay first appeared in *Upping the Anti: A Journal of Theory and Action* Number 10, May 2010.

the defiance that Dylan had intended to foment. But when I looked closer, something else came into view. The redaction also suggested that the song could not be swallowed whole. For those who still remembered what it *used to* sound like, the bank's remix filled the song with meaning. Somehow, by trying to defang it, capitalism made the worn-out tune precious again. In 2007, I had a similar experience when, against my better judgment, I sat through *Juno* 'til the very end. Watching the credits roll, I snapped to attention as I heard Kimya Dawson's "Loose Lips" performed with the line "fuck Bush and fuck this war" relegated to oblivion.

II

What is the relationship between capitalism and forms of cultural radicalism? For many, the answer is simple: the mainstream takes without giving. Our only hope is to save ourselves by going underground. But when we follow our desires—when we cultivate alternatives to drowning in pabulum—we discover that our efforts are easily co-opted. Macabre and vampiric, capitalism gains vitality by devouring all that exceeds it. Every beating heart is thus fair game. Pulled into the market, our imaginative élan hits us like a boomerang. The process, as we experience it, is by now familiar. First, we carve out spaces where we might *really* live despite the deadening weight of cultural entropy. Then, as though it had been waiting for us to make our move, the market catches on and turns the music of rebellion into Top 40 bubblegum. Godard's courageous cinematic experiments become the playbook for advertisers struggling to stay one step ahead of the dull commodities they peddle.

Is it any wonder that we're so protective of our scenes? Suspicious of tourists, we set up tribunals to scrutinize the brave or curious few who wander in off the street. Only slowly do we warm to them. This would be fine if it weren't for the fact that, officially, we're a proselytizing bunch committed to broadening our reach. But gathered on this beach of the tumid mainstream, we can't help but adopt the closed postures of the frightened and outcast. On guard against those who would cheapen what we hold most dear, we cling tightly to all that defines us so that it doesn't get plucked from our hands.

If radical politics was just about giving voice to the most complete version of ourselves we could muster, these postures—though ultimately self-defeating—might at least make sense. But this has never been all that we espouse. And, by standing on guard against the loathsome mainstream, we end up cutting ourselves off from many of the very people with whom our movements must connect. It's a pressing contradiction, and one that has yet to be resolved. Hardly surprising, then, that a film like *The Matrix*, which deals with this problem directly, should continue to resonate more than ten years after the fact.

> The Matrix is a system, Neo, and that system is our enemy. But when you are inside and you look around, what do you see; businessmen, lawyers, teachers, carpenters. The minds of the very people we are trying to save. But until we do, these people are still a part of the system and that makes them our enemy.[1]

Intellectually, we understand the need to connect with people beyond our scenes. Nevertheless, we find it difficult to start from the standpoint of the world as we find it. This is because we perceive the content of this world to be indistinguishable from its master, our enemy. Hating capitalism, we subsequently find those who seem at home amidst its wonders to be suspect. Seduced by Manichean simplicity or emboldened by the relative size and stability of our scenes, we lose sight of the fact that capitalism itself is contradictory. And more: people's current allegiances to mainstream cultural forms may very well arise from capitalism's constant appeal to that which lies beyond it. If this is the case, then it's necessary to come to terms with the deep ambivalence underlying people's identification with the status quo. This ambivalence is both a terrain of struggle and an invitation to engage. But seduced by our scenes and contemptuous of the mainstream, we often miss it.

III

Considered together, the ambivalence underlying people's identification with the status quo and capitalism's unending cooptation of radical content suggests that "the mainstream" may actually harbor a secret desire to connect with *us*. Since the beginning of the twentieth century, the profit motive has led advertisers to focus less on their product's restricted use value and more on the promise it was said to fulfill. The success of this approach became incontestable when, in

1929, Edward Bernays staged a publicity stunt designed to get wom-
en to become smokers. Enlisting a group of young women to defy
taboo by lighting up cigarettes while marching in New York City's
Easter Day parade, and prompting the press to describe their act as a
declaration of freedom, Bernays effectively bound the commodity to
the promise. Immediately thereafter, the number of women smokers
increased dramatically.

Sublime though it may be, smoking would never yield the freedom
it promised. Nevertheless, as a kind of compensatory proxy for wom-
en's seemingly unattainable desires, the cigarette provided a cathartic
deferral or partial resolution. And though people may have come to
the realization—as they have with many commodities—that *the idea* of
smoking is more pleasurable than smoking itself, the absence of plausible alternatives for realizing the promise is often enough to keep people
hooked. In this way, a psychic addiction underwrites a chemical one.[2]

However, people's acceptance of capitalism's limited horizon
should not be confused with the idea that they find the world bound
by that horizon to be sufficient. If anything, feelings of lack seem to
grow apace with disposable income. Nevertheless, allegiance to capitalism remains assured by the fact that—at present—capitalism alone
offers tangible answers to the question: how will my desires be realized, even if only partially?

This is not "false consciousness." Rather, it is practical consciousness for those with little reason to believe that the word "reality"
could pertain to anything other than the irrefutable—capitalist—
world they encounter with their senses. The trick for radicals, then,
is not to denounce mainstream consumption or the desires that
stimulate it but rather to reveal the consumed object's inadequacy
when measured against the desire it promises to fulfill. As with the
nineteenth-century movement of industrial workers, which needed
to move from Luddite iconoclasm to factory council appropriation
before it could consummate its struggle, contemporary radicals need
to overcome our ascetic repudiation of the commodity so that we
might engage its generative contradictions directly.

IV

We're still a long way off. Advertisers continue to be far better than us
at recognizing that it's the secret desire for an actual revolution that

Fig. 1 (above, left): Poster for Britain's Churches Advertising Network (1999)
Fig. 2 (above right): Che Guevara

leads consumers to identify with a "revolutionary" new product (a product denoting a freedom it will always fail to yield).[3] Still, it can't go on forever, and the contradictions underlying capitalism's strategy of stimulating desire show signs of nearing their threshold. With the commodity's inability to fulfill the promises it whispers becoming increasingly apparent, advertisers have upped the ante by supplementing their declarations with visual citations drawn directly from the archive of revolutionary movements. This dynamic reached what may have been its acme when, in 1999, Britain's Churches Advertising Network issued a poster that forged a connection between Jesus Christ and Che Guevara [Figures 1 and 2]. Aimed at generating interest in Easter mass, the poster draws on Alberto Korda's iconic *Guerrillero Heróico* (1960) to stimulate the viewer's identification with Christ as a revolutionary figure.

The result is stunning. It made no difference that, if followed to its logical conclusion, the posited identity between Christ and Che *should* have compelled parishioners to turn against the very church being promoted in the ad. Storming the altar, they *should* have found it nearly impossible to suppress the urge to cry out (as Christ did when he cast the moneychangers out of the temple), "my house shall be called the house of prayer; but ye have made it a den of thieves!" None of this happened. As a compensatory proxy mobilized in response to a world defined by restricted horizons, "Che Jesus" effectively positioned the church itself as the actualization of Christ's revolutionary commitment. By the Churches Advertising Network's own admission, the campaign was very successful.[4]

On the surface, it may seem that the ad's resonance owed more to its recapitulation of postmodernism's addiction to irony than to its citation of content drawn from the revolutionary archive. However, such a characterization ignores the fact that, today, "irony" itself operates as a strategy for the organization and management of desire. In other words, irony makes it possible to reiterate stories infused with longing without acknowledging their implications.[5] By forging a path that leads imperceptibly from enunciation to disavowal, irony saves us from having to come to terms with the demands placed upon us by the stories we continue to love in spite of ourselves. In the case of "Che Jesus," Christ becomes harmless through his ironic association with Che. This allows viewers to embrace the image without having to own up to the demands it places upon them. Meanwhile, the fact that Alberto Korda's original photo has continued to resonate precisely on account of its own overt Christological citation disappears entirely.

V

With minor variations, this process can be detected underlying all mainstream citations of radical culture. These citations stimulate a longing to consume by fostering identification with promises that can, in fact, never be realized through consumption. However, while this process underwrites capitalism's uncanny ability to endlessly reproduce itself through substitution and deferral, it also constitutes a gamble. By speaking in the name of that which lies beyond it, capitalism whets an appetite that it can't satisfy. The trick, then, is to intensify dissatisfaction with partial resolutions without giving up on desire. This does not mean searching for more appropriate substitute objects. On the contrary, it means recognizing—as Max Horkheimer did—that "the critical acceptance of the categories which rule social life contains simultaneously their condemnation."[6]

To be sure, by making consumption the only means by which promises can effectively be realized, capitalism continues to maintain the upper hand. And, so long as it's able to "resolve" the inevitable disappointment it generates by substituting new commodities for ones that have lost their luster, it will continue to do so. But despite this apparent stability, we should not lose sight of the fact that the whole system is built on a fault line.

One of our most pressing challenges, then, is to determine how to decouple the desire that stimulates consumption from the consumable object in which it gets trapped. This process, which Walter Benjamin considered analogous to splitting the atom,[7] is crucial since it simultaneously meets two central objectives of the class struggle. First, it helps to release the tremendous human energy trapped in the ruins of our society (a society that, despite constant cinematic anticipation, has yet to collapse) so that it might be channeled into the process of revolutionary change. Second, by releasing and redirecting this energy, it deprives capitalism of the blood upon which it feeds.

How do we split the atom? To begin, we must first develop a new attentiveness to all the implicit and explicit citations of radical content in mainstream culture. This means recognizing those radical themes that sometimes find latent expression in cultural artifacts whose manifest content appears to be apolitical. It also means not rejecting those more overt citations that sometimes crop up in "political" artifacts that nevertheless strike us as lamentable.

Of these two tasks, contemporary radicals have found it far easier to engage in the former. The recent fascination with zombie movies (which, as a genre, oscillate between extreme Left and extreme Right perspectives)[8] can be understood at least in part as an expression of our newly intensified desire and capacity to find traces of the political within the cultural. Nevertheless, and in stark contrast to this intellectual generosity, it remains difficult for radicals to relate to mainstream social artifacts that express "political" content directly but in a fashion considered to be inadequate.

VI

When Michael Moore's *Fahrenheit 9/11* came out in 2004, radical commentators did all they could to outflank it on the left. Activist blogs and online news sources quickly filled up with scathing indictments. Among the film's most vocal detractors, journalist Robert Jensen condemned both Moore and the many leftists who spoke highly of his film. That they could do so, Jensen intoned, "should tell us something about the impoverished nature of the left in this country."[9] This was because, in his estimation, *Fahrenheit 9/11* was "a bad movie."[10] The substance of Jensen's critique had to do with the film's recourse to what he called "subtle racism"[11] and to its unselfconscious reiteration of dangerous American myths.

With respect to the film's subtle racism, Jensen highlighted how—in an effort to make visible the *de facto* unilateralism of Bush's war—Moore's depiction of the "coalition of the willing" drew heavily on images emphasizing the technologically backward character of the endorsing nations. Of greater significance, Jensen also pointed out that the "victims" of the domestic war on terror featured in the film were overwhelmingly white. According to Jensen, this decision effectively erased the experiences of those countless many—primarily people of color—who were interrogated and detained in the months following 9/11.[12]

These aspects of the film are indeed troubling. But what bothered Jensen most was that, in the film's concluding scene, Moore seemed to reiterate the myth that the American military was a global force for good. Speaking of those who are forced by limited prospects to join the military, Moore recounts how "they offer to give up their lives so that we can be free … and all they ask in return is that we not send them in harm's way unless it's necessary." In light of the debacle in Iraq, he asks, "will they ever trust us again?" According to Jensen, "it is no doubt true that many who join the military believe they will be fighting for freedom." Nevertheless,

> we must distinguish between the mythology that many internalize and may truly believe, and the reality of the role of the U.S. military. The film includes some comments by soldiers questioning that very claim, but Moore's narration implies that somehow a glorious tradition of U.S. military endeavors to protect freedom has now been sullied by the Iraq War.[13]

The capacity to read what's implied is a good skill. However, in this case, Jensen's desire to condemn seems to have prevented him from recognizing that Moore's conclusion may very well encourage viewers to conclude that the soldiers *won't* trust "us" again. In its very structure, the film's conclusion sets up a conflict between the myth (and the promise it extends) and the brutal reality that will always tarnish it. In light of this contradiction, the question thus becomes: if we desire the promise of the myth that all might live with freedom, and if US militarism is not the means by which this promise will be realized, then what must we do to assure that it becomes a reality? Although it's impossible to tell whether or not this was Moore's intention, the conflict between myth and reality can easily be extracted from the material provided.

However, rather than seeking to "complete" the film by recognizing (as Horkheimer did) that the critical acceptance of the categories which rule social life contains simultaneously their condemnation, activist critiques like Jensen's aimed instead at rendering it politically inadmissible. Mainstream audiences didn't get the memo; from the 20-minute standing ovation it received when it premiered at Cannes to the staggering number of copies sold when released on DVD a year later, *Fahrenheit 9/11* resonated strongly with millions of viewers. It remains the top-grossing documentary of all time.

Radicals often responded by asserting that we were to the left of Michael Moore. We reveled in our scathing indictments, which proved—once and for all—that our vision was purer than Moore's (as though this was a challenge; as though this was *the* challenge). Meanwhile, most viewers, deeply affected by the film, neither knew nor cared what we thought. We were talking to ourselves. Again. But what form of critical engagement could have pushed viewers to "complete" the film? By what means might people learn to decouple their desire for freedom from the myth in which it's currently ensnared?

There's no easy answer to this question. And any resolution will require more than merely intellectual interventions. Nevertheless, the uncertainty we confront whenever we're forced to consider *what must be done* should not prevent us from lamenting the fact that, in this case, we didn't do much at all. Enamored by our social marginality, many of us retreated to our blogs. If it occurred to us to leaflet people after the show, we rarely got our act together to do so.

VII

The radical scene's tendency to celebrate its own marginality has made it difficult for us to relate to significant mass cultural phenomena. When, by chance, millions of people end up liking what we like, we take it as a sign that we've done something wrong. How, we ask, could people so invested in the comfort of their own ransacked lives identify with cultural offerings tuned to the pitch of a wheezing tear gas canister? True, we have acknowledged a few crossover successes: Bruce Springsteen remained cool even after Ronald Reagan declared that he liked him, and Rage Against the Machine was welcomed to the stage of the Los Angeles anti-DNC protest in 2000 even though they'd undoubtedly been the soundtrack to countless frat-house conflagrations. But despite these occasional signs of generosity, we have yet to figure out how to co-opt capitalism.

If this problem was clear before, the release of *Avatar* during the final weeks of 2009 made it crystallographic. True to form, many radicals have condemned the film. And this is a shame, since condemnation will not bring us closer to understanding why *Avatar* has stimulated more audience interest than any other Hollywood blockbuster in history. Whether measured in terms of box office receipts or the tremendous amount of online discussion it has inspired, it's useless to deny the film's mass cultural resonance. Indeed, both the intensity and sheer volume of popular discussions suggest that it has successfully overcome the restricted bounds of "entertainment." Less than a month after its release, we reached a moment of decisive inversion. The film itself became the stable referent. People began to interpret their life through *Avatar*'s lens.

Following a story that appeared on CNN in January 2010, *The Huffington Post* reported that *Avatar*-related online discussion boards had become *ad hoc* peer counseling hubs. On these boards, filmgoers struggled with the unforgiving greyness of the world they confronted upon leaving the theater. These feelings of dread were compounded by the dysphoria that arose from people's identification with the Na'vi as ego ideal (the image of themselves as they ought to be). And, because the film presents the Na'vi as natural and harmonious extensions of the world they inhabit, people's struggle for the realization of their ego ideal has put them into direct conflict with their own wasted lives. According to *The Huffington Post*, one viewer described how they had been depressed ever since they saw the film. "Watching the wonderful world of Pandora and all the Na'vi made me want to be one of them," they lamented.[14]

A response such as this one may seem idiosyncratic—testament more to the personal troubles of a science fiction shut-in than to any real social issue. Nevertheless, it's important to consider how, whether or not this was its intention, *Avatar* helped to set up a conflict between many people's persistent but unrealized desire for happiness and the imperfect world in which they live. To be sure, the overwhelming response to conflicts of this kind has been therapeutic or managerial. Nevertheless, the fact that it's experienced as "conflict" at all should alert us to its importance as a site of struggle. In order to orient to this site, it's useful to consider Walter Benjamin's analysis of what, following Freud, he identified as wish images. Describing how people's utopian longing can help to jumpstart the process of social transformation, Benjamin recounted how, "corresponding in the collective consciousness to the forms of the new means of production ... are images in which the new is intermingled with the old."

> These images are wishful fantasies, and in them the collective seeks both to preserve and to transfigure the inchoateness of the social product and the deficiencies in the social system of production.... These tendencies direct the visual imagination, which has been activated by the new, back to the primeval past. In the dream in which, before the eyes of each epoch, that which is to follow appears in images, the latter appears wedded to elements from prehistory, that is, of a classless society.[15]

When applied to Cameron's film, Benjamin's analysis suggests that, by operating in the fantastical register, *Avatar* proposes a resolution to contemporary earthly concerns by staging a return to the site of trauma. As noted by several commentators, this site is none other than the conquest of the Western hemisphere by European powers. Returning to this point with the assistance of allegory, the viewer is given the opportunity to imagine how (if they play their cards right) *this time* the outcome might be different.

Is *Avatar*, then, simply an over-financed rehearsal of *Dances With Wolves*, *Pocahontas*, and *The Last Samurai* as many commentators have proposed? No. What distinguishes these three films from *Avatar* is that, as historical narratives obliged to adhere to the contexts that fill them with meaning, they all end in failure. Barring a revisionism so grand as to overwrite the advent of the modern world system, it could not be otherwise.[16] And so, while Kevin Costner's improbable but deeply affective bond with the Sioux may have redeemed *him*, it could not save the people of the plains from eradication. Only

Avatar—precisely because of its status as speculative fiction—is able to envision redemption as a process with a definitive, resolved, end.[17]

As wish image, the Na'vi stimulate people's longing for a better world by standing in as fulfillment of the unrealized promise of the (mythic) past.[18] As in Benjamin's account, this fulfillment is achieved through of a fusion of the old and the new. In *Avatar*, the fusion is made explicit through the literal connectivity shared by the creatures of Pandora. The Na'vi transfer data through the organic equivalent of fiber-optic cables growing directly from their skulls. James Lovelock's Gaia hypothesis thus finds imaginative concretion through one of the internet era's central fantasies.

Amplifying their significance, these connective links are also explicitly eroticized. Not only is Sully, the film's protagonist, told to avoid playing with its tendrils lest he go blind, the leaked script for the extended love scene (not shown in the cinematic release) has the depicted characters "linking up." And so, while immersion in collaborative networks is normally understood—especially since the publication of *Civilization and its Discontents* in 1930—as demanding the suspension of pleasure, on Pandora connectivity and pleasure magically coincide. In this way, *Avatar* rehearses an image of redemption that echoes Herbert Marcuse's greatest hopes from 1955's *Eros and Civilization*. It's no wonder that (whatever its distance from genuine erotic experience) some online commentators have begun speculating about the possibility of Na'vi porn.

The wish image's social significance arises from its ability to give the desire for redemption a concrete referent. Nevertheless, in and of itself, the wish image does not suggest anything about *the means* by which redemption might be achieved. And so, while it stimulates desire and provides a compelling vision of what the future might hold, it's far from inevitable that the energy drawn to the wish image will be directed toward making that vision a reality. It's therefore entirely possible that *Avatar*—the commodity—will remain the posited "resolution" to the desires it provokes.

In this scenario, the film becomes a kind of repetition compulsion, an expression of capitalism's never-ending process of substitution and deferral (good enough, until something better comes along). Indeed, the depression recounted by repeat viewers not able to gain access to "the real thing" through the film suggests that no other path seemed evident. And while—in and of itself—the film would never be enough, most viewers were left with nothing but consumption-related choices: watch the film again despite its incapacity to deliver on the promise, subject the promise to forms of ironic disavowal, or find some other consumable thing that might *really* do the trick.

VIII

As expressions of our longing for redemption, wish images have often been used to revitalize the commodity form. In order for this *not* to happen, it's necessary for us to imagine how our longing for actualization might be decoupled from consumption and reestablished as a central category of production. As Marx noted in *Capital*, the definitive feature of the human labor process is that the image of the thing to be produced exists in the mind of the producer prior to its concretion. In that field of production known as "politics," this means that the wish image ceases to be a seduction (as happens in the sphere of consumption) and becomes instead the basis for decisive action.

It's therefore not surprising that Indigenous people—people for whom the connection between politics and production often continues to be more explicit than it's become for the cosmopolitan inhabitants of the global north—have begun to draw upon images from *Avatar* to sharpen the focus of their confrontations with constituted power. The website *Survival* recently reported on several of these generative citations.[19]

In one report, a Penan man from Sarawak recounted how "the Na'vi people in 'Avatar' cry because their forest is destroyed." According to the interview subject, the situation for the Penan was the same, since "logging companies are chopping down our big trees and polluting our rivers, and the animals we hunt are dying."[20] Similarly, a Kalahari Bushman described how *Avatar* "shows the world about what it is to be a Bushman, and what our land is to us. Land and Bushmen are the same."[21] Other groups have gone still further by transposing the film from the register of generative analogy into that of resource for action.

Appealing to James Cameron for assistance through an ad placed in the film industry magazine *Variety*, the Dongria Kondh tribe in India highlighted the connection between *Avatar* and their own struggle against Vedanta Resources, a mining company determined to extract bauxite from their sacred mountain.[22] Acting even more directly, a group of Palestinian protestors in Bil'in recently dressed up like Na'vi to highlight the connection between the struggle on Pandora and their own experience of dispossession.[23] In an uncanny instance of art-imitating-life-imitating-art, IDF soldiers were captured on film firing tear gas at the demonstrators. In this way, the structural analogy between Israel and *Avatar*'s "sky people" became irrefutable.[24]

But despite these creative appeals to the film's resonant images (appeals that have come from Indigenous people themselves), many radicals continue to be reluctant to acknowledge the film's importance. To be sure, there have been some notable exceptions: Evo Morales welcomed *Avatar* as a "profound show of resistance to capitalism and the struggle for the defense of nature."[25] Similarly, in an overwhelmingly positive report for socialistworker.org, Nagesh Rao concluded that it was significant that "millions of moviegoers around the world are flocking to a film that unflinchingly indicts imperialism and corporate greed, defends the right of the oppressed to fight back, and holds open the potential for solidarity between people on opposite sides of a conflict not of their choosing."[26] Nevertheless, within North American radical scenes, assessments such as these have remained rare.

IX

Why? In order to answer this question, it's necessary to highlight the numerous ways in which the film's representation of people in struggle differs sharply from radical ideals. Along with its suggestion that people with disabilities (should) want to be "cured" and its uncritical woman-as-prize plot device, *Avatar* infuriates us because the oppressed Na'vi are exoticized and incapable of saving themselves. Worse, the film relies upon the heroic intervention of a white outsider to bring resolution. Annalee Newitz did much to stimulate discussion about the latter frustration with her influential "When Will White People Stop Making Films Like 'Avatar,'" an article first published on the website io9.com.[27] In that piece, Newitz proposes that *Avatar*, like *Dances With Wolves*, is best understood as a fantasy about race told from the perspective of white people. According to Newitz, "these are movies about white guilt."

> Our main white characters realize that they are complicit in a system which is destroying aliens, AKA people of color—their

cultures, their habitats, and their populations. The whites realize this when they begin to assimilate into the "alien" cultures and see things from a new perspective. To purge their overwhelming sense of guilt, they switch sides, become "race traitors," and fight against their old comrades. But then they go beyond assimilation and become leaders of the people they once oppressed.[28]

Newitz concludes that this is "the essence of the white guilt fantasy." In her account, this fantasy involves more than the desire to be absolved of crimes or to join the side of the righteous; instead, "it's a wish to lead people of color from the inside rather than from the (oppressive, white) outside."[29] In other words, according to Newitz, *Dances With Wolves* and *Avatar* encourage white people to imagine that it's possible to simultaneously be absolved of their guilt while maintaining a version of the superiority and privilege associated with their current position.

These dynamics will no doubt sound familiar to many radicals (indeed, Newitz's article circulated as broadly as it did precisely because it rang so true). And there's no doubt that the fantasy of painless redemption described in the piece constitutes a real obstacle to meaningful solidarity. It's therefore both surprising and unfortunate that, when measured against the issues she's highlighted, Newitz's proposed resolution falls as flat as it does. "I'd like to watch some movies about people of color (ahem, aliens), from the perspective of that group, without injecting a random white (erm, human) character to explain everything to me," she reports.

> Science fiction is exciting because it promises to show the world and the universe from perspectives radically unlike what we've seen before. But until white people stop making movies like Avatar, I fear that I'm doomed to see the same old story again and again.[30]

How are we to understand these comments? First, Newitz positions herself as a connoisseur of radical difference. Next, she notes that the repetition compulsion that overtakes white people while working through their fantasy of overcoming guilt without losing status prevents her from realizing her own desire. In other words, the unacknowledged preoccupation with white guilt (a phenomenal experience with an incontestable material basis) gets in the way of realizing the desire to indulge in the pleasure of unmediated engagement with the Other. The logical—but politically untenable—resolution to the problem therefore must be: overcome guilt! Enjoy what the universe has to offer! What at first appeared to be a radical critique thus turns into a reiteration of pedestrian multiculturalism.[31]

X

Newitz hits the mark when she claims that *Avatar* provides a clear view of white people's racial fantasies. However, her injunction to simply produce films that "show the world and the universe from perspectives radically unlike what we've seen before" leaves the problem unresolved. This is because white people's compulsion to tell the same story over and over again corresponds directly to the unresolved nature of the material circumstances in which they find themselves. Or, more directly: because white people *are* guilty, it's inevitable that knowledge of that guilt will return like a repressed phenomenon—even if only in symptomatic form. Consequently, until we find a means of resolving the history of injustice and oppression we've contributed to or benefited from, any "overcoming" will be nothing more than deferral. But why do white fantasies take people of color as their object?

In order to answer this question, it's useful to begin by noting, as David McNally does, that "bourgeois culture is constituted in and through a process in which bodiliness is ascribed to outcast others…"

> Bodies appeared outside bourgeois society, therefore, as attributes of foreign or alien social types. These non-bourgeois others … were feminized, racialized, and animalized… All of these bodies underwent simultaneous processes of sexualization and degradation.[32]

Obverse to the racialization and animalization of people of color, Europe's white bourgeois subjects began to envision themselves in increasingly disembodied ways. Modeled after the Christian mystery, which posits spirit as residing *in* but not being *of* the body, Richard Dyer notes that this conception of whiteness impelled those possessed by it toward unattainable transcendental omniscience (what McNally, later in his analysis, calls "idealist abstraction").[33] The fact that such transcendence is—practically speaking—unattainable did not prevent white people from becoming disconnected from the ground of corporeality.[34]

By imposing a constitutive tension in being, the spiritual conceits of whiteness have historically stimulated a tremendous capacity for limited forms of self-realization. However, they have also produced a systemic anxiety that cannot be resolved within the terms available to whiteness itself. In response, and in an effort to "resolve" the anxiety brought on by their premature and always-partial ascendance to the universal, white people have often developed a chronic desire for gross particularity.

Given their association with the body in the white imagination, it's hardly surprising to find that people of color have been enlisted as the imagined resolution to white lack. Whether in the moment of domination (where the deference of the dominated confirms the being of the dominator) or of Romantic allure (where the posited corporeality of the person of color is invested with the power to save those who have lost their way), people of color—as categorical abstractions—have offered the same respite to white people that commodities have offered to capitalist consumers more generally. In the moment of their "consumption," they are substitute objects, deferred actualizations.

Anti-racist theorists have been right to point out that white people's racial fantasies are harmful to those they take as their object. However, these fantasies must also be understood as wish images. Although distorted by their immersion in the sphere of consumption, these images denote a legitimate desire to overcome capitalism's expulsion of the body. In this way, they lay claim to the promise of a mythic past—a moment before the fall—when human experience was envisioned as whole. Marking the highpoint of the historical division between mental and manual labor, such reconciliation is impossible in the bourgeois world.

To the extent that it rehearsed these racial fantasies, and to the extent that these fantasies resonated with people, *Avatar* provided an opportunity for radicals to turn identification with the film into disaffection with the world. Even at its worst, the film's contradictions invited us to pry it apart, to wrest the desire that animates consumption from the inevitable limits of the consumed object itself. Had we proceeded in this way, we *could* have begun to incite change through the illumination of what Marx described as "mystical consciousness that is unintelligible to itself." From there, we *could* have highlighted the extent to which "the world has long dreamed of possessing something of which it has only to be conscious in order to possess it in reality."[35] That "something" is a world free of exploitation, a world where, through activity, people themselves put an end to repetition and deferral.

For the most part, however, radicals left mystical consciousness to its own devices. We were not prepared to harness the massive public interest in *Avatar*. And, by succumbing to familiar habits, we lost an opportunity. The mode of intervention considered above can be applied to any commodity; however, there are moments—strategically speaking—when its application will be especially significant. Mass cultural resonance is one way to recognize these moments. Before the next one is upon us, let's not be afraid to try splitting atoms.

MATTER'S MOST MODERN CONFIGURATIONS

Rivera, Picasso, and Benjamin's Dialectical Image

> "Human history is like paleontology. Owing
> to a certain judicial blindness even the best
> intelligences absolutely fail to see the things which
> lie in front of their noses. Later, when the moment
> has arrived, we are surprised to find traces
> everywhere of what we failed to see."
> —Karl Marx

I

When engaging in materialist analysis, conventional wisdom instructs us to pay attention to bread and butter, bricks and mortar. This is no doubt important; however, a more nuanced understanding of the precise attributes of "matter" demands that we come to terms with the fact that solid objects are—for the most part—empty spaces bound together by energetic relays. Such relays are at play in history as well. There, people struggle to assemble material fragments so that they might actualize the desires with which they've become infused

---

This essay first appeared in *Scapegoat: Architecture / Landscape / Political Economy*, No. 2, 2011.

through the course of the struggle for freedom. Foregrounding such relays does not put us at odds with materialist analysis. Quite the opposite: when properly understood, they reveal themselves to be constitutive of it.

II

In Convolute N of *The Arcades Project* and in his essay on the concept of history, Walter Benjamin provided a brief but compelling account of the dialectical image.[1] According to Benjamin, images became dialectical when they produced a moment of historical cessation in which a viewer could come face to face with "a revolutionary chance in the fight for the oppressed past."[2] By constellating the fragments of historical memory, these images enjoined the viewer to consider what would be required to act upon history as such. Here, the *promise* of finally fulfilling the desire for happiness and the *means* by which that fulfillment might be achieved become visible all at once.

For Benjamin, dialectical images revealed how the unrealized promise of the past—a promise often conceived in mythic or religious terms—might come to fruition through action upon the profane conditions of the present. And, as Susan Buck-Morss has pointed out, such a vision of reconciliation is itself "an ur-historical motif in both Biblical and classical myth."[3] However, unlike other forms of engagement with mythic anachronism, dialectical images do more than rediscover past themes "symbolically, as aesthetic ornamentation."[4] Instead, by impelling profane reckoning, they enjoin the viewer to actualize unrealized promise by forging a constellation between the past's wishful motifs and "matter's most modern configurations."[5] Thus it was that Neil Armstrong set foot on the moon under the sign of Apollo.

In what follows, I consider Diego Rivera's *Man at the Crossroads* (1933) [Fig. 1] and Pablo Picasso's *Guernica* (1937) to highlight how they intuitively gave Benjamin's conception a concrete visual form.[6] To be sure, these images did not produce the cessation of happening that Benjamin had hoped for. Nevertheless, from the standpoint of formal analysis, they are coherent visual approximations of the dialectical image. As such, they are useful reference points for those seeking to illuminate—and thus to make vulnerable—the properly architectonic dimensions of late capitalism's ersatz depthlessness. And, once

Fig. 1: Diego Rivera, *Man at the Crossroads* (1933)

this has been accomplished, we can begin to consider how an image worthy of Benjamin's concept might be produced *today*.

The need for such a production arises not solely from the fact that—as Fredric Jameson has noted—it is now easier to imagine the end of the world than it is to imagine the end of capitalism.[7] With the dialectical image, the very conception of "anti-capitalism" reaches a point at which the habit of positing resistance as a merely logical negation of the constituted world is repudiated once and for all. Because it forces us to recognize the extent to which everything is already present (the extent to which the problem is not one of "matter," but of its configuration), the dialectical image enjoins its viewers to confront the decision demanded by politics from a point wholly intrinsic to their own desires for freedom. Here, the collective subject of history finds its nominating "we" first and foremost through the encounter with an experience of lack that—though experienced individually—remains universal right up until the moment of its dissolution.

III

Man at the Crossroads was an enormous mural that stood nearly 5 meters tall and 11.5 meters wide. Gathered on the right side of the image are the forces of socialist revolution. Workmen look on from the bottom quadrant. Marx, Trotsky, and others gather behind a banner exhorting the workers of the world to unite. Immediately behind these figures, the viewer confronts a statue of Caesar holding a broken column emblazoned with a swastika. The statue's head has come off and the workers are using it as a stool.

In the top right quadrant of the image, peasant women line up alongside workers carrying red flags as they march in procession.[8] In the space behind the statue, demonstrators confront soldiers in gas masks. Suspended mid-ground, a group of athletes looks leftward with determination and élan.

In the bottom left quadrant of the mural, seated spectators gaze into a kind of looking glass. Behind them sits a statue of Jupiter with its hands cut off. The lightning that these hands once wielded has been channeled into a machine displaying an x-ray image of a human skull. Beside the x-ray stands Charles Darwin surrounded by animals. Congregated on the same mid-ground as Jupiter, a group of men stand about pensively. Behind them, a conflict unfolds between demonstrators and police riding horses. A line of soldiers wearing gas masks consumes the top left quadrant of the image. Above their heads flies a squadron of bombers similar to those that will destroy Guernica in 1937—three years after Rivera's mural was itself destroyed.

In the middle of the image stands the time machine. Evoking the liberating potential of technology, the time machine also recalls Ezekiel's Old Testament vision, in which the development of productive forces is anticipated in dream form. According to Ezekiel, "when the living creatures moved, the wheels beside them moved; and when the living creatures rose from the ground, the wheels also rose." This was because "the spirit of the living creatures was in the wheels."[9] Under capitalism, this dream would find a perverse—but potentially liberating—concretion.

The time machine is set in a circular form bisected by two ellipses that divide it into four quadrants. In the bottom quadrant, plants from different parts of the world reach roots into the exposed geological substratum of natural history. The top quadrant comprises the bulk of the time machine's machinery. It appears to be assembled from components derived from different technological phases in the history of production. Occupying opposite poles, natural history is counterposed to the "new nature"[10] of human history while simultaneously being connected to it through the mediating figure of Man. In the left quadrant, representatives of the idle rich play cards and sip martinis. Opposite these figures, workers representing different races gather together with Lenin.

The ellipsis bisecting the image from top left to bottom right contains the microscopic elements of the world. In the ellipsis bisecting the image from top right to bottom left, a telescopic view replaces the microscopic one. The viewer is confronted with the enormity of the universe and its celestial bodies. In the center of the image sits a worker with hands on a set of controls. Wearing overalls and heavy gloves, he turns his eyes upward and assumes a posture that suggests Renaissance-era devotional painting, socialist realism, or both. Caught between the poles of natural and human history, the telescopic and microscopic expanses of the universe, and the antithetical terms of the class struggle all contracted to a single point, Rivera's Man occupies a space of absolute tension and non-resolution. Rendered in its barest schematic form, the mural looks something like this:

Considered in this way, *Man at the Crossroads* abides by the dialectical image's defining characteristics. For Buck-Morss, such images "can perhaps best be pictured in terms of coordinates of contradictory terms, the 'synthesis' of which is not a movement toward resolution, but the point at which their axes intersect."[11] The image's accumulated tensions cannot be resolved by teleological fiat. Instead, the task falls to the viewer who comes to realize that the moment of reckoning cannot be suspended indefinitely.[12]

But while the formal confluence between Rivera's image and Benjamin's conception is striking, the mural's initial impact owed less to its composition than to the fact that it was denied an audience in the lobby of the Rockefeller Center. "Rockefellers Ban Lenin in RCA Mural and Dismiss Rivera," announced *The New York Times* on April 10, 1933.[13] Almost immediately, diverse sections of civil society began to mobilize. According to journalist Pete Hamill, responses included "protests, picket lines, fiery editorials," and "press conferences."[14] For his part, "Diego made an impassioned speech at a rally in Town Hall" while "liberals drew parallels between the brainless censorship of Stalin's 'socialist realism' and that of the Rockefellers."[15] On June 15, 1933, the socialist newspaper *Workers' Age* ran a photo of the mural along with an article by Rivera. At that moment—and as Benjamin predicted a dialectical image might—Rivera's mural threatened to disappear irretrievably.[16]

For several months, the unfinished work lay beneath a heavy cloth that had been hung to conceal it. Then, under cover of darkness on February 9, 1934, Rockefeller had the mural destroyed. The image, however, did not disappear. For months, it remained an important point of discussion in Left and liberal circles both in New York and elsewhere. Later in 1934, Rivera reproduced the mural in the *Palacio de Bellas Artes* in Mexico City. Renamed *Man, Controller of the Universe*, the image began to find resonance amongst new audiences. No longer simply the focal point of a fight around artistic expression and no longer just an impressionistic trace caught by snapshot, the image began to come into its own. Around the same time, the liberal façade of the Rockefeller enterprise began to crack.

IV

From the standpoint of the present, the conflict between Rockefeller and Rivera appears inevitable. Why did a captain of industry imagine that a communist artist would produce an image appropriate for his building's lobby? In order to answer this question, it's useful to consider the circumstances that led to the conflict itself. On November 7, 1932, Rockefeller assistant Raymond Hood sent a telegram to Rivera inviting him to paint a mural in the Rockefeller Center. According to Rockefeller, the mural was to depict "Man at the crossroads" as he looked "uncertainly but hopefully towards the future." Rockefeller further indicated that the mural was to depict "human intelligence controlling the powers of nature."[17]

In a written submission for the project, Rivera described how he would address the theme: "my painting will show human understanding in possession of the forces of nature, which are expressed by a bolt which cuts off the fist of Jupiter and is transformed into useful electricity which helps to cure man's illnesses, unites men through radio and television, and gives them electricity and motive power."[18] Further into his description, Rivera described how the right side of the image would be given over to "workers coming to a real understanding of their rights in relation to the means of production which has resulted in a plan to do away with tyranny, personified by a statue of Caesar which is disintegrating and the head of which lies on the floor."[19] Mesmerized (and having already been brushed off by Picasso and Matisse), Rockefeller allowed the plans to proceed.

By February 1934, the mural was destroyed. Justifying his decision, Rockefeller pointed to the image of Lenin that Rivera incorporated into the mural after the commission had been approved. And Rockefeller may indeed have felt duped. But even though Lenin was never explicitly mentioned in the written submission, it's hard to imagine how a mural that set out to depict proletarian cooperation and the liberating potential of electricity could have yielded anything else. After all, hadn't it been Lenin who proclaimed that communism was "soviet power plus the electrification of the whole country"?[20] For anyone taken by historical details, his appearance in Rivera's mural seems as inevitable as Rockefeller's bewilderment seems shocking.

The conflict becomes clearer when considered from the standpoint of the dialectical image. Both Rockefeller and Rivera knew what it meant to be at the crossroads. Both knew that the relationship between labor and nature was of central importance when traversing the gulf between present and future. Agreement ended, however, when consideration turned to the precise *means* by which that gulf would be traversed. If Rockefeller had envisioned "human intelligence controlling the powers of nature," he could not envision how, at its logical conclusion, this control needed to extend to the "new nature" of technological forces—the means of production—as well.

V

Like *Man at the Crossroads*, *Guernica* [Fig. 2] is an enormous canvas standing nearly 3.5 meters tall and nearly 8 meters wide. And, like Rivera's mural, *Guernica* is divided into three sections and cut into four quadrants by lines that seem to emanate from its center. On the right, a figure with arms outstretched screams from an open window. Flames engulf the building. Another figure stretches a long arm into the middle of the canvas. Holding an oil lamp, the figure illuminates the scene below. Moving from right to left across the bottom of the canvas, a woman hobbles along the ground. Her breasts are exposed and her knee is painfully contorted.

On the left side of the image, a woman holds a dead infant close to her chest. Its eyes are slits. Evoking Michelangelo's *Pietà*, the woman's head is thrown upward in a cry of anguish. Her eyes are frantic. Behind the woman stands a placid bull staring into the space occupied by the viewer. To the right of the bull, a bird flutters in agitation

Fig. 2: Pablo Picasso, *Guernica* (1937)

on top of a table that's barely distinguishable from the background against which it's set. Beneath the woman with the dead infant, the viewer confronts the outstretched hand of a fallen soldier. Moving toward the center of the canvas, the arm gives way to the soldier's head. His eyes are frozen. His mouth is a scream. Moving still further rightward, the viewer discovers that the soldier's head has been severed. His other arm has likewise been severed. In his hand, he still clutches a broken sword.

A horse takes up the image's center. Pierced by a lance and about to fall over, it's depicted with its head thrown back, mouth open, and eyes staring wildly. The woman crawling right to left across the bottom of the canvas has the horse's head in her sightline. The figure staring with arm outstretched from the window looks down upon the same scene in horror. Distinct from all the other figures in the image, the horse is covered in vertical brushstrokes. Nearly uniform in their execution, they occupy a connotative space caught somewhere between horsehair and ledger marks tallying the dead. Above the horse's head glows an incandescent light. Both visually and connotatively indeterminate, the light is a blazing sun, an explosion, an eye, a suspended bare light bulb.

Although the arrangement of *Guernica*'s contents suggests a plausible foreground, mid-ground, and background, the image itself remains nearly completely flat. Prying its figures from the scene in which they find themselves is difficult. One is left with the impression that there is no space to breathe. For Robert Hughes, this kind of visual organization was a defining characteristic of early cubism. During this period, Picasso's images had "very little air in them."[21] And though *Guernica* was not cubist in any conventional sense, its reiteration of certain cubist representational strategies nevertheless managed to give the whole scene an airless, claustrophobic, and topographical quality. For art historian Frank D. Russell, *Guernica* "brought Cubism into the open and evoked a broad concern with the language of modern art."[22] Practically speaking, this meant that the viewer was drawn into an indeterminate zone in which distinctions between inside and outside, content and context, began to fall apart.

The institutionalization of the avant-garde during the postwar period made *Guernica*'s topographical perspective commonplace. And, as Fredric Jameson has noted, Picasso's work now tends to strike postmodern viewers as more or less "realistic."[23] Nevertheless, when it first appeared in 1937, *Guernica's* claustrophobic topography was shocking. Describing the scene at the Paris World's Fair where the work was first exhibited, Spanish Pavilion architect Josep Lluís Sert recalled that, when confronted with *Guernica*, "the majority didn't understand what it meant." Nevertheless, "they did not laugh… They just looked at it in silence."[24]

As its title affirms, *Guernica* is a historical painting; however, the depicted events stand in relation to the history they refer to in an indeterminate way. For John Berger, *Guernica* is striking because "there is no town, no aeroplanes, no explosion, no reference to the time of day, the year, the century, or the part of Spain where it happened."[25] Moreover, the canvas offers "no enemies to accuse" and "no heroism" to admire.[26] But despite this indeterminacy, Berger is convinced that even an uninitiated viewer would know that *Guernica* was a work of protest. How?

> It is in what has happened to the bodies. … What has happened to them in being painted is the imaginative equivalent of what happened to them in sensation in the flesh. We are made to feel their pain with our eyes. And pain is the protest of the body.[27]

Although Berger goes on to recount a number of misgivings about the work, his assessment of *Guernica* coincides with Benjamin's conception of the dialectical image in several important respects. This is so not least because, in *Guernica*, the title (which refers to a concrete, profane reality) becomes a kind of caption that turns the image as a whole—an image that, for Berger, was "a protest against a massacre of the innocents at any time"[28]—into what Buck-Morss imagined Benjamin would have understood as an allegorical emblem, "a montage of visual image and linguistic sign, out of which is read, like a picture puzzle, what things 'mean.'"[29] Illuminated in this way, the unique event provides passage into the realm of a more universal meaning. The fragment becomes metonymic, and decisive action at the point of tension opens the possibility of action upon history as such.

Even though the specific details it recounts have begun to fade from our collective memory, *Guernica* has continued to speak to people. This resonance no doubt owes to the fact that its illuminated fragments contain traces of a more universal experience. According to radical arts collective Retort, "the experience and preserved memory of blast and firestorm is one of the central strands of twentieth century identity."[30]

Consequently, by depicting this scene, *Guernica* stimulates "the repressed consciousness of modernity's ordinary costs."[31] Thus it was that April 26, 1937 became constellated with our own catastrophic present.

VI

How did Rockefeller—the man who destroyed Rivera's mural—end up donating *Guernica* to the UN? Recounting how he came to buy a tapestry reproduction of the image in 1955, Rockefeller remained silent on the question of political content and instead weighed in on the merit of reproductions. Having learned from architect and collaborator Wallace Harrison that a "huge tapestry … had been made from a maquette which Picasso had designed after the original painting," Rockefeller could not help but to respond in conventional bourgeois fashion: "When I saw the tapestry, I bought it immediately."

> [Art historian and first director of the Museum of Modern Art] Alfred Barr was disturbed by my purchase of what he had heard was just a distorted copy of one of the greatest paintings of the twentieth century. … However, when Alfred actually saw the tapestry for the first time, he completely changed his mind.[32]

In 1985, Rockefeller's estate bequeathed the tapestry to the United Nations. Hung outside the Security Council chambers in New York, the offering was no doubt meant to be emblematic of Rockefeller's commitments. Those commitments were idealistic. But they were material, too: the Rockefeller family had been directly responsible for financing both the Museum of Modern Art (which housed the *Guernica* canvas between 1958 and 1981) and the Wallace Harrison-designed United Nations compound, which was built on the ruins of a slaughterhouse worthy of Upton Sinclair. Reporting on the area in the real estate section of *The New York Times*, Jerry Cheslow recounts how, "by the turn of the twentieth century,"

> Turtle Bay had become a seedy, overcrowded warren of tenements and deteriorating row houses, many of them homes to German, Irish, Polish and Italian immigrants. Many of the residents toiled in the stock pens, garages, coal yards and slaughterhouses on what is now the site of the United Nations.[33]

In this way (and in truly Benjaminian fashion), Rockefeller's "cultural treasures" cannot be contemplated without horror. "They owe their existence not only to the efforts of the great minds and talents who have created them, but also to the anonymous toil of their contemporaries."[34]

On February 5, 2003, Colin Powell presented U.S. plans for war on Iraq at a press conference outside the United Nations Security Council chambers. Instead of *Guernica*, however, the backdrop for the event was a blue shroud that could not help but announce what it concealed. As with the veiling of *Man at the Crossroads*, the veiling of *Guernica* brought the image to the attention of millions.

As before, people responded with outrage and incredulity. In the February 5, 2003 edition of *The New York Times,* columnist Maureen Dowd commented that Mr. Powell couldn't "seduce the world into bombing Iraq surrounded on camera by shrieking and mutilated women, men, children, bulls and horses."[35] The problem was no less evident to activists on the street. Scanning the anti-war scene, Retort took note of how "many a placard on Piccadilly and Las Ramblas rang sardonic changes on Bush and the snorting bull."[36] Shrouded and in danger of disappearing irretrievably, *Guernica* flashed up at a moment of danger like *Man at the Crossroads* had before it.

VII

Investigating *Man at the Crossroads* and *Guernica* together in this way highlights a number of important points concerning materialist analysis and how it might best be conducted. First, it shows how these two works, although rarely considered together in the literature of art history, are nevertheless bound to one another through an intriguing historical relay. Almost from their inception, both works lived a double life caught somewhere between original and reproduction. Both mediated controversy and both became tied in various ways to the Rockefeller legacy. As part of this legacy, both works were shrouded at a moment of danger. In both cases, the act of shrouding led to significant political commentary and mobilization.

In addition to these biographical connections, the works also share a number of significant compositional features. Most evident among these is the significant role that scale plays in their perceptual organization. Here, the viewer is immediately confronted with the fact that both images approach dimensions akin to those of the cinema's famous silver screen. This is no small matter since, as Berger has noted, film was the dominant art form of the early twentieth century.

> Technically, the film depends upon electricity, precise engineering, and the chemical industries. Commercially, it depends upon an international market. ... Socially, it depends upon large urban audiences who, in imagination, can go anywhere in the world: a film audience is basically far more *expectant* than a theatre audience. ... Artistically, the film is the medium which, by its nature, can accommodate most easily a *simultaneity of viewpoints*, and demonstrate most clearly the *indivisibility of events*.[37]

If there's anything that can be said about *Man at the Crossroads* and *Guernica*, it's that they are cinematic in precisely these ways. As popular monumental works conceived for presentation in the Rockefeller Center and at the Paris World's Fair, both engaged with sites designed to foster mythic identification with the promise of the commodity form. These sites owed their existence to the integration of world markets and the advent of the mass urban audience. Epistemologically, both images convey the simultaneity of viewpoints and the indivisibility of events. Finally, both images place the viewer in a position of unbearable tension and expectation.

However, unlike in cinema (which has temporal duration), the cessation of happening engendered by the images' single frame execution places responsibility for resolving this expectation squarely on the viewer's shoulders. Because there is no "after" to which the viewer can orient except the one that she herself creates, cinematic expectation gives way to expectation of one's self.

Consequential as these effects were, however, it's important to note that Rivera and Picasso did not limit themselves to merely reiterating cinematic gestures. Had they restricted themselves in this way, their efforts would likely have remained quaint but fruitless attempts to refurbish easel painting and its supernova outgrowths in the face of their inevitable decline. But this is not what happened. Instead, Rivera and Picasso fused cinematic conventions with those of the medieval triptych. By holding the two forms in tension, they discovered (as Benjamin himself did around the same time) that "the materialist presentation of history leads the past to bring the present into a critical state."[38]

In other words, by finding traces of contemporary desires for self-realization buried in the refuse of the mythic past, and by showing how these desires might at last be actualized through matter's most modern configurations, Rivera and Picasso discovered the trick of contracting historical time to a single, decisive moment. Here, the religious is not an antithesis to the material (as is normally assumed) but rather its wishful anticipation.

The triptych was popular in European religious art during the fourteenth and fifteenth centuries. As with religious art more generally, it fused the devotional with the instructive. During the early-twentieth century, surrealist identification with Dutch painter Hieronymus Bosch (1450–1516) revived interest in the form. Painting at the end of the fifteenth and beginning of the sixteenth century, Bosch depicted the human struggle with sin. In contrast to other Renaissance artists, he did not see earthly struggles leading to angelic ascent. Instead, Bosch saw corporeal desire lowering people to the level of beasts. In his work, sinners occupy the same plane as demons.

Bosch's work—and especially his *Garden of Earthly Delights* [Fig. 3]—resonated with the surrealist desire to explore the dark side of human experience. And since this desire occasionally led Bosch to depict judges, clergymen, and the propertied classes in a critical fashion, his work remained open to radical interpretations. In the *Garden*'s "hell" panel, the seven deadly sins directly embody the failing that defeated them. Sitting amidst the condemned, greed shits coins, gluttony is forced to throw up again and again, and pride becomes transfixed by her reflection (supplied by a mirror affixed to another figure's ass).

Neither Rivera nor Picasso produced triptychs in the conventional sense; nevertheless, both drew heavily on the form's structure and thematic organization. Commenting on Picasso's understanding of the triptych's significance, Russell recounts how "a hinged panel is by its nature a sort of dismemberment, a planned rupture."

In *Guernica*, this aspect of triptychs is brought to the surface in theme as well as in form, the one panel hinged at the pinched neck of the lightbearer, the other at the shrunken and hacked-off neck of the warrior—neither personage permitted to cut across the boundaries, the painter preferring to lop heads rather than cover over the formal clarity of his plan, part of the plan being of course these acts of mutilation.[39]

Proceeding in a somewhat different fashion, Rivera's use of the triptych is no less deliberate. In *Man at the Crossroads*, the partitioning of the picture plane allows for a formal and spatially coherent organization of the image's key antagonisms. But despite these novel strategies for realizing the simultaneity of viewpoints and the indivisibility of events, what remains most significant about these formal citations is that, by invoking the triptych, both Rivera and Picasso managed to infuse their images with significant (though significantly profaned) religious connotations.

Indeed, it's hard to ignore the extent to which both *Man at the Crossroads* and *Guernica* are saturated with the Passion. As profane ambassadors of the Christian mystery of death and resurrection, Rivera's Man and Picasso's horse (figures occupying the central "panel" of their respective images) are illuminated by a kind of stereoscopic process. The "old" sacred is enlisted to fill the "new" profane with consolidating meaning. In the process, both reach a point of unbearable tension. It is the point at which a materialist analysis capable of grasping the energetic relays that course between the constellated fragments of historical memory deposits us—whether we're ready or not.

VIII

Describing Rivera and Picasso's works in theological terms may seem fanciful, an unfortunate side effect of trying to find a common interpretative basis for wildly divergent subject matter; however, a broader appraisal of their work confirms that they were no strangers to religious citations. For Rivera, this affinity can be traced back to Mexico's Chapingo chapel where, in 1927, he painted what many consider to be his greatest work. According to Rivera biographer Patrick Marnham, the reasons for such a characterization are self-evident: "The ingenuity of Rivera's blasphemy is due to the way in which … he adapted the technique of Renaissance devotional art to the desecration of a religious building and its transformation into a place of anti-religious devotion."[40]

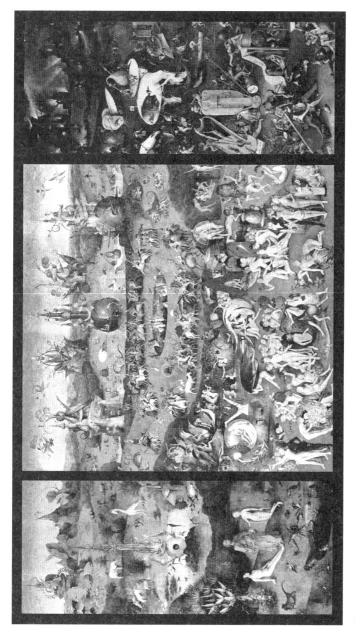

Fig. 3: Hieronymous Bosch, *Garden of Earthly Delights* (1490–1510)

Although Marnham doesn't mention Benjamin, he nevertheless reveals the extent to which Rivera's work approximates Benjamin's "messianic" materialism. Here, the dream forms of an unfulfilled past discover the means by which they might be actualized through matter's most modern configurations. At Chapingo, Marnham notes, Rivera "came closest to recreating the medieval function of religious art: art as an instrument of conversion, the highest form of propaganda…"

> Rivera's images in Chapingo were … intended to remind people of their past, to direct their conduct in the present, and to describe their future. If, in the Middle Ages, the past was evoked in legends and visions, the present was divided into virtuous and vicious behaviour, and the future contained punishments and rewards, in Rivera's art the same pattern was applied, but the visions were moved from the past to the future since the system he was advocating was Utopian rather than Arcadian.[41]

Drawing deep from the archive of mythic symbols, Rivera forged a bond between religion—what Marx, in his critique of Hegel's *Philosophy of Right*, called the "general theory" of the world[42]—and the profane means by which the promise of that "theory" might be actualized. God thus gives way to Man, who comes face to face with what Benjamin took to be his "*weak* Messianic power."[43] But no *telos* will guarantee the outcome. Because figures like Rockefeller must remain invested in mythic resolutions (since these underwrite the logic of the commodity form), the very promise of the "new nature" must itself be wrested from myth through decisive action.

Rivera made his understanding of this dialectical relationship explicit in 1932's *Detroit Industry* murals. There, an infant's inoculation is depicted in a style reminiscent of Renaissance-era Nativity scenes (complete with three wise men—now medical scientists—in the background). On the south wall's "automotive production" panel, Rivera incorporated another mythic citation by rendering an industrial stamping press in the likeness of the Aztec goddess Coatlicue. In Aztec mythology, Coatlicue nurtures humanity even as she demands sacrificial victims. From the vantage of the assembly line, it's hard not to recognize her as a mythic anticipation of the brutal contradictions of industrial production. Like Benjamin, who was fascinated by the "correspondences" that arise "between the world of modern technology and the archaic symbol-world of mythology," Rivera seized upon figures like Coatlicue to illuminate the dangers (but also the promise) trapped in matter's most modern configurations.[44]

Like Rivera, Picasso did not shy away from mythical citations. Along with his regular recourse to Greek mythology,[45] he also drew both directly and indirectly on Christian themes. Russell fully grasped the significance of these latter citations when he described *Guernica* as a "modern Calvary…detonated by sudden entrances and exits."[46] Here, the old and the new come together in an explosive admixture. Consequently, "the picture in its episodes is timeless, archaic. The timetable of the Spanish Republic is here widened to include all time." Furthermore, it's "in certain Biblical outlines" that *Guernica*'s true meaning and significance is to be "uncovered."[47] It therefore follows that the image is "a dedication to the past and to the future."[48] Russell concludes by observing that *Guernica* might best be understood as "a structure salvaged carefully from the rubble of the past, dedicated to the idea of a resurrection and to a future."[49] Although he is never cited, an assessment more in keeping with Benjamin's insights would be difficult to produce.

IX

Concurrent with their remarkable synthesis of the cinematic and the religious, *Man at the Crossroads* and *Guernica* also resolve the antithetical terms of the early-twentieth century conflict between the "formalist" strategy of montage and the narrative conventions of socialist realism. By forcing relationships between discrete and discontinuous objects, montage highlights social relations that might otherwise go unnoticed. Skeptical of its potential, Georg Lukács nevertheless conceded that montage could, on occasion, become a powerful political weapon.[50] Nevertheless, Lukács doubted that the mere organization of fragments could ever yield a clear conception of the social totality. At best, montage was an epiphenomenal expression of the *experience* of fragmentation that seemed to define capitalism in the period immediately prior to the advent of consumer society. In contrast, and because it was specifically concerned with reflecting social relations, Lukács felt that realism avoided succumbing to "whatever manifests itself immediately and on the surface."[51]

These tensions are not easily resolved, and it's beyond the scope of this investigation to work them out in any detail. However, it's important to note that Rivera and Picasso's images suggest a plausible means of overcoming the impasse. Although mobilizing different representational strategies, both works successfully incorporate formalist and realist attributes into singular, unitary constructions that nevertheless remain replete with tension.

In Rivera's mural, figures occupying different historical moments and discontinuous geographical spaces are brought into improbable proximity. Similarly, the figures populating *Guernica* look like outcasts from the morning paper. For art historian Ellen Oppler, these figures are "paper cut outs, posterlike, resembling the stark images of news photos or flickering newsreels."[52] In both cases, discrete fragments are filled with new significance as a result of relationships established between nodes in the constellated whole. But alongside these experiments in montage, both works achieve the kind of narrative cohesion favored by realists.[53] In order to understand how, it's necessary to move beyond the picture plane to consider the means by which the viewer becomes implicated in the depicted scene.

Here, it becomes evident that—though neither work has a protagonist in the conventional sense—both images achieve narrative coherence by forcing the viewer to assume "protagonist" responsibilities. In other words, by outsourcing resolution, they induct the viewer. Whether confronting the absolute non-resolution of the world's accumulated contradictions or witnessing the catastrophic aftermath of aerial bombardment, the viewer is given nothing with which to identify except her own *weak* Messianic power. Expressed synchronously with montage's fragmentation, realism's encapsulating anthropological narrative seems to move the scene toward a cessation of happening that can only be resolved through the viewer's decisive action on history itself.

Of all the attributes conspiring to make these works dialectical images, the viewer's placement before the depicted events is perhaps most significant. In his consideration of *Guernica*, surrealist artist and Picasso biographer Roland Penrose gives us a sense of why this might be the case; in his estimation, Picasso had found a "universal means of conveying the emotions centered around a given event" and "arrived at a timeless and transcendental image."

It is not the horror of an actual occurrence with which we are presented; it is a universal tragedy made vivid to us by the myth he has reinvented and the revolutionary directness with which it is presented.[54]

As a description of profane illumination, Penrose's account highlights the point at which the depicted event opens onto the universal and makes history itself the object of a redemptive labor process. Both the challenge and the possibility of redemption fall solely upon the viewer. Nothing in the image itself can resolve the tensions it unleashes. The demand is unsettling. It explains the tremendous resonance that *Guernica* continues to enjoy. It also explains the denunciations that began circulating even before the paint had dried.

In *Man at the Crossroads*, natural history and human history confront one another at a moment just prior to their potential resolution. Overlying this temporal synchronicity is a spatial one. Antagonists in the class struggle are brought to the point of inevitable confrontation. As "controller of the universe," the Man in *Man at the Crossroads* must resolve the tension. However, because he is caught at a point of absolute historical arrest, he can only fulfill this mission if you, the viewer, intercede.

X

Rivera and Picasso's works closely approximate aspects of Benjamin's dialectical image. For this reason, they must be considered central reference points for anyone interested in producing such an image today. However, despite the fact that they became important rallying points in the struggle against constituted power, the works themselves never prompted the "leap in the open air of history" that Benjamin had hoped for.[55] In other words, if they were dialectical images from the standpoint of analysis, they did not yet constitute such images from the standpoint of politics.

Based on this assessment, it may be tempting to conclude that Benjamin's conception—though provocative—is ultimately unsuited to the unforgiving world of *realpolitik*. However, since the proverbial moment "when the chips are down"[56] underlying Benjamin's philosophy is not yet upon us (and since, in Benjamin's estimation, that final instance would have "retroactive force"[57]), it remains more fitting to see these images as *one more* ruin, *one more* fragment, *one more* unrealized promise in need of actualization. What, then, in matter's most modern configurations, would allow us to rise to the occasion?

III

PROGRESS

(THE FIRST REVOLUTIONARY MEASURE TAKEN)

OBITUARY IN ABSENTIA

"The historian is the herald who invites
the dead to the table."
—Walter Benjamin

I

In 1925, T.S. Eliot saw the writing on the wall. The world would end, he thought, "not with a bang but a whimper."[1] In our own time, 2012 was destined to become the year of the Great Mayan Apocalypse—a centuries-old declaration of calendrical oblivion, finally come to collect. Some, determined to secure front-row seats to the greatest show on earth, stormed the Yucatan like the vile offspring of Duane Hanson and Burning Man. Time to go out with a bang, they exclaimed. But as the sun broke the horizon on December 22, it became clear that the world, in its obstinacy, would trundle on. No apocalypse this year, Yucatan reveler. Better luck next time.

A cataclysmic letdown, one might say. Then again, maybe *this* is what the end looks like. Maybe this unendurable *persistence* is the whimper that Eliot foretold.

It's not so hard to believe. Back in 1938 when Orson Welles made radio history with his adaptation of H.G. Wells' *War of the Worlds*, naïve Americans came face to face with catastrophe. The story's news-bulletin format was enough to authenticate the Martian invasion and provoke widespread panic. Seventy-four years later, a

---

This essay first appeared on the website *Truthout* on January 4, 2013. http://www.truth-out.org/speakout/item/13714-2012-obituary-in-absentia.

generation plagued by survival sickness seized upon the Mayan expiration date as a gift, an invitation to lay hold of one Real thing before finally, mercifully, perishing. Hollow and stuffed, we were denied this small reprieve. Still, the promise of oblivion became marketing gold. Over the course of one year, the ruin of the world became the image of the ruin of the world, and premonitions of our demise became a desiccated charnel waxworks.

Sensing an opportunity to be both the voice of reason and to cash in, venerable outlets like *The Guardian* set about debunking the myths upon which our forebodings were based. Conveying the results of his fact-finding mission among the Mayans, journalist Shankar Chaudhuri could not help but adopt the venerable postures of pious anthropology. "Throughout our trip," he reported, "we encountered many ordinary Mayans from every walk of life to check out their reaction to the supposedly doomsday prediction."[2] In his estimation, "most" of the Mayans with whom he spoke were "largely baffled by the question," while others "flatly denied that there was any reason that the world would come to an end."[3] Thus assuaged by his native informants, Chaudhuri concluded that "the image of the apocalypse" could therefore best be understood as a projection of "our own society's subconscious fears, insecurities and fantasies."[4]

Predictably, the story wraps where it should begin. What *are* these subconscious fears, insecurities, and fantasies? And how do they arise from our current condition? Why have we come to long so desperately, collectively, for an end? And what would we do if we discovered we were already there, on the edge of this tumid river, enduring with a whimper? Blame the promoters, if you will, but The Great Mayan Apocalypse was a bigger bust than Woodstock '99. Nevertheless, the fantasies it traded in were real. One look at last year's obituaries is enough to know why 2012 made us long for final, tranquil, release.

II

"One small step for man, one giant leap for mankind." Neil Armstrong died on August 25, 2012. The first man on the moon fell down dead. He'd had a long life, and he saw the world as no one before him had. A lunar perspective, circa 1969: looking down on the planet at precisely the moment when the new and integrated space of global multinational capitalism began to congeal.[5] It was the beginning of the end.

In an obituary posted on their website, NASA sought to revitalize the utopian reflex that—once upon a time—made it self-evident that space travel should happen under the sign of Apollo. By their reckoning, Armstrong's words from the Sea of Tranquility were "the climactic fulfillment of the efforts and hopes of millions of people."[6] And more: "Armstrong and fellow astronaut Edwin 'Buzz' Aldrin were there as representatives of all humans."[7] All of the world, under one sun, united in reason and warmth.

A beautiful image, to be sure. But small consolation when your city's on fire. Apollo may have been the god of light, but he also brought the plague. By April 29, 1992, Armstrong's utopia finally succumbed to globalization's basest form. Like a storm that could be seen from space, the L.A. riots revealed Apollo's Janus face. And at the center of the hurricane lay Rodney King's bruised and bloodied body, immortalized by George Holliday in a fit of scopophilia. It would be enough. The cops got off, and the city erupts. In light of what Mike Davis called "a future already looted,"[8] the riot appeared to L.A.'s underclass like "a magic dispensation."[9] Consequently, the looting that followed abided by "a visible moral economy."[10]

A jubilee that did not last, the riot's "bang" fell silent. Bush I, Bush II, Iraq, Iraq, Recession.

Floating in a swimming pool (the closest us mortals get to feeling like we're in space), Rodney King dies. It's June 17, 2012. A few months earlier, in a *New York Times* interview marking the riot's twentieth anniversary, he recounted how a cop once told him that people would know Rodney King a hundred years from now.[11] And maybe they will. But 2012 witnessed no commemorative riot, no jubilant redistribution, no revitalization of Armstrong's naïve and distant lunar hope.

When second-wave radical feminist Shulamith Firestone died in her sweltering East-Village apartment in late August, there was no Holliday with a camera, no one to note (let alone ease) her passing, no one even to mark her time of death. Like hagiographies penned for those we'd forsaken, the obituaries that followed were cloying. "A painter by training, Ms. Firestone never anticipated a high-profile career as a writer," wrote Margalit Fox in *The New York Times*. "The crush of attention … soon proved unbearable, her sister said." Thus it was that, "in the years that followed, Ms. Firestone retreated into a quiet, largely solitary life."[12]

No mention is ever made of our collective failure, of the gulf between our willingness to concede Firestone's brilliance and our incapacity to realize a single one of her goals. Under venal conditions such as these, who in their right mind wouldn't retreat? The upstart visionary who smashed out *The Dialectic of Sex*[13] as Armstrong cast wistful glances across the void had, by the 1990s, fallen victim to the empty duration that now engulfs us all. In 1998's *Airless Spaces*, the problem thus became: "getting through the blank days as comfortably as possible."[14]

This is the way the world ends, has already ended.

III

The death I call my life is difficult to look at. It would be easier to accept if I could embrace it in one bleak vainglorious hurrah. Blow up the world. Cue the Great Mayan Apocalypse. But while these options—or options such as these—have not yet been eclipsed, they remain as distant as wish fulfillment. How, then, might we write our obituary *in absentia*? How shall we come to terms with our end?

One option might be to make it a means. Following Christopher Hitchens and Nadine Gordimer, Jeffrey Eugenides recently suggested that, for writers struggling to make the most of their talents and avoid the perils of market and fashion, it was necessary to imagine that they were writing "posthumously."[15] Write like you're already dead, he proposed, and rediscover the vital energy that led you to pick up a pen in the first place. The idea caught on and—in less than a week—more than 5000 people had recommended the procedure to their Facebook friends.

Modest beginnings, maybe. But if this movement takes off, I'll pledge my allegiance unreservedly. Besides, there's more than art at stake. After all, the question of oblivion applies to politics as well. "Since atomic war would divest any future of its meaning," Albert Camus told an interviewer in 1957, "it gives us complete freedom of action. We have nothing to lose except everything… This is the wager of our generation."[16]

That was before the Sea of Tranquility and *The Dialectic of Sex*, before the L.A. riots and last year's deaths. Still, the sentiment continues to resonate. At a time when the cruel and stupid ways our enemies conspire to "divest any future of its meaning" have proliferated beyond measure, there's only one justifiable stance: dare to embrace complete freedom of action, knowing you're already dead. There's no guarantee, but it might be enough, to end this insufferable whimpering.

OCCUPATION, DECOLONIZATION, AND RECIPROCAL VIOLENCE

The Wish

A lot can change in two months. When intrepid activists descended on Zuccotti Park on September 17, 2011, few expected that they would spend the night. Within a month, their occupation had spread to dozens of other outposts across the land. A month later, most of the parks and squares had been cleared. Officially undaunted, the occupiers clamored throughout 2012 to gain purchase in stormier, windswept fields. But it was no use; in a movement called "Occupy," the struggle and the encampment were one.

Sooner or later, even great eulogies become historical footnotes. What, then, can be learned from Occupy now that its arc can be traced in a single meager paragraph? According to Walter Benjamin, adopting a position downstream from an event's source could provide an analytic opportunity.[1] From such a position, he maintained, the critic might judge a current's force. Now that Zuccotti is a wasteland in a wasteland again (so sterile that even the office workers in adjoining towers won't eat lunch there), we can take stock of what we learned—and make lists of the questions that still demand answers.

This essay first appeared in Gavin Brown et al. (eds.), *Protest Camps in International Context: Spaces, Infrastructures and Media of Resistance* (Bristol: Policy Press, 2017). An earlier version appeared as "'Occupation' Between Conquest and Liberation," *Situations: Project of the Radical Imagination*, Vol. VI, nos. 1 & 2, Fall 2015/Winter 2016.

Why, for instance, did the movement's renunciation of kleptocracy spread at such an epidemic rate, and how did a continent beset by tent cities in the fall have little more to confront than a barricade's worth of hasty anthologies and slapdash monographs come spring? On the surface, the struggle to understand a movement's rise and fall seems to demand an analysis of the swirling vortices that guide the circulation of struggle. But while such an approach might help us to understand Occupy's degeneration from lighting rod to empty signifier, it's also true that it's likely to overlook the importance of foundational political *concepts*. However, once political concepts—and, indeed, the meaning of politics itself—are foregrounded, both the movement's contagious appeal and its rapid decomposition become instantly comprehensible.

Indeed, not since *The Port Huron Statement*[2] has an American movement been so successful in revitalizing our engagement with the conceptual bedrock of politics. Among these concepts, perhaps the most cherished was "democracy" itself. Ringing out with People's Mic choirs, the movement's General Assemblies could not help but remind us of the church-basement enthusiasm that, for Tocqueville, was the very heart of *Democracy in America*.[3]

Even before there was "democracy," however, there was "occupation." Perhaps more than any other term, noun or verb, it was occupation's destiny to spark debate—and these debates were as important as they were divisive. Reviewing them from our current downstream position, it becomes clear that movement fights about occupation's meaning allowed us to grapple, albeit indirectly, with a fundamental question who's answer continues to elude us: what does it mean to be political today?

The rapid diffusion of protest encampments during the fall of 2011 gives an indication of how generative "occupation" had been. Nevertheless, the ferocity (to say nothing of the unresolved character) of movement debates suggests that this resonance owed largely to the conceptual indeterminacy of the concept itself. In many cases, "occupation" became what Benjamin would have called a wish image—a vision capable of stimulating the longing for the promise of a future happiness by recalling traces of unrealized promise buried in the (mythic) past.[4]

Little wonder, then, that the late-capitalist disarticulation of social space (with its carcinogenic profusion of dead and transitory zones) stimulated recollections of an era when it was thought to be possible to foster a collective, exuberent "we." Eden, Winstanley's squatted wastelands, the Tennis Court Oath: each prior iteration becomes a spark with the power to push the approximate present into the actualized future [Figures 1 and 2]. Boomeranging through the past to stimulate its energetic élan, the wish image provides a vision of liberation that impels people to *act*. But how, and on what basis? The wish image doesn't say, and the concept has yet to find its object.

Although their sources are varied, wish images have consistently emerged from the Romantic current that has buoyed social movements since the end of the eighteenth century. In the immediate aftermath of Wall Street's catastrophic meltdown, movement Romanticism and the wish image "occupation" revealed their profound affinity.

Drawing on Mao (or maybe, sadly, Tyler Durden) and writing as The Imperative Committee, some participants in the 2009 occupation of The New School issued a manifesto proposing that, as far as they were concerned, "an occupation is not a dinner party, writing an essay, or holding a meeting." Instead, it was "a car bomb."[5] Conceived as the prelude to a messianic rupture in capitalism's base immediacy, it therefore followed that "the coming occupations will have no end in sight."[6] A little more than two years later, as Occupy Wall Street began showing signs of being possessed by what George Katsiaficas has called the "Eros effect,"[7] activist Conor Tomás Reed proclaimed in the movement-based journal *Tidal* that, "for many of us, 'occupy' has become a verb to be sung."[8] This desire owed primarily to the fact that *the word itself*, when wielded by the right people, seemed to turn the world upside down.

> This rowdy crowd word, at once descriptive and prescriptive, aims to body-flip the logic of imperialism on its head. A radical people's occupation of public space doesn't erect checkpoints; it tears them down. Instead of usurping others' resources, we heartily pool our own for free distribution.[9]

From Mikhail Bakhtin's celebration of the medieval carnival[10] to Naomi Klein's approving observation that the movement against globalization responded "to corporate concentration with a maze of fragmentation; to globalisation with its own kind of localisation; to power consolidation with radical power dispersal,"[11] the idea that struggle restores balance by reversing valuations has been as persistent as it

Fig.1 (top): Jaques-Louis David. *The Tennis Court Oath* (1789)
Fig. 2 (bottom): Wasim Ahmad. OWS General Assembly (March 17, 2012)

has been seductive. In the Western political tradition, such inversions can be traced back to Scripture, where—in The Book of Acts—it is revealed that riots broke out in Thessalonica after Paul preached the Good News to unbelievers, who lamented: "These that have turned the world upside down are come hither also … and these all do contrary to the decrees of Caesar, saying that there is another king, one Jesus."[12]

No sooner had the crop of new believers begun to savor their regicidal fantasies of deposing the One Percent's Caesars, however, others began to take issue with occupation's new ubiquity. In their view, "occupation" seemed irreparably tarnished by its association with the acts of conquest it was thought normally to denote. In their estimation, not only did the movement's preferred nomenclature alienate those who had endured histories of colonial violence at the hands of occupying forces, it also ensured that movement efforts would fail. How, they asked, could a liberation struggle win if it rallied behind conquest's banner?

The Anti-Colonial Critique

Barely a week into Zuccotti's Bakhtinian body flip, statements began appearing on the Internet calling attention to the fact that the mobilization had failed to address the *colonial* occupation that wrote America's story into the annals of humankind in letters of blood and fire. In a widely circulated *Racialicious* article, Indigenous writer and activist Jessica Yee suggested that—by encouraging "organizers, protestors, and activists" to "'occupy' different places that symbolize greed and power"—the movement had signaled its insensitivity to the fact that "The United States is already being occupied." She went on to clarify: "This is Indigenous land. And it's been occupied for quite some time now."[13]

In response to the movement's careless framing, Yee enjoined protestors to consider how, instead of "more occupation," what was needed was "decolonization." Moreover, since "colonialism affects everyone," it was in everyone's interest to participate in its undoing. This was all the more true since, by her reckoning, "colonialism also leads to capitalism, globalization, and industrialization." "How," she asked, "can we truly end capitalism without ending colonialism?"[14]

Although its defining attributes remained unspecified, "decolonization" quickly became occupation's antithesis. And with the contest thus established, Yee's call gained traction in many cities. Over the course of a few short months, activists positioned within, alongside, and in opposition to the growing Occupy movement initiated projects and set up websites with names like "Decolonize Canada," "Decolonize North America," "Decolonize Oakland," "Decolonize Occupy," "DeColonize the 99%," and "Decolonize The World."

In the best interpretations, Yee's article was read less as an injunction to shut down movement operations than as a call to deepen them by exposing the primary contradiction underlying American experience. Thus it was that, on December 4, 2011, members of Occupy Oakland's People of Color caucus put forward a motion encouraging participants in that city's General Assembly to consider dropping "Occupy" and adopting "Decolonize" as their watchword. "We want to open our movement to even greater participation," their proposal asserted. "For many of us, including our local native communities, the terms 'occupy' and 'occupation' echo our experiences under colonial domination and normalizes the military occupations that the U.S. is supporting in places such as Iraq, Palestine, and Afghanistan."[15]

Speaking in favor of the motion, activists argued that the proposed name change would allow them to gain traction in communities affected by colonial occupation and conquest. In turn, such base-building would help the movement to grow. Although the motion ultimately failed, the meeting's transcript reveals broad support for the "name change" position.[16] According to one participant, "the historical context of 'occupy' doesn't fit with the goals of this movement." According to another, "the term occupy is racist" and, as a result, "few people of color [were] involved" in movement activities. One participant reported how, "as a Jewish person," they could not "support Palestinian people in a movement named 'Occupy,'" while another expressed concern that, by "using the language of our oppressors," the movement would be "weakened" in a fundamental way.[17]

Sentiments like these were not a west-coast anomaly. Speaking at a public forum two months after the eviction of Toronto's Occupy encampment on November 23, 2011, Indigenous Environmental Network organizer Clayton Thomas Mueller added his voice to those calling for the movement to change its name. "No Native person ever called this movement 'occupy,'" Mueller said, "and certainly no Palestinian ever did."[18] On April 24, 2012, the authors of the POC

Open Letter to the Occupy movement were even more direct when they declared that "*Occupation is a failed political strategy.*" And more: "*Liberation through occupation is impossible.*"[19]

Adopting a slightly more concilliatory tone in their retrospective analysis of movement gains, Baltimore-based authors Lester Spence and Mike McGuire conceded that, "to the extent the fight against financial capital *is* a war," the term occupation helped to emphasize "the fundamental nature of the struggle." Nevertheless, since "occupation" also "denotes ... white settler colonialism" and "has a deeply regressive meaning,"[20] they concluded by exhorting "future iterations" of the movement to "use symbols that reflect the realities of settler colonialism and refrain from using language that denotes 'occupation.'"[21]

When viewed as a strategic proposition, Spence and McGuire's recommendation seems to make sense. Nevertheless, across the continent, efforts to rename the movement met with resistance. For many radicals, this resistance was enough to confirm their suspicion that the movement and its participants were irreparably racist. Such assessments should not be discounted; however, it's equally important to consider how the reluctance to dispense with "occupation" might also have owed to the inadequacy of the proposed alternative. If the movement's use of "occupation" was overly Romantic and insensitive to histories of conquest, it was equally true that the call to "decolonize" (Yee) tended to lack the "descriptive and prescriptive" (Reed) clarity of "occupation" as a tactic of "war" (Spence and McGuire)—and, hence (and following Clausewitz[22]), of *politics* itself.

The call to "decolonize" the Occupy movement was motivated by the sincere hope that America's history of violent conquest might finally, mercifully, be undone. But while there's no reason to suspect the motivations that compelled people to call for an end to the indiscriminate use of the term "occupation," this should not lead us to conclude that the *analytic* basis of their exhortation should likewise be beyond scrutiny.

Returning to Yee's *Racialicious* article, the attentive reader is immediately struck by the important conceptual work accomplished by two distinct but interrelated rhetorical gestures. In the first, the movement's occupations are—by virtue of their common nomenclature—rendered as conceptual equivalents to the occupation that inaugurated colonialism in the Americas. Consequently, in the second, "occupation" is posited as the logical antithesis to decolonization, which is in turn held to be the only logical response to the founding violence of occupation.

These rhetorical moves reiterate conceptual habits that are pervasive among American radicals. Most evident in movement discussions about "violence," such habits usually lead us to take note of what our enemy does and then to propose that—as a reflection of our opposition to their rule—we will do the exact opposite. In this way, resistance becomes a process of conceptual negation, of siding with the *representational* antithesis of the thing we oppose. "They have power," said Melanie Kaye/Kantrowitz; "we won't touch it with a ten-foot pole."[23]

So it is that we find ourselves launching assaults from the antithetical side of the conceptual divide. But what content might be attributed to such a negation? Yee never says. Although she briefly considers the tactical repertoire associated with "occupation" (e.g. occupying places that "symbolize greed and power"), no such repertoire gets elaborated with respect to decolonization. An oversight, maybe; or maybe an admission that the conceptual distinction cannot hold. Indeed, no less an authority than Frantz Fanon made clear that, when conceived as a *practical* and not merely a conceptual act, decolonization is in fact much closer to occupation than Yee's comments would allow.

Like the OWS enthusiasts who cheered their movement's messianic reordering of the world, Fanon begins his decolonization treatise on a Romantic note by proposing that, "if we wish to describe it precisely," we would do well to recall "the well-known words: 'The last shall be first and the first last.'"[24] But there's more: in a world cut in two, the will to decolonize first finds expression in the desire to *occupy the occupiers*. "The look that the native turns on the settler's town is a look of lust, a look of envy," says Fanon. "It expresses his dreams of possession—all manner of possession: to sit at the settler's table, to sleep in the settler's bed, with his wife if possible."[25] Comments like these may raise questions about Fanon's feminist credentials. Just as important, however, are those questions that might be raised concerning his implicit philology. It would not have surprised him—if he didn't know it already—that, throughout the sixteenth century (the very centerpiece of modern colonialism's "age of discovery"), the terms "occupy" and "occupation" were closely associated with acts of sexual possession.[26]

Liberation owes nothing to negation; instead, it is the fruit of reciprocity. Opposition to militarism calls on us to disavow "class war" about as much as our conviction that picket lines mean "don't cross" demands that we cede abortion clinics to the placard-wielding zealots who showed up first. Thus far, the history of American racism has made it harder to accept the same with respect to occupation; however, our collective failure to acknowledge occupation's inescapability as a necessary form of reciprocal violence has prevented us from advancing beyond the representational satisfactions associated with conceptual negation.

For the movement's Romantic enthusiasts, these satisfactions took the form of innocence as they carved out micro-zones of autonomy while beseeching the State to safeguard their right to burlesque its sovereignty. For movement detractors, representational negation proved instead to be a reliable alibi. Responding to a force they didn't create but couldn't ignore, the most satisfying option was to declare that force inadmissible.

History, meanwhile, records numerous instances in which radicals have embraced occupation as a term and tactic of explicitly *anticolonial* resistance. Though it may not have been their intention, these movements helped to reveal occupation's centrality to *all* forms of political action—whether carried out in the name of conquest *or* of liberation. Considered at their threshold, such acts make clear that politics without occupation is, in fact, inconceivable. Will it be *their* occupation or *ours*—and, if it is ours, what will we produce? These profane questions (only hinted at by the Occupy movement's regicidal wish images) are, in the final instance, the only ones that matter. A brief consideration of the 1968 occupation of Columbia University and the 1969 occupation of Alcatraz make clear the extent to which this is the case.

The Occupation of Columbia University

In the spring of 1968, Columbia University was in tumult. The American student movement was at the height of its powers, and Students for a Democratic Society had not yet begun its downward spiral into sectarian rivalry. In fact, the group had begun forging meaningful alliances with other forces standing in opposition to the war in Vietnam and to the ongoing attacks against Black people at home. It was in this context that the SDS chapter at Columbia University began to organize campaigns on two distinct but interrelated fronts. Along the first, they attacked the University for its participation in the

Military Industrial Complex and, in particular, for its involvement in the Institute for Defense Analysis. Along the second, they began to challenge Columbia's encroachment into Harlem and Morningside Heights. In particular, they mounted opposition to University plans to erect a gymnasium in Morningside Park.

Although the planned structure would occupy a large portion of the available green space (a prized possession in northern Manhattan), planned usage was scheduled to be restricted to Columbia affiliates. Serving the adjoining neighborhoods of Harlem and Morningside Heights, the park was considered important territory by local residents, who perceived the development to be a form of colonial encroachment. In an article in the April 27, 1968 edition of *The New York Amsterdam News*, Victor Solomon of the Harlem chapter of CORE made these feelings clear when he declared: "Harlem is a colony and is being treated like one."[27]

By the end of April, the two SDS campaigns culminated in the occupation of several university buildings. For almost a week, protesters seized and held five separate structures and declared them to be "free" space. At the center of the occupation was Hamilton Hall. Not only was it the first building to be seized, it was also held exclusively by Black students and community-based militants. When police finally raided the buildings, they took great care not to be seen using force to remove the occupiers from Hamilton Hall. At a rally held on the day of the arraignment hearing for students arrested during the occupation, one participant underscored his support for "the students who have been carrying this struggle for the Harlem community against imperialistic, colonialistic attitudes of Columbia University that is trying to ... turn Harlem into a colony."[28]

How did all of this transpire? To get a sense of the dynamics that marked those days, it's useful to turn to the pages of Columbia's student newspaper, *The Columbia Daily Spectator*. In addition to the breadth of the paper's occupation-related coverage, the publication's status as a daily produced by amateur journalists conspires to yield a relatively unedited account of the events. By following the story unfolding on the *Spectator's* pages, one can detect the eruption of anxieties concerning the meaning of politics even as they are coded in the careful tones in which white people talk about race.

On April 23, activists staged a demonstration in opposition to the construction of the gymnasium at Morningside Park. Charging that the new structure would intensify the university's encroachment into Harlem and Morningside Heights, the campaign coincided with the concurrent demand that the university become disentangled from the Institute for Defense Analysis. Writing about the demonstrations, *Spectator* journalist Michael Stern recounted how, after marching to the construction site in Morningside Park, "protesters, led by members of Columbia's Students for a Democratic Society and Students Afro-American Society, tore down sections of the metal fence surrounding the site and fought with police for several minutes."[29] Stern continues: "After reiterating the charges that Columbia was discriminating against the community by building the gym on park land and refusing the community full use of the building's facilities, [SDS leader Mark] Rudd proposed that the crowd return to Columbia."[30]

Upon returning to the university, the demonstrators began a spontaneous sit-in at Hamilton Hall, an academic building just off of the University's sprawling central green and adjacent to College Walk, the main artery bisecting the campus at 116th Street (which also bisects Morningside Park, immediately to the East of the University's walls). As the day wore on, the demonstrators made clear that their plan was to stay. According to the *Spectator*, "at the midnight hour last night, several hundred of the demonstrators who had occupied Hamilton Hall since early yesterday afternoon, were readying themselves for an all-night camp-in in the corridors and the classrooms of the building."[31] According to the report's unnamed author, "the unexpected and unprecedented siege of Hamilton Hall began ... when more than 400 students and non-University demonstrators, exhilarated by the destruction of the fence surrounding the site of Columbia's new gymnasium, jammed into the building's tiny lobby and demanded to see 'the Man.'"[32]

Although they had been central to the action at the construction site, the occupation of Hamilton Hall was not the work of SDS alone. For their part, political organizers from Harlem saw the occupation as an opportunity to help curb the university's encroachment into their territory. It therefore came as little surprise that—in the early hours of April 24—"black very militant community leaders" decided "to blockade the building and close it down." The decision to move from "camp-in" to occupation thus arose not from white activists but rather from their "very militant" counterparts. In response, "the white students inside the building decided ... to go along with the plans for barricading the building."[33] For some, this development was cause for apprehension. According to *Spectator* reporter Robert Stulberg, "the demonstration, which was initially sponsored by Students for a Democratic Society and the Student Afro-American Society, has apparently come under the control of black very militant community leaders." In Stulberg's estimation, participants in the occupation included "members of the Harlem chapters of the Student Nonviolent Coordinating Committee, the Congress of Racial Equality, and the militant Mau Mau Society."[34]

As the occupation developed, it yielded a nascent form of sovereign contestation. Owing to a recognition of the limits of demand-based politics and, at the same time, to the precariousness of their own claim to territorial control, the occupation produced intense negotiations about demands and the precise conditions under which they might be met. As Stulberg reported, "the demonstrators … stated yesterday afternoon that they will not leave until all of their demands are met, and they will not send a group to negotiate their demands until the University agrees to give the demonstrators amnesty." He continued: "Among the list of six demands are requests that the University stop construction of the new gym in Morningside Park, sever its ties with the Institute of Defense Analysis and allow open hearings for all future judicial cases on campus."[35]

Although they generally follow the repertoire laid down by modern social movements, these demands are interesting because they show how, in addition to underscoring the activists' opposition to the University's involvement in colonial violence both at home and abroad, they also set out to contest the configuration of sovereign power. This is achieved in an indirect manner, by trying to use existing laws to undermine the reach of the law itself. Thus it was that what began as a "camp-in" staged to leverage demands developed into a civil war in miniature, in which control over territory became the means by which the struggle for sovereign determination of the law was sought.

The unease that this shift caused found expression in the pages of the *Daily Spectator*, where an op-ed entitled "A Day of Warning" listed things about the anti-gym demonstration that needed to be condemned. Rounding out the piece, the author concluded by noting that "control of the protest in Hamilton Hall has, to a great degree, passed from Columbia students into the hands of people who are not members of the University community but are outside agitators whose interests and goals may bear little relationship to the ends desired by the demonstrators." Despite the critical tone, however, the op-ed endorsed the call for an end to the gymnasium's construction—provided, of course, that it could be achieved through "discussions with all interested community groups."[36] In the end, the threat of "outside agitators" and Black "militants" concealed a more fundamental anxiety about the waning power of political-representational norms and the emergence of a new (but also more primitive and honest) political scene in which anti-colonial resistance took the form of occupation, struggle for territorial control.

According to the *Spectator*, "the arrival of these militants raises another serious problem for the University: whether to call in city police to empty Hamilton Hall." On the one hand, "since they are taking part in an illegal demonstration inside a University building, the black leaders are trespassing on Columbia property." Consequently, "the University could attempt to have them removed by police on these grounds." On the other hand, with the political polarization intensified, "any violence which might erupt from such a confrontation … could have repercussions far beyond the ivy-covered walls of the University" and, as such, needed to be seriously considered.[37] By outlining the problem in this way, the *Spectator* effectively demonstrated how, with the emergence of a sovereign contestation between constituted power and a usurping one, it is constituted power that must work to maintain representational norms since doing otherwise concedes that an exceptional circumstance has, in fact, arisen.

The occupation of Hamilton Hall quickly led to both territorial and political polarization, with the anti-colonial forces of occupation squaring off against their colonizing counterparts. The headlines of the April 25 issue of the *Spectator* reveal how the sense of invasion had taken hold. "Faculty Recommends Halt to Gym Construction: Campus Closed Down, SDS Holds [President] Kirk's Office," read the banner above the fold. Meanwhile, in another headline, the paper made the following ominous proclamation. "Outsiders Influence SDS Action."

Such warnings did little to prevent the action from spreading, however. Indeed, the front page confirmed that, since they last went to print, "Protestors Occupy 2 New Buildings." Penned once again by Robert Stulberg, the article explains: "During the course of the day, which was marked by several near-violent outbreaks, members of Students for a Democratic Society barricaded themselves inside the office of President Grayson Kirk, while militant black students and community protesters remained in control of Hamilton Hall."[38] For their part, "the administration decided to seal off the campus after receiving reports that militant black organizations in Central Harlem were planning to stage a mass protest at Columbia."[39]

> According to Victor Solomon, chairman of Harlem CORE, the Harlem community will demonstrate at Columbia today and everyday that black militant students and community members continue to hold Hamilton. Mr. Solomon said yesterday that a sound truck will travel through Harlem this morning to attract local people to Columbia.[40]

In their Editorial, the *Spectator* staff recounted how, "faced with unsubstantiated rumors of community residents marching on Columbia to protest, the University all but sealed off the campus and locked many University buildings." In this way, they lent "credence to the charge that the administration considers the University to be a fortress surrounded by unfriendly natives."[41] But where the rumors unsubstantiated? On April 27, the paper's front-page headline read: "Brown and Carmichael Appear at Hamilton." According to Arthur Kokot, "Black militant leaders H. Rap Brown and Stokeley Carmichael forcibly entered the campus early yesterday afternoon, after which Mr. Brown told a gathering of over five hundred students assembled outside of Hamilton Hall, 'if the University doesn't deal with the brothers in there, they're going to have to deal with the brothers in the streets.'"[42] Kokot's story continued:

> Mr. Brown and Mr. Carmichael entered the campus at 1:10 p.m. after breaking a police line defending the Amsterdam Ave. entrance to College Walk. They were immediately surrounded and escorted to Hamilton, by a group of forty black high school students and several other black persons. ... Mr. Brown emphasized the fact that black students are in control of Hamilton. ... The two black leaders had been aided in entering the campus by a group of approximately one hundred male and female young black students from several Manhattan high schools who had entered the campus around 11:20.[43]

On the evening of April 29, 1000 cops are called onto campus to empty the occupied buildings. The lead story in the April 30 issue of the *Spectator* reads: "In a brutal bloody show of strength from 2:30 until 5:30 this morning, New York City police, at the request of the Columbia administration, cleared the five buildings held for the past week by student demonstrators." The paper then goes on to give an in-depth account of how each building was evicted. Here, it's significant to note that no violence was used to clear Hamilton Hall: "while police resorted to violence at other campus buildings to remove demonstrating students, a small detachment of the Tactical Police Force—without billy clubs—peacefully removed about a hundred black students from Hamilton Hall."[44]

The Occupation of Alcatraz

One year later, between 1969 and 1971, several hundred Indigenous activists occupied Alcatraz Island. According to movement participant Adam Fortunate Eagle, "Alcatraz was a powerful symbol."[45] However, the action's significance did not arise primarily from the symbolic realm. For members of Indians of All Tribes, seizing the island was worthwhile in large part because it was thought to have "enough facilities to give it some real potential."[46] In other words, the objective was not simply to *hold* the space but to *produce* something with and within it. As Fortunate Eagle recounts, activists hoped that the island's "potential" could be used to "galvanize the urban Indian community and reach out to the Indians on the reservation."

> We developed our ideas of the practical, historical, and political reasons why Alcatraz should become Indian, and what exactly we would do with it. All of our thoughts were later incorporated into proclamations made at the takeover.[47]

Despite being a member of the "local native communities" invoked by the Occupy Oakland People of Color Caucus in the preamble to their December 4, 2011 motion, Fortunate Eagle remained unfazed by the "echo" of "colonial domination" in the terms "occupy" and "occupation." Indeed, as far as he was concerned, the homology between "their" occupation and "ours" was an important political discovery. And it's precisely for this reason that the activists that landed on Alcatraz are—in Fortunate Eagle's account—referred to as "the occupying force," and that their arrival is described reverentially as "the takeover."[48] The homology between "their" occupation and "ours" can be extended. Despite Reed's *Tidal* insistence that "a radical people's occupation of public space doesn't erect checkpoints,"[49] activist scholar Hannah Dobbs has noted that Indians of All Tribes secured Alcatraz by—among other things—painting "giant 'no trespassing' signs, including one that read … 'Warning Keep Off Indian Property.'"[50]

Based on accounts such as these, it's clear that (regardless of the practice's apparent self-evidence today) positing resistance as the conceptual negation of the oppressor's terms was not yet hegemonic in 1969—or even in 1992, when Fortunate Eagle published his reflections; or even among "local native communities," despite the fact that this is where the allergy to "occupation" is ostensibly strongest.

For Carl Schmitt, politics presupposes "the distinction of friend and enemy." Here, the political enemy is "existentially something different and alien, so that in the extreme case conflicts with him are possible."[51] In this way, the goal of politics becomes: repulsing one's opponent "in order to preserve one's own form of existence."[52] Although tainted by his association with fascism, Schmitt's formulation is nevertheless instructive when considering anti-colonial encounters. In Fortunate Eagle's account, deliberation enabled activists to "agree on a name we could use to structure the occupying force and sign the proclamations—'Indians of All Tribes.'"[53] Apart from the telling reference to his Indigenous compatriots as an "occupying force," Fortunate Eagle's testimony highlights how the inauguration of politics is marked by the emergence of a "we"—a "form of existence," to use Schmitt's apt but misunderstood phrase.

Having landed on Alcatraz, Indians of All Tribes declared: "We, the native Americans, re-claim the land known as Alcatraz Island in the name of all American Indians by right of discovery."[54] Though the proclamation's gestural mimesis was no doubt meant to be—and indeed was—humorous, its political implications are impossible to ignore. For one, the "we" that did the reclaiming amounted to a new people—a group that came together through reclamation and would not likely have emerged without it. Moreover, by making the claim on behalf of "all American Indians," the occupiers effectively erased prior national divisions in an effort to conceptually extend the boundaries of their "we." Finally, by appealing to the "right of discovery" (and thus drawing on a European colonial legal contrivance to legitimize their possession), Indians of All Tribes demonstrated that the realization of their sovereign claim required that the legal claims of others be nullified.[55]

Having established the basis of their entitlement, the Indians of All Tribes proclamation enumerated the uses to which the island would be put. Significantly, all proposed uses concerned the development of the people's form of existence. These included: a center for Native American Studies, an American Indian spiritual center, an Indian Center for Ecology, a Great Indian training school, and—finally—an American Indian museum.

Marked as it was by the weight of sovereign assertion, it's not surprising that the proclamation led Fortunate Eagle to consider the similarities between the actions of the occupiers and those that marked the conquest of the Americas. "I thought of the Mayflower and its crew of Pilgrims who had landed on our shores 350 years earlier. The history books say they were seeking new freedom for themselves and their children, freedom denied them in their homeland."

> It didn't matter that Plymouth Rock already belonged to somebody else; that was not their concern. What did concern them was their own fate and their own hopes. What a sad commentary on this country that we, the original inhabitants, were forced to make a landing 350 years later on another rock, the rock called Alcatraz, to focus national attention on our own struggle to regain the same basic freedom.[56]

Alcatraz marked a watershed moment in Indigenous struggles in the United States. As historian Troy R. Johnson reports, there were more than 65 major Indigenous occupations or actions in support of occupations in the period between 1969 and 1975. Many of these actions, which involved occupying abandoned military bases, explicitly mixed the struggle for legal recognition with the struggle to create new forms of Indigenous existence along post-national lines.

Citing the 1868 Sioux treaty right to occupy former Indian lands scheduled by the government to be declared "surplus," United Indians of All Tribes occupied Fort Lawton on March 8, 1970. According to Johnson, "Indians from Alcatraz Island made up the majority of the occupation force."[57] On the same date, 14 activists also occupied Fort Lewis, Washington.[58] On April 2, 1970, another attempt was made to occupy Fort Lawton. According to occupation participant Bernie Whitebear, "Alcatraz was very much a catalyst to our occupation here. … If it had not been for their determined effort … there would have been no movement here."[59]

On May 1, 1970, Pomo Indians occupied Rattlesnake Island near Clear Lake California. Against the objections of the lumber company then claiming title to the land, they were "allowed" to stay.[60] On May 9, 1970, approximately 70 Mohawks from the St. Regis Indian Reservation occupied Stanley Island in the St. Lawrence River, posted a "no trespassing" sign, and reclaimed the island—along with its nine-hole golf course.[61] According to Ward Churchill, "Mohawks from St. Regis and Canghawaga [Kahnawake]" partook in a similar action on May 13, 1974, when they "occupied an area at Ganiekeh [Moss Lake], in the Adirondak Mountains." After declaring the site to be "sovereign Mohawk territory under the Fort Stanwix treaty," they "set out to defend it (and themselves) by force of arms."[62]

Implications

Although they were important moments of anti-colonial struggle in America, the occupations of Columbia and Alcatraz were not anomalies. Moreover, they reveal that, rather than being decolonization's antithesis, occupation has historically been a central tactic in the struggle to achieve it. The fight to determine what liberation might mean must first contest what—following Weber—we might call the state's monopoly on the legitimate use of occupation. Although it often remained insensitive to the colonial experiment from which it remained inseparable, the Occupy movement's wish images revealed that regicide was its guiding star. And, had they reached it, they would have opened clear lines along which decolonization forces might have advanced.

Instead, the wish image remained unclarified. And occupation (the concept without content) was set upon by decolonization, its contentless antithesis. Had the conceptual problem been addressed, and had the strategic lines been more carefully drawn, our eulogy may have been a ballad instead. Having missed our opportunity, the least we can do is ensure that this footnote gets consulted.

THE WORK OF VIOLENCE IN THE AGE OF REPRESSIVE DESUBLIMATION

"Law and order are always and everywhere the
law and order which protect the established
hierarchy; it is nonsensical to invoke the absolute
authority of this law and this order against those
who suffer from it and struggle against it—not
for personal advantages and revenge, but for their
share of humanity. There is no other judge over
them than the constituted authorities, the police,
and their own conscience. If they use violence,
they do not start a new chain of violence but try
to break an established one. Since they will be
punished, they know the risk, and when they are
willing to take it, no third person, and least of
all the educator and intellectual, has the right to
preach them abstention."
—Herbert Marcuse

This essay first appeared in Andrew T. Lamas, Todd Wolfson, and Peter N.
Funke (eds.), *The Great Refusal: Herbert Marcuse and Contemporary Social
Movements* (Philadelphia: Temple University Press, 2017).

I

Recounting the feudal origins of high bourgeois culture in *One-Dimensional Man*, Herbert Marcuse noted how people's historic inability to reconcile form and content, heart and mind, "is" and "ought," tended to prompt generative encounters with alienation. By stimulating what amounted either to recollections or anticipations of yet-to-be realized happiness, these sublime agonies supplemented the positivist instrumentality of official bourgeois culture even as they stood against it. At their logical conclusion, they compelled the aesthetic (in both of its overlapping but distinct senses) to indict the world as it was given.[1]

This feudal inheritance, Marcuse noted, was "an outdated and surpassed culture" that could only be recaptured through "dreams and childlike regressions." Nevertheless, he did not hesitate in noting that—precisely by virtue of its non-resolution—this culture was, at the same time, an intoxicating vision of a "*post*-technological" and reconciled future. Indeed, for Marcuse, feudal society's "most advanced images and positions seem to survive their absorption into administered comforts and stimuli; they continue to haunt the consciousness with the possibility of their rebirth in the consummation of technical progress."[2]

Confronting these passages half a century after they were penned cannot help but yield an uncanny effect. It is not easy, for instance, to overlook the degree to which what was once true of the bourgeoisie's encounter with feudal culture seems equally well to apply to our own encounter with Marcuse today. On first blush, the intellectual figurehead of the American New Left confronts us as an endearing anachronism, a source of wishful stimuli that (like a latter-day Walt Whitman ready to "charge [us] full with the charge of the soul"[3]) cannot help but swaddle us in childlike innocence. Great Refusal! Eros! Abolition of the performance principle!

Almost immediately, however, the pleasure of this initial response is troubled by the realization that it has been a long time since we have been innocent. Extending the Marcuse-Whitman analogy, we might even deduce that there is no way for the body electric to escape. Like the rest, it is (we are) plugged into—and thus drained by—this society's erotic economy. As with feudal culture for the bourgeoisie, the initial promise of infantile regression we find in Marcuse gives way to a renewed sublime agony. Correspondingly, the encounter with innocence reveals itself to be ambivalent—as does the child-like regression itself, which in one moment underscores (and even seems to justify) postmodernism's fêted man-child before suggesting a hazardous course toward the realization of an unfulfilled promise. Nowhere does this tension become more evident than in Marcuse's discussion of political violence.

On the one hand, Marcuse cries out in opposition to the prosaic horrors that turn violence into workaday "aggressiveness" (those forms of antisocial social cohesion that enact a calculated regression from the deepest chambers of technorational society's wind-up heart).[4] On the other hand, regressions of this sort prompt a desire for conse-quential action that cannot be contained by repressive desublimation's proxy resolutions. By following these desires through to their logical conclusion, actors might reconnect to (and thus assume ownership over and responsibility for) the capacity for violence that stands as precondition to genuine human being.[5] Through its unbearable non-resolution, the sublime ransacks the past to devise viable images of a future happiness. In Marcuse, this ambivalence finds its most acute expression in his treatment of violence, which he disavows on account of the inadequacies of its proxy before finally embracing it as a pro-fane, political-ontological inevitability.

II

In John Cameron Mitchell's 2006 cult classic film *Shortbus*,[6] the own-er of a postmodern, post-9/11 sex club lovingly describes his creation by noting how "it's just like the '60s, only with less hope." For more than twenty years, Fredric Jameson has alerted us to the fact that the postmodern condition is inseparable from such nostalgic echoes.[7] And, following Walter Benjamin, we might envision that echoes of this sort could be of use when guiding our desires toward desirable resolutions.[8] But while such echoes indicate a superficial continuity between two moments, it is necessary to acknowledge (as the sex club owner did) that, today, the search for resolutions to human desires is more fruitfully pursued by abandoning hope.

To be sure, the resolutions to the feeling of constitutive lack available in the 1960s tended to be much further from the hopeful cultivation of a new sensibility than adherents often held them to be.[9] Nevertheless, the counterculture remained valuable precisely on account of its ability to constitute an antithetical "we" (a mode of existence capable of repolarizing one-dimensional society in order to bring it—whether or not it had been the counterculture's intention— to the brink of civil war). From this vantage, the promise lay not in the counterculture's positive, affirming content, but rather in its capacity to muster a Great Refusal—to produce a moment of pure negation capable of liberating humanity's productive capacities and setting them along a different course.

The counterculture betrayed its moment. By focusing inward on the cultivation of a positive content rather than determining what would be required to move from self-affirming rebellion to the self-abolition required by revolution, the counterculture's degeneration echoed the limitations that Jean-Paul Sartre had noted in Charles Baudelaire's sublime tantrums a generation earlier.[10] In this way, it assured that it would be reabsorbed by the status quo—and that its energies would serve to revitalize (rather than to abolish) it.[11] What was true of the counterculture also holds for Marcuse, who played a central role in revitalizing Left politics by binding movement activities to the resolution of libidinal drives. Reading his texts, one cannot help but note how he enveloped critical theory's negative dimensions[12] in a positive normative vision in which human biology itself abetted revolution.[13] Although Marcuse sometimes acknowledged this ambivalence explicitly, one cannot help but be left with the impression that it was surely the positive vision (that Whitmanesque stroll through some new Eden) and not the powerful negative thrust of his critical theory that drew the movement to him.

Today's new cycle of struggle seems to cry out for Marcuse's return. The enthusiasm in the streets and squares since 2010-11 has signaled a kind of resurgence of political optimism that, with few exceptions, has not been witnessed since the 1960s. Nevertheless, closer investigation reveals that this renewal is inflected with a different temperament—one that might lead us to conclude that it, too, is "just like the 1960s, only with less hope." As can be attested by the now-regular devolution of bacchanalian exuberance into protracted civil war (e.g., Tahrir Square, Taksim Square), this ambivalence is political; however, it is ontological, too. Whether tacitly acknowledged or explicitly embraced, the disavowal of hope by contemporary social movement actors must be seen as a move away from deferred gratification and proxy resolutions and toward concrete reckoning.

Meanwhile, the echoes persist. Many of the ideas that Marcuse put forward as cautionary tales in *One-Dimensional Man* had become the profane features of everyday life by the time Jameson published his groundbreaking book on postmodernism.[14] Indeed, it is impossible to read many of Marcuse's observations without being struck by the feeling that they are prescient first drafts, thematic sketches destined to find their way to center stage a generation later. Consider, for instance, to how retrospectively *avant-la-lettre* Marcuse can sound in a passage such as this: "The good urge to épater *le bourgeois*," he writes, "no longer attains its aim because the traditional 'bourgeois' no longer exists, and no 'obscenity' or madness can shock a society which has made a blooming business with 'obscenity.'"[15] To be clear, Marcuse's point was that the traditional bourgeois "no longer exists" because one-dimensional society obliterated the sublime culture it had inherited from the feudal era through a process of radical social dispersion. Recounting the desublimated sexuality that found pervasive expression in the literature of his time, for instance, Marcuse reports that it had become "part and parcel of the society in which it happens, but nowhere its negation," as might have previously been the case with the sublimated sexuality of the Romantics. "What happens" in this literature, he concluded, "is surely wild and obscene, virile and tasty, quite immoral—and, precisely because of that, perfectly harmless."[16] To get a sense of this dismal blossoming's contemporary manifestations, it suffices to recall how, in *Postmodernism*, Jameson observed that the "offensive features" of contemporary aesthetic production "no longer scandalize anyone and are not only received with the greatest complacency but have themselves become institutionalized." Indeed, they are "at one with the official or public culture of Western society."[17]

Alternately, and following Marcuse, we might recall how one salient feature or modernist art was that it tended to respond "to the total character of repression...with total alienation." For Marcuse, expressions of this sublime tendency could still be found in the work of figures like John Cage. "But," he wonders, "has this effort already reached...the point where the oeuvre drops out of the dimension of alienation...and turns into a sound-game, language-game—harmless and without commitment, shock which no longer shocks, and thus succumbing?"[18] As clear anticipations of Jameson, such comments alert us to the prescience and enduring value of Marcuse's insights; however, they also underscore the profound inadequacy of a purely representational approach to the problems we now confront. At their threshold, these problems take the form of an intractable tension between complicit aggression and a potentially liberating violence that always seems just out of reach.

III

Revolutionary at its inception, the regime of representational politics that came into being through bourgeois victory in the late eighteenth century has degenerated into a form of repressive desublimation. Politics, a thing with grave consequences, previously unavailable to the masses (politics as a form of productive activity, always and necessarily entailing a violence before which the sovereign must stand unflinchingly as final arbiter), is now widely disseminated through representation. This "resolution" to the problem of genuine being, which gives access to the thing without demanding responsibility for its consequences, allows us to feel the satisfaction of participation (of acting out, of acting as if) without having to deal with the substance to which it refers. Meanwhile, the productive violence of politics itself continues to be hoarded by the state, which claims a monopoly on the legitimate right to use it.

Through the course of the twentieth century, however, it became clear that this proxy would never satisfy the desire for the Real (that *thing* which escapes symbolization, and which cannot be represented) that it inadvertently stimulates. In response to our growing impatience, we are now placated with unending opportunities for what Marcuse called "aggressiveness"—forms of violence that are primarily representational, cathartic, and complicit in the reproduction of a highly managed labor force.[19] Like the commodity sphere they subtend, however, these satisfactions are prone to wearing thin. Meanwhile, the violent transformation of social reality brought about by a state politics at war with our interests enjoins us to muster a response.

Since the advent of the bourgeois public sphere, this response has occasionally found expression in the activities and campaigns of modern social movements. An effective means of exploiting the contradictions between what Marx called "the substance" and "the phrase" of the bourgeois revolution,[20] these movements tallied significant victories over the course of the nineteenth and twentieth century. Nevertheless, because they were conceived as demand-based formations that sought greater recognition from constituted power and because, consequently, they staked their claim in the public sphere,[21] they have tended to become complicit in the reproduction of the bourgeoisie's representational paradigm.[22] This schizoid position has been a source of tremendous anxiety; and the wholesale erosion of the public sphere (a "structural transformation" that began more than a century ago[23] but that ended with a whimper under neoliberalism's shadow) has only exacerbated the problem.

In response, forces committed to social justice but antagonistic toward the established social-movement repertoire have struggled to devise means of contesting state power that are not contingent upon its recognition. Inevitably, these have involved a scramble to reconnect with violence—that force now known primarily by way of repressive desublimation (through which the state supposedly enacts the will of those it represents) or through the proxy of aggression (which remains indexed to the perpetuation of the status quo). Recounting the death of politics under such conditions, the anonymous French insurrectionists in Tiqqun stated it thus: "violence is what has been taken away from us."[24] To be sure, the efforts of groups like Tiqqun to reconnect with violence have thus far remained tactically inconclusive.[25] Nevertheless, they have proven to be extremely important from the standpoint of political pedagogy.

This has certainly been the case with respect to state responses, which have consistently sought to reiterate the representational fiction upon which bourgeois authority first found legitimation; however, it has also been true for social movement participants themselves. Here, on the one hand, we find those who are seduced by the promise of a politics beyond representation, a politics freed from the aggressive distortions of repressive desublimation. In the United States, this group has been nurtured by CrimethInc., which has argued that "a small group that behaves confidently as if they are living in a different world can call into question things everyone else takes for granted; if they take their departure far enough at the right time, they can make the impossible possible by persuading others that it is so on the strength of their own conviction."[26] On the other hand, we find those whose psychic structure has been fundamentally reordered by the representational paradigm. Instead of a Great Refusal, these forces respond to movement violence by entrenching themselves all the more deeply into the existing regime—despite the fact that, through the contemporary normalization of naked force, this regime no longer seeks to legitimate itself through reference to once sacred, self-evident truths.

As symptoms of the cultural logic of late capitalism, these two tendencies echo those noted by Marcuse in his Introduction to *One-Dimensional Man* more than fifty years ago. In that text, Marcuse recounted how the triumph of industrial society was such that it could manage qualitative transformations for the foreseeable future even as it appeared to be riven by forces that heralded its dissolution.[27] As was true for Marcuse in his own time, it is too soon to know which of these tendencies will prevail. Will social movements continue along a path of incremental tinkering that ends by legitimating the opposition (our enemy, constituted power), or will they resolve their contradictory stance by disavowing representational seductions and embracing the properly martial elements that continue like hollow devotions to find expression in even the most staid mobilization (e.g., the march, the drum, the banner, the blockade)?

Although the answer cannot be known in advance, recent events are enough to suggest that the latter option alone points to liberation.[28] In order for it to be realized, it is necessary to first highlight and then foster those pedagogical moments when protest turns violent and when violence tears at the representational screen that envelops us all. Through these tears, it is sometimes possible to glimpse another politics and, in turn, another world. Such visions make clear that our enemies are twofold. On the one hand, we confront the ambassadors of constituted power, the purveyors of representation, and the peddlers of repressive desublimation. On the other, we face erstwhile allies committed to social justice but seduced by representation's siren song. Of these two enemies, the former is inestimably more important; however, we shall not muster the force to confront them effectively until the latter is first addressed.

In what follows, I draw on Marcuse's observations about repressive desublimation, social movements, and violence to understand the tremendous hostility that frequently accompanies violent eruptions at contemporary political demonstrations. In particular, I am interested in what social-democratic and labor-bureaucratic responses to black bloc violence reveal about the aggrieved parties. Through a consideration of such erstwhile-ally responses to black bloc street fighting during protests against the G20 in Toronto during the summer of 2010 and in the subsequent actions of Occupy demonstrators in Oakland, I propose that black bloc violence can play an important pedagogical role in clarifying the meaning of politics in an era stricken by repressive desublimation.

To understand why, it is necessary to consider three interrelated dynamics. First, black bloc actions make a direct claim on the productive character of violence while simultaneously undermining its repressively desublimated aggression-based proxies (though they are always, tellingly, denounced as having more in common with the latter). Second, they are seductive to those who feel that their desire for real life and real consequences is not being (and cannot be) met by current, repressively desublimated, arrangements. Finally, they expose the ineffectual fiction that underwrites the social-democratic identification with representational politics. To be sure, the black bloc poses these problems (stimulates these promises) without being able to resolve them through the means to which it currently lays claim. Nevertheless, by its ability to point out *the possibility* of an outside to this "comfortable, smooth, reasonable, democratic unfreedom,"[29] it has already proven felicitous.

IV

Unlike previous mobilizations against global summits, I mostly had to sit out the G20 in Toronto. Along with being in the final throes of dissertation writing at the time, I was also preoccupied with arranging details for the release of *Black Bloc, White Riot*, which was scheduled to come out later that summer.[30] These considerations, however, did not prevent my roommates from assuming prominent roles in the Toronto Community Mobilization Network, the main organizing body for the protests. In the lead-up to the actions, I did what I could to share the materials and lessons I had amassed from similar mobilizations in the past; mostly, however, I stayed out of their way.

That was how things stood until the early morning of June 26, when I received a phone call. It was my roommates, and they had just learned that there was a warrant out for their arrest on charges of conspiracy. All of a sudden, I was in the midst of a "Miami model" moment, and my roommates were calling on me to help them work through it.[31] Since, miraculously, cops had yet to show up at our door, I urged my roommates to make their way home so that they could prepare to enter police custody on the best possible terms. By the end of the morning, they—along with more than a dozen others—had been picked up and branded as ringleaders, part of the "main conspiracy group."[32]

The events that unfolded subsequently made clear that whatever conspiracy may have existed could be set into motion without my roommates or any of their co-accused being present. That afternoon, Toronto was thrown into tumult. And though they numbered in the thousands, the police lost control of the streets. A black bloc broke into the financial district and set cop cars on fire. Through their agitation, they opened a path through police lines that allowed other demonstrators to approach a fortified summit site additionally protected by the exceptional suspension of the rule of law.[33] With my roommates in detention along with hundreds of others at some sketchy East-end warehouse that the cops had turned into a dungeon, I began keeping track of responses to the events that had unfolded.

Writing in *Canadian Dimension*, author Adam Davidson-Harden critiqued the black bloc by claiming that it had helped to legitimate the state's security efforts. Moreover, by suppressing discussion of protestor grievances, it ultimately provided cover for the G20 and its agenda. "The black-clad mob…has left a lot of people not only in the general public but in the wider nonviolent social/global justice movements in Canada feeling disgusted, demoralized and dispirited," he wrote. In his view, this was "just the result you want if your goal is to marginalize and stifle dissent."

> While the more numerous non-violent voices were indeed heard on the streets and at Queen's Park (25,000 in the main march!), they weren't "heard" in the more meaningful, mass sense as loudly as the same reels of destruction overplayed in the media, and the same accounts of destruction and violence witnessed to on the ground by journalists, activists and citizens. The blocistes … take the discursive space away from the broader movements, inviting and indeed compelling the public (through the media, of course) to only focus on the violence of smashing, burning, destroying, throwing, hitting … which are all pointless, repulsive, destructive, and frightening.[34]

This assessment would be reiterated by Sid Ryan of the Ontario Federation of Labour (OFL) who, in a *Toronto Star* article entitled "Thousands Stood Up for Humanity," asserted that—despite the fact that the message on June 26 had been "clear"—it was tarnished by the black bloc, whose actions violated democratic norms. In contrast, Ryan noted that the OFL worked explicitly to maintain such norms. In practical terms, this meant working "diligently to ensure that our democratic right to lawful assembly would be respected, and that citizens could participate in a safe and peaceful event."

> To this end, we liaised with the Toronto Police and cooperated at every turn. On the day, hundreds of volunteer marshals facilitated what was an extraordinarily successful event, given the tension that had pervaded the city in the days before.

"Shamefully," however, "a small number of hooligans used the cloak of our peaceful and lawful demonstration to commit petty acts of vandalism in the streets of Toronto." According to Ryan, and "despite their stated goal of challenging the anti-democratic nature of the G20, these actions actually undermined democracy." As a result, "the weeks and months of effort to educate and activate ordinary people on issues of social, environmental, and economic justice … went up in flames."[35] This position was further elaborated in a media statement by Canadian Labour Congress (CLC) President Ken Georgetti: the CLC "abhors the behaviour of a small group of people who have committed vandalism and destroyed property." Noting that the CLC worked in conjunction with others to organize "a peaceful demonstration," he insisted: "we cooperated with police … and had hundreds of parade marshals to maintain order."

> Our rally and march were entirely peaceful from start to finish. It appears that a small group of anarchists, who are unknown to us, became involved in some violent and destructive activities as the day progressed.

In conclusion, Georgetti issued the following resolute declaration: "We condemn these actions and we will continue to exercise our democratic right to free expression in a peaceful manner at all times."[36] Finally, Canadian Union of Public Employees (CUPE/Ontario) President Fred Hahn and Secretary-Treasurer Candace Rennick added their voices to this chorus when, in an official statement, they decried the events as amounting to "nothing short of the abandonment of the rule of law, both by a small group who took part in the protests, and by a massive and heavily armed police force who were charged with overseeing them."

> Due process, civil liberties and the right to peaceful protest have been the victim. And it's a sad day when some of those, who feel powerless to change the direction of their elected leaders, find in that feeling of powerlessness an excuse to break the law and vandalize the property of their fellow citizens and who, in so doing, silence the legitimate voices of so many others whose commitment to protest and dissent is matched by their rejection of violence and vandalism.[37]

This line of reasoning was not restricted to social democratic and labor leaders, however. In a post filed on June 28, 2010, blogger Milan Ilnyckyj complained that the black bloc had come to "dominate the news coverage" and obscure "legitimate messages from activist groups." Moreover, these actions seemed doomed "to justify the expense and intrusion of the heavy-handed security that now accompanies these events." Summing up his position, he noted that the black bloc "just distracts from serious discussions" by acting out its "incoherent rage." As a result, and "given how effectively the violent minority drowns out important messages," the task befalling sensible people involved "finding some way to keep a lid on them."[38]

For scholars and activists who have followed the debates surrounding the black bloc since its eruption on the streets of Seattle in 1999, perspectives like those recounted above will no doubt sound familiar. Indeed, they reflect positions that are widely held by social-movement commentators and participants. Moreover, they rely upon a series of well-established rhetorical conventions. To get a sense of how pervasive this narrative and conceptual coherence has become, it suffices to briefly revisit some of the commentary that erupted around black bloc participation in the Occupy movement. Here, alongside journalist Chris Hedges' widely cited and vitriolic denunciation (in which he likened the black bloc to a "cancer"[39]), one finds comments like those by John Blackstone of CBS News who wondered whether the black bloc might be "hijacking Occupy Oakland." In a report published on November 4, 2011, he noted that, "by destroying property and challenging police," the black bloc (despite its small numbers) might "hijack the message of otherwise peaceful protests." The consequences, for Blackstone, were clear: "Those intent on violence may be on the fringes, but once the trouble begins, they often get the spotlight. In Oakland, city officials have warned that more violence could bring another order to close down the Occupy encampment."[40]

One day later, Sheila Musaji filed a story with *The American Muslim* in which she declared without equivocation that the black bloc and its tactics were definitely "hurting the Occupy Movement."[41] Quoting from personal correspondence with San Francisco Bay-area blogger Rashid Patch, Musaji helped to cultivate the impression that the black bloc was comprised primarily of "angry, uncaring, sadly damaged" youth. By Patch's account, participants in the black bloc "were never socialized, perhaps barely housebroken. Often seriously abused as children, they are responding in kind to the world." But while "these are the kind of people who turn into Charlie Mansons—or followers of the Charlie Mansons," Patch nevertheless found some of them to be "astonishingly intelligent, brilliantly creative, and terribly, terribly bitter about every aspect of life." Patch continued:

> They are a symptom of society's madness and violence. Some of them take on that role consciously, and argue with great fervor that their vandalism is a logical political response to the conditions of their life—that violence is the only rational response to a pathological society.[42]

V

What are we to make of such comments? Clearly they raise both strategic and tactical questions that cannot be ignored. After all (and even according to the accounts of its participants), the black bloc actions in Toronto were improvisational at best.[43] In addition to these concerns, however, the statements cited above also give symptomatic expression to a peculiar conception of the political and to the anxious social-democratic allegiance that underwrites it. Even though it is asserted in defiance to the status quo, this conception accords with the bourgeois logic of representation. In the end, it amounts to a form of repressive desublimation. When considered from this vantage, it becomes clear that at least part of the hostility directed toward the black bloc arises from the fact that, through its actions, it brings this complicity to light.

In order to substantiate these claims, it is useful to review Marcuse's comments on repressive desublimation to confirm that the dynamics he describes coincide with those underlying bourgeois representational politics and the social-movement commitment thereto. In Marcuse's account, by opening up previously inaccessible fields of potential self-resolution, repressive desublimation amounted to a "liquidation of two-dimensional culture." However, "this liquidation … takes place not through the denial and rejection of the 'cultural values'" that organized the bourgeoisie's ascent to class dominance (values that explicitly made use of the aesthetic as a field for the cultivation of sublime and transformative experiences of alienation) but rather through their "wholesale incorporation into the established order, through their reproduction and display on a massive scale."[44] While sublimation helped to highlight the inadequacy of the world, desublimation worked to provide the desired object without the accompanying resolution. When applied to politics, repressive desublimation turns a dynamic founded on antagonism[45] into a perverse form of inclusion. To give but one example, one might highlight (as Marcuse himself did) how bourgeois representational politics produces situations where opposition to the system becomes evidence that the system itself is working. As Marcuse noted in "Repressive Tolerance,"

> The exercise of political rights (such as voting, letter-writing to the press, to Senators, etc., protest demonstrations with a priori renunciation of counterviolence) in a society of total administration serves to strengthen this administration by testifying to the existence of democratic liberties which, in reality, have changed their content and lost their effectiveness. In such a case, freedom (of opinion, of assembly, of speech) becomes an instrument for absolving servitude.[46]

Meanwhile, the profound distrust expressed by those who have aligned themselves with representational politics toward those who enact the Great Refusal by embracing violence (and, hence, Being itself) directly alerts us to the significance of those political actors and their acts. This significance owes not to tactical efficacy (which is always debatable) but rather to the fact that the act itself repolarizes the political universe, calls the self-evidence of one-dimensionality into question, and forces those who would abide by representational politics' repressively desublimated stipulations to account for the inevitable contradictions arising from their claim to secure political freedom through unfree means. "Under a system of constitutionally guaranteed...civil rights and liberties," Marcuse notes, "opposition and dissent are tolerated unless they issue in violence."

> The underlying assumption is that the established society is free, and that any improvement, even a change in the social structure and social values, would come about in the normal course of events, prepared, defined, and tested in free and equal discussion, on the open marketplace of ideas and goods.[47]

The violence that sometimes takes place at demonstrations calls these presumptions into question. And though the melee may come to be representationally contained, the fact of the rupture produces pedagogical and therapeutic effects that cannot be ignored. The ensuing nervousness arises not from the chaos per se (indeed, the chaos might be quite minimal) but from the fact that such violence reveals that the commitment to representational politics is as likely to lead to liberation as are the forms of self-expression opened by repressive desublimation.

This is the pedagogical value of the Great Refusal. For Marcuse, such a refusal amounted—in its pure negativity—to a "protest against that which is."[48] Through acts of negation aimed at repolarizing the political universe while confronting the lack inherent in existing reality, people discover "modes of refuting, breaking, and recreating their factual existence."[49] The sequence of events described in this passage is far from arbitrary; carried out at the conceptual level and involving the objectification and reparsing of the material world, the act of refuting must come first. Indeed, it accords with the role assigned by Marx to "imagination" in his discussion of the human labor process in Chapter VII of *Capital*.[50] Refutation is then followed by the act of "breaking"—the necessarily negative political-productive act required to prepare the way for subsequent acts of creation and recreation, the transformative reconfiguration of "existing reality."

However, only with the erection of the barricade (the polarizing two-dimensional expression of the "gut hatred"[51] or "biological hatred"[52] that Marcuse held to be indispensable to the cultural revolution) does "the gesture ... of love"[53] underlying efforts to productively transform society emancipate itself from the plastic confines of its contemporary repressive desublimation. Considered from this perspective, it becomes evident that the animosity generated by the black bloc owes to its capacity to highlight the extent of people's ongoing identification with a fraudulent reality. "To discuss tolerance in such a society," writes Marcuse, "means to re-examine the issue of violence."

> Even in the advanced centers of civilization, violence actually prevails: it is practiced by the police, in the prisons and mental institutions, in the fight against racial minorities. ... This violence indeed breeds violence. But to refrain from violence in the face of vastly superior violence is one thing, to renounce a priori violence against violence, on ethical or psychological grounds (because it may antagonize sympathizers) is another.[54]

Reviewing Marcuse's comments makes clear that, whatever his misgivings about "aggressiveness" as an outgrowth of repressive desublimation, he was open to considering violence a productive social force. Indeed, he maintained that this force needed to be protected from bourgeois ethics and representational politics. In the hands of constituted power, violence becomes the means by which the status quo is endlessly reproduced. By seizing hold of violence in a moment of Great Refusal, insurgent forces signal the possibility that another production is possible. Society is repolarized, and one-dimensionality dissolves. In contrast, "with respect to historical violence emanating from among ruling classes, no such relation to progress seems to obtain."[55]

THE BATTLE FOR NECROPOLIS

Considered from the standpoint of the commodity form's totalizing reach, the enthusiasm for the commons expressed by contemporary radicals suggests that fundamental social change may once again be on the agenda. Nevertheless, the celebration of the concept's promise has thus far tended to coincide with an eschewal of the difficult practical demands it also entails. Consequently, many "actually existing" experiments in commoning have contributed more to the edification of their miniscule participant bases than they have to the eradication of capitalist enclosure. To be sure, such experiments can be valuable sources of information. However, when conceived as ends in themselves, they risk becoming a sideshow to the struggle demanded by the concept that animated them. It is in opposition to this tendency that we must commit to the battle for necropolis.

On the surface, referring to our struggle for the commons as a "battle" (describing it in the language of territorial war) seems at odds with the practical character of most contemporary campaigns. Indeed, many of these seem more concerned with finding reprieve in the cracks opened by neoliberalism's overreach than at provoking direct confrontations with power. Meanwhile, even our most promising experiments in (for instance) urban agriculture suggest that the

---

This essay first appeared in Mary Dellenbaugh, Martin Schwegmann, Markus Kip, et al. (eds.), *Urban Commons: Moving Beyond State and Market (Bauwelt Fundamente 154)*. (Basel: Birkhäuser, 2015).

struggle for the commons is currently motivated less by concerns with production *per se* than by the urge to recover neglected aspects of our humanity. Here, the inconsequential yields of our harvests are nothing when compared to the genuine relations we cultivate despite living in a time when such bonds have, for the most part, gone fallow.

But if the longing for human connection underwriting the common's current allure makes the language of "battle" seem dubious, matters are made still worse by my insistence that the terrain for which we must fight is necropolis—the city of the dead. Surely, some might say, such a claim can be nothing more than a symptom of the pop fixation on the imminent zombie apocalypse. And, indeed, evidence is everywhere; one need only to think of the stunning set piece in the recent cinematic adaptation of *World War Z* (in which a zombie horde overtakes Jerusalem by crashing down its historic walls) to see that this is the case.

But while the call to wage a battle for necropolis may seem on first blush to be little more than the *cri de coeur* of a science fiction shut-in (and while it may seem inimical to that species of sober analysis demanded by situations such as ours), it is precisely to the themes of *politics as war* and the *persistence of the dead* to which we must turn if we hope to advance our struggles for the commons beyond their current state of wishful anticipation—a state that stimulates our longing for social transformation even as it thwarts the realization of our aims.

When pushed to its logical conclusion, the tension between the commons as wish-fulfilling image and the commons as unrealized practical accomplishment is enough to provoke a reckoning with the more basic (but also more brutal) connection between sovereignty and war. And though it is normally conceived as pertaining to territory, the struggle for the commons reveals that this war must necessarily involve a struggle for *the past* as well. As some readers may already have suspected, my analysis in these matters is indebted to the insights of Walter Benjamin. Familiar to many as a theorist of capitalism's dreamscapes and urban environments, I demonstrate how Benjamin might also be read as a compelling and provocative theorist of the commons. However, because I may have courted naysayers by conceiving of my subject in these unorthodox terms, let me begin by seeing what I can do to show that the premise is not as eccentric as at first it might seem.

The Dead Among Us

What, then, is the connection between the commons and the city of the dead? Let's begin by considering the "right to the city," a slogan first coined by Henri Lefebvre in 1968 and subsequently popularized by groups struggling to derail capitalist efforts to militarize urban spaces and turn cities into theme parks for the rich. Picking up where Lefebvre left off, David Harvey has recently argued that the meaning of such an unwieldy collective "right" boils down to "greater democratic control over the production and use of the surplus" or, more precisely, "democratic control over the deployment of the surpluses through urbanization."[1] In these formulations, cities are posited as both the practical manifestation of a society's accumulated surplus and as a force in the further development of the surplus itself.

According to Harvey, the city fosters the production of social surplus by way of both its historical aggregation and consequent intensification of the productive forces.[2] At the same time, and at the other end of the production cycle, it serves as a catalyst enabling the realization of surplus value through the market. As a terrain of intensified consumption (for individuals, markets, and means of production), the city facilitates the reabsorption of the very surplus it helped to generate through its own intensification of the production process. For this reason, capitalists rely heavily on urban expansion to ensure that the value of commodities does not depreciate through crises of over-accumulation or the failure to reinvest. Consequently, as Harvey notes, the "history of capital accumulation" is ultimately inseparable from the "growth path of urbanization" itself.[3]

In order to understand what this has to do with the dead, it's necessary to ask: what is the social surplus? Returning to Marx's *Capital*, we discover that, along with being the concrete form taken by surplus value immediately prior to its realization through exchange on the market, social surplus is also the practical objectification of dead or expended labor. Indeed, for Marx, "capital *is* dead labour."[4] This sounds menacing, and Marx stokes our fear by adding that, like a vampire, capital "only lives by sucking living labour, and lives the more, the more it sucks." But while skeptical readers might dismiss these lines as poetic indulgence, it's important to note that—in the immediately preceding passage—Marx gives his vampires a concrete dimension. "Capital has one single life impulse," he writes. And that impulse is "to make its constant factor, the means of production, absorb the greatest possible amount of surplus labour."[5]

Here, the means of production become visible in their status as fixed or constant capital, the concrete form through which the social surplus is produced (i.e. extracted from living labor) and ultimately reabsorbed (e.g. through reinvestment, expansion, etc.). Since capitalists perpetually revolutionize the means of production to gain advantage on the terrain of relative surplus value, the ever-changing "fixed" aspect of capital[6] becomes the concrete repository (the tomb, the mausoleum) of dead labor. Moreover, since the production process relies on constant capital (i.e. as means of production) to extract surplus labor and thus to produce social surplus through the contractually concealed exploitation inherent in the working day,[7] such capital also "produces" dead labor on a daily basis. As a result, capitalism pits living labor in the present against the historically accumulated dead labor entombed in constant capital.

From *The Economic and Philosophic Manuscripts of 1844* right through to the exposé of commodity fetishism in *Capital*, Marx makes clear that the estrangement yielded by this relationship is immediate. The worker feels it whenever she confronts the object she created as an alien force. However, by speaking of the aggregate of this dead labor as a social "surplus" (by highlighting its subsequent transposition back into the ever-expanding realm of fixed capital), we are alerted to the fact that the practical manifestations of alienation accumulate over time as well. Conceived in this way, social surplus comes into view as the form taken by the historical *accumulation* of dead labor. This accretion can be traced concretely by considering how, as Benjamin noted, the railway track heralds the subsequent development of the steel girder—which in turn yields the skyscraper, the aesthetic emblem of an alienation accumulated to the point of becoming sublime.[8]

As a social form, the city is a monumental accomplishment. It is built over generations, and each generation inherits both the practical accomplishments of its predecessors *and* the accumulated estrangement that made those feats possible. Ralph Chaplin, author of the famous American labor anthem "Solidarity Forever" (1915) knew this estrangement well. In his account, "It is we who plowed the prairies, built the cities where they trade; / Dug the mines and built the workshops, endless miles of railroad laid." Nevertheless, as a result of the wage relation, capitalism leaves us to "stand outcast and starving

Fig. 1: Hugo Gellert, "Karl Marx, Capital in Pictures," 1934.

midst the wonders we have made." As a popular retelling of Marx's labor theory of value, Chaplin's anthem is without equal—and it's for precisely this reason that he refuses to leave matters as he found them. Consequently, each verse of his battle hymn concludes with the reminder that, despite our outcast status, "the union makes us strong."

Canonized and subject to turgid recitation by today's staid labor movement, the incendiary dimensions of "Solidarity Forever" are now difficult to perceive. It is therefore necessary to retrace its lines in the interest of salvaging their neglected implications. Immediately, we discover that the "we" and the "us" that Chaplin invokes are clearly temporal ones, since no single generation of workers accomplished the various discrete stages of urban-industrial development he describes (the plowing of prairies, for instance, generally predates and enables the subsequent building of "cities where they trade"). Consequently, the "we" that stands outcast and starving is comprised of both the living and the dead. Furthermore, since the surplus labor of dead generations is trapped within the social surplus, the dead themselves are in some way concretely present in the "wonders" being contemplated (the workshops built by the historic "we," for instance, become a site for the extraction of dead labor in the present). In the final instance—and as the WPA-era communist artist Hugo Gellert knew well—these wonders include the city itself [Fig. 1].

If there is a union, then, between the living and the dead (a union that will make both groups strong), the practical task falling to the living is to free the dead from the social surplus so that their estrangement might come to an end. Concretely speaking, this involves learning how to dismantle and reconfigure (rather than merely repossess) the accumulated matter of the built environment so that it might finally coincide with the will of those who produced it. No small task, to be sure. But even if the living rise to the occasion and commit to reconfiguring the social surplus, we must still determine what sort of earthly task can be assigned to the dead. One answer is this: we must allow, and even insist, that the dead remind us of the desire that animated their efforts while alerting us to the many ways that such desires have historically been susceptible to capture and recuperation.

According to John Berger, capitalism's strength can be measured by the degree to which it managed to break the interdependent bond between the living and the dead. Nevertheless, and despite this new disconnect, "the dead inhabit a timeless moment" that amounts to a "form of imagination concerning the possible." Consequently, Berger enjoins us once again to establish a "clear exchange" across the "frontier between timelessness and time." [9] Only then, he insists, might we benefit from the guidance of dead compatriots who never got to see their dreams fulfilled. Similarly, for Walter Benjamin, "there is a secret agreement between past generations and the present one. Our coming was expected on earth."

> Like every generation that preceded us, we have been endowed with a *weak* Messianic power, a power to which the past has a claim. That claim cannot be settled cheaply. [10]

Aligning Chaplin with Berger and Benjamin in this way may lead skeptics to claim that I'm taking liberties with "Solidarity Forever" and its current adherents. Nevertheless, living-dead alliances of the sort I've described featured prominently in the radical working-class culture of Chaplin's time. In Earl Robinson's famous "Ballad of Joe Hill" from 1930, for instance, the narrator learns in a dream that, although he was executed by firing squad in 1915, the eponymous Swedish-American labor organizer and songsmith lived on wherever there was struggle: "From San Diego up to Maine, / In every mine and mill / Where working men defend their rights / It's there you'll find Joe Hill." Drawing on similar themes, Chaplin concluded his own anthem (penned the year that Hill himself was executed) by reminding us how "we shall bring to birth a new world from the ashes of the old." Finally, the two anthems converge when we recall that (according to movement folklore) the ashes from Joe Hill's cremation were distributed among representatives of the international working class to be scattered worldwide.[11]

By reducing the social surplus to ash, the union of the living and the dead prepares the way for a new world to be born. Indeed, it was not Romanticism alone that led anarcho-syndicalist icon Buenaventura Durruti to proclaim in the midst of Spain's civil war that, since workers had built the palaces and cities being razed in the conflict, they were "not in the least afraid of ruins." Seeming to riff on Chaplin directly, Durruti concluded his commentary by observing that, while "the bourgeoisie might blast and ruin its own world before it leaves the stage of history," it did little to change the fact that "we carry a new world here, in our hearts."[12] Whether by ruin or refurbishment, the tremendous accumulation of dead labor in the social surplus furnishes the energy to realize the promise trapped in the city to which we claim a right.

I will concede that setting down the rudiments of a political theology in trochaic tetrameter may seem like a hazardous undertaking.[13] Nevertheless, the conclusion to Chaplin's "Solidarity Forever" makes clear that, to the extent that the social surplus ever constituted a "wonder," its value owed not to the objectified form through which it first found expression but rather to the accumulated aspirations trapped within it as dead labor. Given this fact, the struggle for the urban commons must inevitably be a battle for necropolis.

Benjamin's Common

For readers familiar with Walter Benjamin's work, the arguments re-hearsed above will likely sound familiar. At the same time, however, the association may seem strange. After all, even prodigious eclec-ticism was not enough to lead Benjamin to include the commons amongst his various themes. Be this as it may, a careful reading sug-gests that the commons did feature in his work as an *implicit* refer-ence. In order for it to be made explicit, we must first review his more direct engagement with the dead.

In his famous essay on the concept of history, Benjamin outlined how the human struggle for happiness was emboldened by the efforts of past generations, whose own struggles remained unfulfilled. The relationship becomes especially acute when people realize they are "about to make the continuum of history explode." Consequently, according to Benjamin, Maximillien de Robespierre viewed ancient Rome as "a past charged with the time of the now" and "the French Revolution viewed itself as Rome reincarnate."[14]

But while the past can stimulate people's desire for social change, there's nothing inevitable about this outcome. Just as the oppressed clamor to lay hold of the past to advance their struggles, history's vic-tors use it to substantiate the myth of progress that justifies their power. Although he does not use the term, Benjamin's account of the ensuing struggle suggests that the past itself is best understood as a commons forever in danger of enclosure. Indeed, according to Benjamin, "only a redeemed mankind receives the fullness of its past—which is to say, only for a redeemed mankind does the past become citable in all its moments."[15] Nevertheless, this same past is forever in danger of "becom-ing a tool of the ruling classes" by being subjected to (enclosed within) a narrative "conformism that is about to overpower it." Consequently, "*even the dead* will not be safe from the enemy if he wins."[16]

In the hands of the victors, the past becomes a catalogue of "cul-tural treasures" ("wonders," in Chaplin's sense) that get passed from ruler to ruler. And just as each treasure bears the mark of the barba-rism that underwrote its creation, "barbarism taints also the manner in which it was transmitted from one owner to another." As indexes of desire, such treasures are distorted. They become symptomatic expres-sions of the historical enclosure that enabled their production and transmission. For this reason, Benjamin maintained that they should be considered with "cautious detachment."[17]

At the same time, however, these treasures also contain the promise of *another* outcome, since—like the social surplus more generally—they contain the unrealized aspirations of those generations trapped within them as dead labor. With minimal extrapolation, it becomes clear that *this promise* is the common inheritance that Benjamin enjoins us to actualize in its "fullness." Since they are both its stewards and its prisoners, claiming this common in the present requires that we forge an alliance with the dead.

By bringing the past into contact with "time filled by the presence of the now,"[18] such an alliance enjoins us to "awaken the dead, and make whole what has been smashed."[19] The spatial dimension of the common thus proves to be a trans-temporal one, with past and present intermingled. Given the alliance of the living and the dead upon which it is founded, the institutional arrangements that might prevail in such a common remain difficult to imagine. Nevertheless, as Benjamin maintained, our capacity to realize common dreams is a power upon which the past lays a claim—and "that claim cannot be settled cheaply."[20]

Few will doubt the desperate elegance of Benjamin's formulation. Nevertheless, even the most compelling of arguments requires evidence if it is to be believed. For this reason, it's important to recall those events that can help to emancipate the battle for necropolis from the register of metaphor. Considering the problem from the standpoint of constituted power, one might be reminded of the hundred-plus workers who died during the construction of the Hoover Dam. A "wonder" of anthropocenic proportions set into operation the year Durruti perished, folk wisdom suggests that many of the workers who died building the dam became entombed in the concrete construction itself. Despite the intuitive logic to such claims, the likelihood that bodies disintegrate within the national infrastructure remains small; nevertheless, this does not mean they escaped being trapped in it by other means. One such means is commemoration. If we were to believe Oskar J.W. Hansen's monumental plaque erected at the site, these workers gave their lives "to make the desert bloom" [Fig. 2]. In all probability (and if their situation had allowed it), the workers themselves would have disagreed.[21]

Even the dead are not safe from the victor if he wins. As the past succumbs to historical enclosure, the social surplus becomes tightly bound to the myth of progress. America is a nation of monuments, thought Alexis de Tocqueville. What, then, do these monuments tell us about America? Even the Boston Tea Party becomes an amusement park under the weight of commemoration. Indeed, a recently opened memorial site in Boston Harbor left one reporter marveling at how "the live actors, replicas, artifacts, holography, and … commentary" sprinkled throughout the exhibit "create an environment that is as much theme park as it is museum."[22] How could it be otherwise? America cannot soberly acknowledge the violence that heralded its emancipation from colonial rule without conceding that those it now holds in thrall may be justified in following suit.

Such examples provoke feelings that oscillate between incredulity and vertigo; however, it's important to recall that the dead are not always given up without a fight. In its most rudimentary form, the impulse to wrest the fallen from the powerful finds expression in counter-commemoration. More ambitiously (and taking a page from *Antigone*), history turns its floodlight on those who have struggled to defend the bodies of their fallen kin directly. Historian Ruth Richardson reminds us that, toward the end of the Georgian era, working class communities in England organized to protect deceased loved ones from grave robbers who sold corpses to anatomy schools in what she called "a pitiless example of free trade."[23]

In response to such thefts, these communities formed what amounted to impromptu graveyard defense leagues and often rioted against anatomy schools and other targets. According to Richardson, such organizing was motivated by the feeling that those who robbed graves "were the agents of social injustice, and their trade in corpses made a mockery of the meanings and values popularly invested in customary death practices." Moreover, since the "bodysnatchers" tended to emerge from the ranks of the communities they attacked, they "betrayed the deepest sentiments of their own class by their ruthless trade in human flesh."[24] Reporting on a riot against an anatomy school in Aberdeen in January of 1832, Richardson writes:

> A crowd gathered swiftly, and before long the school was invaded. … The crowd shouted encouragement to those inside in their effort to set the building alight, while at the back some enterprising rioters began an attack on the rear wall, simultaneously undermining its foundation and battering its fabric. In a short time the entire wall collapsed, while the fire inside

Fig. 2: Hoover Dam plaque honoring workers who died during its construction. "The United States of America will continue to remember the services of all who labored to clothe with substance the plans of those who first visioned the building of this dam." The central panel reads: "They died to make the desert bloom."

the building took hold. ... The school was fully demolished by eight o'clock, and the town was quiet by ten in the evening.[25]

By alerting contemporary readers to the central role played by the dead in shaping visions of justice, such struggles are reassuring in their concreteness. At the same time, they highlight the degree to which the dead themselves are most easily comprehended in their status as *bodies*. But while this dimension cannot be overlooked, it's important to recall that the dead are present in the Hoover Dam whether or not they are buried in it. Meanwhile, the struggle against the grave robber is not enough to release the dead from the cultural treasures they haunt as anonymous, toiling echoes. It's easy to perceive bodies as concrete, corporeal presences. Social relations are similarly concrete; however, their trans-local and trans-temporal dimensions make them more difficult to perceive (let alone to grasp) directly. As in other cases where the gap between what can be sensed and what can be stated compels us to resort to mythological resolutions, the battle for necropolis shifts to the field the wish image.

Common Dreams

According to Benjamin, wish images arise when people begin anticipating the future by recalling a past whose promise had yet to be fulfilled.

> In the dream in which, before the eyes of each epoch, that which is to follow appears in images, that latter appears wedded to elements from prehistory, that is, of a classless society." Intimations of this ... mingle with the new to produce the utopia that has left its traces in thousands of configurations of life, from permanent buildings to fleeting fashions.[26]

In seeking a connection between the wish image and the commons, one might be reminded of how it has recently become fashionable for coffee shops in gentrifying neighborhoods to arrange their enterprises around a large common table rather than many small ones. This table (sometimes referred to as a "harvest table") is generally perceived to add value to the coffee-shop experience by encouraging forms of conviviality that would otherwise be impossible. For shop owners, the arrangement makes infinite sense: not only does it intensify the allure of the commodity by infusing it with the ambient promise of community, it can also help to maximize the number of paying customers.

But while we might condemn hipster coffee drinkers for trying to find community through the market (and while we might condemn them for their complicity in gentrification, which is itself a mode of enclosure), it's important to acknowledge that the problem lies not with the desire *per se* but rather with the insufficiency of its posited object resolution. Meanwhile, indulging in a little *recherche du temps perdu* makes clear that the search for community (and even for revolutionary alliance) in coffee shops might not be so outrageous after all.

According to urban sociologist Ray Oldenburg, "third places" like coffee houses are best understood as "levelers." As points between home and work that are distinct from both, third places allow for people to come together across social divisions on the basis of common interests. Connecting the "leveler" concept directly to the peasant insurgents who operated under the same name, Oldenburg notes that coffeehouses established in the seventeenth century were themselves "commonly referred to as levelers, as were the people who frequented them."[27] Moreover, the rules posted inside the doors of London coffeehouses during this period "enforced the leveling of coffee house visitors."[28] By Oldenburg's account, it was a rule that patrons were happy to oblige.

In addition to providing "neutral ground upon which men discovered one another apart from the classes and ranks that had earlier divided them,"[29] third places like coffeehouses provided patrons with warmth. "Warmth," writes Oldenburg, "radiates from the combination of cheerfulness and companionship, and it enhances the sense of being alive."[30] Already by the nineteenth century, however, the warmth had begun to fade. This was because "the openness and equality of the original establishments gave way to partitioned seating and single, large tables were replaced by strategically placed smaller ones."[31] Consequently, "community has become elusive"[32] and contemporary patrons "seeking to gain respite from loneliness or boredom … manage only to intensify those feelings." Little wonder, then, that we should find them sitting "spaced apart from one another … hunching over some invisible lead ball of misery."[33]

Based on Oldenburg's account, it's possible to see how (despite its obvious profit-maximizing function) today's harvest table might help patrons to recall a time when community seemed inseparable from leveling. In this way, it might even sharpen visions of a future happiness by furnishing them with a positive content. By themselves, however, wish images say nothing about *the means* by which that happiness might concretely be realized. As a result, such images tend more regularly to refurbish the status quo by infusing hollow commodities with a new vitality than they do to become dynamos propelling social change. Such ambivalence highlights a challenge that has affected movement-based struggles for the commons as well.

According to Silvia Federici, the commons were so important to the "struggles of the medieval rural population that their memory still excites our imagination, projecting the vision of a world where goods can be shared and solidarity … can be the substance of social relations."[34] But while such visions can help to convince us that arrangements of this kind might be possible once again, it's important to recall that the medieval commons existed alongside private ownership—and that it was *this* form of ownership that made it valuable from the standpoint of social reproduction. As Federici notes, "the commons were essential to the reproduction of many small farmers or cottars who survived only because they had access to meadows in which to keep cows, or woods in which to gather timber, wild berries and herbs, or quarries, fish-ponds, and open spaces in which to meet."[35]

More bluntly, we can say that the commons were by no means antithetical to private property. Instead (and regardless of the degree to which claims on the commons were secured through struggle from below), the commons themselves were an externality that was nevertheless factored into the productive calculations of feudal landowners, who (for their own reasons) did not want their cottars—their source of labor power—to die. Given this arrangement, there's little reason to idealize life on the peasant commons. Nevertheless, as Federici points out, the commons also yielded a remarkable degree of freedom. In her account, "besides encouraging collective decision-making and work cooperation, the commons were the material foundation upon which peasant solidarity and sociality could thrive."[36]

With the advent of enclosure, the bonds of social solidarity fostered by the commons led peasants to fits of riotous excess and to their subsequent denunciation as levelers. By the mid-seventeenth century, this "leveler" tendency became associated with conspiratorial dreams of regicide and declarations of popular sovereignty. But while such developments suggest that the promise inherent in the commons had led levelers of all sorts to confront the profane demands of politics, it's important to recall that (with the notable exception of the landholding class itself) claims on the commons were rarely issued directly in the name of those who asserted them.

Sovereignty as Wish...

Even as enclosure intensified, the overwhelming tendency among outcast forces was to frame their struggles as attempts to restore conditions thought to have been prescribed by God. In 1649, a group of peasants in Surrey came together under the banner of the Diggers. Outraged at enclosure and motivated by a peculiar reading of Christian scripture, they occupied wastelands, denounced landlords, and struggled to find their way back to Eden. According to the group's leader, Gerrard Winstanley, "they that are resolved to work and eat together, making the Earth a Common Treasury, doth joyn hands with Christ, to lift up the Creation from Bondage, and restore all things from the Curse."[37] The scene is well known, and the outcome is as tragic as the Digger's efforts were courageous. What's less often noted, however, is how Winstanley's experiment could not be carried out in the name of the earthly force that stood to gain from it. Instead, the action proceeds under the watchful eye of Christ, with whom the Diggers imagined they had joined hands. The weight of sovereign responsibility is thus transposed, and profane self-interest is glossed in transcendental conceit.

We can hardly blame them. It's hard to assume the burden of sovereignty, and movements in the present have on the whole fared no better. Moreover (and even after the disenchantment of the world heralded by capitalism's triumphant ascent), Christianity remains an amazing compendium of wish images. Winstanley's reading of scripture was unorthodox, to be sure; however, it doesn't take much to find evidence of a communist tendency guiding the Christians of biblical times. Consider, for instance, the *Book of Acts*, where it is written:

> And the multitude of them that believed were of one heart and one soul: neither said anything of them that aught of the things which he possessed was his own; but they had all things in common. … Neither was there any among them that lacked: for as many as were possessors of lands or of houses sold them and brought the prices of the things that were sold, and laid them down at the apostles' feet: a distribution was made unto every man as he had need.[38]

According to Karl Kautsky, early Christian communism operated primarily through interventions at the level of consumption. For this reason, work and families (not to mention possessions) were denounced in an effort to circumvent worldly concerns and forge a brotherhood in Christ.[39] As the sect grew and began attracting "wealthy and cultured persons," however, Kautsky found that "many a Christian propagandist began to feel the need of putting the Christian doctrine more amiably in order to attract these people."[40] This impulse is most evident in the Gospel of Saint Matthew, where an "astute spirit of revisionism has wiped out every trace of class hatred."[41] Nevertheless, even today, the fraternal bonds forged by the Apostles persist in their allure. As Kautsky notes, "however much certain influential circles of the Christian congregation … sought to obliterate its proletarian character, the proletariat and its class hatred were not obliterated thereby."[42] And even as the church evolved into a menacing force looming over the medieval era, the saintly renunciation of earthly property persevered as a compensation, a supplement, and—as Winstanley's legacy attests—a spur to action too.

As wish image, the Christian common was already inseparable from the necropolis in Ancient Rome, where believers who had not yet overcome their status as a marginal cult began carving out catacombs to bury their dead. Interpreted by nineteenth-century Romantics as a kind of conspiratorial underground, the Christians of the catacombs were said to congregate, say mass, and make arrangements for their mutual safety. In *Martyr of the Catacombs*, an anonymous novel penned at the height of the Romantic era, the seductive allure of nocturnal necropolitan conspiracy is indulged to what may be an unhealthy degree. According to the author, "the vast numbers who dwelt below were supplied with provisions by constant communication with the city above. This was done at night. The most resolute and daring of the men volunteered for this dangerous task."[43]

Marveling at the catacombs themselves, the author recounts how the Christians descended willingly into their depths, "carrying with them all that was most precious to the soul of man, and they endured all for the great love wherewith they were loved."[44] In this way, they forged a connection with the dead as well. "Witness these gloomy labyrinths," the author enjoins, "fit home for the dead only, which nevertheless for years opened to shelter the living." In addition to this alliance, the catacombs also provided a means for the past to make its way into the present. For the author of *Martyr*, the results are inspiring.

> The walls carry down to later ages those words of grief, of lamentation, and of ever-changing feeling which were marked upon them during successive ages by those who were banished to these Catacombs. They carry down their mournful story to future times, and bring to imagination the forms, the feelings, and the deeds of those who were imprisoned here. As the forms of life are taken upon the plates of the camera, so has the great voice once forced out by suffering from the very soul of the martyr become stamped on the wall.[45]

Predating Benjamin's observation that wishes leave their mark on "thousands of configurations of life" by more than half a century, the account of history as resonant image conveyed by this passage is nothing

Fig. 3: Jean-Victor Schnetz, *Funeral of a Young Martyr in the Catacombs of Rome* (1847)

short of extraordinary. Still, it's important to recall that the anonymous author of *Martyr* was not alone in having succumbed to the seductions of those "tender greetings of affection, of friendship, of kinship, and of love" that "arose amid the moldering remains of the departed."[46] Indeed, similar sentiments found compelling visual expression in the paintings of the neo-classically trained Romantic Jean-Victor Schnetz. A student of Jaques-Louis David, Schnetz's *Funeral of a Young Martyr in the Catacombs of Rome* (1847) [Fig. 3] splits the difference between the enthusiasm that led him to lionize the fighters of the July Revolution in a work that rivaled Delacroix's own submission on the theme[47] and the neoclassicism of his teacher (whose *Sermant des Horaces* stimulated Jacobin sentiment in its own special way).

Distorted by their transposition into the hagiographic register, contemporary readers can be forgiven for doubting the historical accuracy of these Romantic glosses on catacomb life. Nevertheless, few can doubt that the idea of the commons as an *underground* (existing within and alongside, but also beneath the established world) has persisted as an enduring wish image. Indeed, versions of it can be seen in sources as varied as St. Augustine's *City of God* and Victor Hugo's *Hunchback of Notre Dame*.

In the latter work, hallucinogenic recollections of the medieval commons are enlisted as a kind of antithesis to—and compensation for—the bourgeois world despised by the Romantics. In the novel's Court of Miracles, conceptual distinctions are torn down with the same enthusiasm that toppled fences and hedges during the enclosure riots. For Hugo, the Court of Miracles was "a city of thieves, a hideous wart on the face of Paris; a sewer, from which escaped every morning ... that stream of vices ... which always overflows in the streets of capitals." Meanwhile, it was also "a lying hospital where the bohemian, the disfrocked monk, the ruined scholar ... were transformed by night into brigands."

> The limits of races and species seemed effaced in this city, as in a pandemonium. Men, women, beasts, age, sex, health, maladies, all seemed to be in common among these people; all went together, they mingled, confounded, superposed; each one there participated in all.[48]

Hugo's description allows us to witness the ease with which the Romantics fused their love of the medieval commons to the promise of political conspiracy. From this volatile admixture sparked wishful anticipations of a triumphant underground—a zone marked indelibly by social dissolution and, ultimately, by signs of death. *Hunchback* was penned nearly two centuries ago. Still, Hugo's sensibility (like that of the Romantics more generally) continues to find expression in the countless celebrations of the common-as-underground that infuse today's radical counterculture with mythic significance. To get a sense of this dynamic, one might recall the protest encampment described in *Expect Resistance*, CrimethInc.'s swashbuckling homage to those who live like they mean it:

> When I showed up the occupation was already in full swing. It looked like the outpost of a medieval army: banners painted

with inscrutable proclamations, cauldrons of stew steaming over an open fire, sooty-faced barbarians conferring in the crisp morning air. It seemed inconceivable that something like this existed in my own century, let alone my zip code.[49]

Such accounts are inspiring. Not only do they stimulate the imagination and provoke our longing for happiness by bringing the mythic past into the present, they also provide a concrete vision of what might be accomplished in the small autonomous spaces we carve out of the hostile enclosures in which we find ourselves trapped. But while our struggles are often animated by recollections of the mythic past, such recollections do little to clarify how the desired outcome is to be practically achieved. Indeed (and as was mentioned previously), the wish image's indeterminacy makes it highly susceptible to capture.

As we begin coming to terms with this dynamic, we might recall the degree to which Ancient Rome spoke to the Romantics as they launched their rebellion against capitalist ascent. Percy Shelley made his indebtedness clear when, in an 1818 letter to Thomas Love Peacock, he recounted how Rome was "a city … of the dead, or rather of those who cannot die, & who survive the puny generations which inhabit & pass over the spot which they have made sacred to eternity."[50] The trick, as Shelley saw it, was therefore to forge an alliance with the dead so that we might overcome our puniness and potentially become sacred once again.

Fully a generation earlier, Rome had been a wish image for the Jacobins, who zeroed in on its republicanism as a model for their own aspirations. Considering the "conjuring up of the dead of world history," Marx recalled how the heroes of the French Revolution "performed the task of their time … in Roman costumes and with Roman phrases."[51] This dramatic citation, however, did not exhaust Rome's wish-image scope—or its political range. In the 1930s, dead Romans were once again invoked, this time by the Nazis, as they slouched toward Germania. In the hands of Albert Speer, the Pantheon became the model for the *Volkshalle*.

In the face of such indeterminacy, it's important to consider what must be done to push our struggles beyond wishful anticipation. How shall the dead be freed from the social surplus, and how shall they be spared from perpetual induction into armies whose mythologies are at odds with their interests? How, following Benjamin, shall we awaken the dead and make whole what has been smashed? Such questions require programmatic answers; however, before such answers can be devised, it's necessary for matters to be clarified conceptually. And this means returning once more to the problem of sovereignty.

...And as Profane Necessity

What, then, is the relationship between sovereignty, the commons, and the city of the dead? In order to answer this question, it's useful to return to *Rebel Cities* where, in an oblique attack on the Romanticism that dominates contemporary Left scenes, Harvey proposes that the common is best understood as "an unstable and malleable social relation between a particular self-defined social group and those aspects of its actually existing or yet-to-be-created social and/or physical environment deemed crucial to its life and livelihood."[52] Although he evades direct reference, this definition betrays a significant indebtedness to the concept of the political outlined by Carl Schmitt. Indeed, Harvey's account of the "self-defined social group," its "physical environment," and those aspects deemed "crucial to its life and livelihood" neatly reiterate Schmitt's insistence that politics arises from the relationship between a people, a territory, and what he called its form of life or "mode of existence." [53]

Given this congruity, it's not surprising that Harvey's account also reiterates Schmitt's friend-enemy distinction. For Schmitt, politics presupposes a "distinction of friend and enemy" in which the political enemy is "existentially something different and alien, so that in the extreme case conflicts with him are possible."[54] As a result, politics itself requires that the enemy be "repulsed" so that one might "preserve one's own form of existence."[55] Here, the collective subject constituted through the friend-enemy antagonism preserves its form of existence by repulsing the enemy in order to secure control of contested terrain. Only then is it possible to determine which social relations will prevail. Standing at the opposite end of the political spectrum, Harvey adopts a nearly identical position when he notes how, "at the end of it all, the analyst is often left with a simple decision: whose side are you on, whose common interests do you seek to protect, and by what means?"[56]

Answering such questions demands that we determine who we are, where we operate, and what kinds of social relations we would like to see prevail within our territory. To the extent that we find ourselves plagued by the vampirism of constant capital, "we" are none other than the living in league with the dead. Although our territory is not yet defined, we know that it is potentially as expansive as the planet and as microscopic as the finest machined parts in the wonders against which we're pitted. Since we are not yet sovereign, we know that our enemy has determined the social relations that prevail in our territory. As a result, we, the living, are pitted against the dead as a mortal adversary—but it doesn't have to be that way.

Along with its *Trauerspiel*-like *frisson*, one practical implication of this assessment is that the question of territory reveals itself to be necessarily *prior* to considerations regarding the mode of production. As a result, our prefigurative experiments in commoning are likely to amount to nothing if we don't control the territory upon which they occur. From this realization arises a second, more challenging one: enclosure is not the antithesis to the commons we consider it to be. Rather it is the practical means by which the commons can be achieved in a world populated by enemies. As Harvey notes:

> In the grand scheme of things (and particularly at the global level), some sort of enclosure is often the best way to preserve certain kinds of valued commons. That sounds like, and is, a contradictory statement, but it reflects a truly contradictory situation. … The production and enclosure of non-commodified spaces in a ruthlessly commodifying world is surely a good thing.[57]

Our opposition, then, should not be to enclosure *per se*, but rather to the fact that the world's existing enclosures were not erected by us or in our interests. Our struggle for the commons, then, presupposes the constitution of a political "we" capable of fighting for the control of territory. Only then does it become possible to consistently intervene at the level of social relations. And only then does it become possible to break apart and reconfigure the built environment so that the aspirations of the dead might finally be fulfilled.

"How does one organize a city?" Responding to his own question, Harvey is unequivocal: "we simply do not know."[58] The scale and the social fragmentation of contemporary urban environments exacerbate the problem, to be sure, and the fratricidal rivalries of Left forces don't help much either. But if Harvey's impasse suggests the need for further investigation, it also encourages us to consider what might be learned by forging an alliance with the dead. At very least, our counterparts in this union can tell us what *didn't* work—and what they had most longed for before being interred in the surplus.

NOTES

Introduction

1   I served on the Advisory Board of *Upping the Anti: A Journal of Theory and Action* between 2005 and 2006 (Issues one and two) and on the Editorial Committee between 2006 and 2012 (Issues three through thirteen). http://uppingtheanti.org/journal/.

2   Raymond Williams, *Marxism and Literature* (Oxford: Oxford University Press, 1977), 128.

3   Raymond Williams, *Keywords: A Vocabulary of Culture and Society* (London: Fontana Press, 1976), 87.

4   Sigmund Freud, *Civilization and its Discontents* (London: The Hogarth Press and the Institute of Psychoanalysis, 1975), 76.

5   Although, as diagnosis, "neurosis" was weeded out of American psychology with the publication of the DSM III in 1980, the term continues to permeate popular discourse and popular judgment. Concurrently, although the DSM revision seemed to echo broader social trends toward de-pathologizing what were recognized to be functional states, it is worth considering what might have been lost as a result of the redaction. As Fredric Jameson has made clear, neurotic social dispositions (as opposed to postmodern, schizophrenic ones) are strongly correlated to what he has identified as "hermeneutic" or "depth model" modes of social analysis including the dialectical, the existential, and the semiotic. In contrast to the postmodern fascination with the surface, these modes presupposed that what was on the surface was not the whole story. It is in keeping with this insight that I have revitalized usage of the term here. Fredric Jameson, *Postmodernism, or, The Cultural Logic of Late Capitalism* (Durham: Duke University Press, 1991), 12.

6   To the best of my knowledge, citations of Simmel's work do not appear directly in any of the major texts within the Situationist canon; however, Simmel's influence on Georg Lukács is an established fact, and *Society of the Spectacle* is inconceivable without *History and Class Consciousness*. Georg Simmel, "The Metropolis and Mental Life" in *Georg Simmel on Individuality and Social Forms* (Chicago: University of Chicago Press, 1971), 324–339.

7   Frantz Fanon, *The Wretched of the Earth* (New York: Grove Press 1963), 316.

8   Jean-Paul Sartre, "Preface" in *The Wretched of the Earth*, (New York: Grove Press

1963), 20.

9   Ray Oldenburg, *The Great Good Place: Cafés, Coffee Shops, Community Centers, Beauty Parlors, General Stores, Bars, Hangouts and How They Get You Through The Day* (New York: Paragon House, 1989), 184.

10   In this sense (and though she would disavow the psychoanalytic language), the common experience of neurosis amounts to what Dorothy Smith describes as the "bifurcation of consciousness" that inaugurates the process of social mapping at the heart of institutional ethnography. See Dorothy Smith, *The Conceptual Practices of Power: A Feminist Sociology of Knowledge* (Toronto: University of Toronto Press, 1990).

11   As Walter Benjamin conceived it, such universality owes not to the "additive" accumulation of data (as in historicism's "universal history") but rather to the "constructive principle" by which discrete configurations crystalize to become entrypoints into "a revolutionary chance in the fight for the oppressed past." Here, one finds "in the lifework, the era; and in the era, the entire course of history." Walter Benjamin, "Theses on the Philosophy of History" in *Illuminations* (New York: Schocken Books,1990), 262–263.

12   "Lilla Watson," *Wikipedia*, n.p., n.d., https://en.wikipedia.org/wiki/Lilla_Watson.

13   Recently, "the neurotic turn" has even become the title of an edited collection exploring the concept's enduring relevance. Charles Johns (ed.), *The Neurotic Turn: Interdisciplinary Correspondence on Neurosis* (London: Repeater, 2017).

14   Walter Benjamin, "Theses on the Philosophy of History," 256.

15   Max Horkheimer, "Traditional and Critical Theory" in *Critical Theory: Selected Essays* (New York: Continuum,1995), 208.

16   According to Guy Debord, one of the most beguiling features of the society of the spectacle was that it "reunites the separate, but reunites it *as separate*." Guy Debord, *Society of the Spectacle* (Detroit: Red and Black, 1983), 29.

17   C.L.R. James and Grace C. Lee, *Facing Reality* (Chicago: Charles H. Kerr, 2006).

18   Herman Hesse, *Siddhartha* (New York: New Directions, 1951), 53.

19   The theme of absolution—of the perfect identity between all things and the corresponding eradication of desire and want—is a recurring motif in many religious traditions; however, it's important to note that this same theme also found expression in the resolutely anti-Christian work of Friedrich Nietzsche when he forced his reader to contemplate the meaning of life in the face of eternal reccurence. Recounting a scenario in which the reader is confronted by a demon who announces that life must be relived endlessly exactly as it has hitherto been lived, Nietzsche asks: "how wouldst thou have to become favorably inclined to thyself and to life, so as *to long for nothing more ardently* than this last eternal sanctioning and sealing?" Friedrich Nietzsche, *Joyful Wisdom* (New York: Frederick Ungar

Publishing Co., 1960), 271.

20 Max Weber, *The Protestant Ethic and the Spirit of Capitalism* (New York: Routledge, 2001).

21 To cite but one recent example, political organizer Ejeris Dixon noted how activist "call-out culture," although ostensibly designed to maintain movement norms, often had the opposite effect: "Some call-outs are necessary, and truth-telling is not designed to be pretty. But some call-outs are disingenuous and even manipulative. I've worked on several processes to support groups to transform issues raised through call-outs. In some cases, the folks making the call outs are not interested in change. Sometimes this is because people are too traumatized to stay engaged. And sometimes people are actually interested in the demise of the organization or group." Ejeris Dixon, "Our Relationships Keep Us Alive: Let's Prioritize Them in 2018." *Truthout*, February 8, 2018, n.p., http://www.truth-out.org/opinion/item/43444-our-relationships-keep-us-alive-let-s-prioritize-them-in-2018.

22 In "One Way Street" Benjamin pointed out that, in his estimation, "significant literary work can only come into being in a strict alternation between action and writing." For this reason, "it must nurture the inconspicuous forms that better fit its influence in active communities that does the pretentious, universal gestures of the book—in leaflets, brochures, articles, and placards. Only this prompt language shows itself actively equal to the moment." Walter Benjamin, "One-Way Street" in *Reflections* (New York: Schocken Books, 1978), 61.

23 Pierre Missac, *Benjamin's Passages*, (Cambridge, MA: The MIT Press, 1995), 23.

24 As Benjamin noted when assembling material for his *Arcades Project*, "I needn't *say* anything. Merely show." Walter Benjamin, *The Arcades Project* (Cambridge, MA: Harvard University Press, 2003), 460.

25 Theodor Adorno et al., *Aesthetics and Politics* (London: Verso, 2002), 129.

26 Walter Benjamin, "Surrealism" in *Reflections* (New York: Schocken Books, 1978), 182.

27 Walter Benjamin "The Concept of Criticism in German Romanticism" in *Walter Benjamin: Selected Writings, Volume I, 1913–1926* (Cambridge, MA: Harvard University Press, 2004), 158.

28 Walter Benjamin, "Theses on the Philosophy of History," 263.

29 Walter Benjamin "The Life of Students" in *Walter Benjamin: Selected Writings, Volume I, 1913–1926* (Cambridge, MA: Harvard University Press, 2004), 37.

30 Walter Benjamin, "Central Park" in *The Writer of Modern Life: Essays on Charles Baudelaire* (Cambridge, MA: Harvard University Press), 161.

31 Walter Benjamin *The Arcades Project*, 474.

32 Ibid.

33 Ibid.

I • Catastrophe

Chris Hedges vs. CrimethInc.

1   JA Myerson, "Interview With Chris Hedges About Black Bloc." *Truthout*, February 9, 2012, n.p., http://www.truth-out.org/opinion/item/6587:interview -with-chris-hedges-about-black-bloc.

2   CrimethInc., "Black Bloc Confidential." CrimethInc., February 20, 2012, n.p., https://crimethinc.com/2012/02/21/black-bloc-confidential.

3   Chris Hedges, "Black Bloc: The Cancer in Occupy." *Truthout*, February 6, 2012, n.p., http://www.truth-out.org/opinion/item/6510:black-bloc-the-cancer-in-occupy.

4   Rebecca Solnit, "Throwing Out the Master's Tools and Building a Better House: Thoughts on the Importance of Nonviolence in the Occupy Revolution," *Common Dreams*, November 14, 2011, n.p., https://www.commondreams.org/views/2011/11 /14/throwing-out-masters-tools-and-building-better-house-thoughts-importance #.TsGgAZO6AFM.facebook.

5   Ibid.

6   Walter Benjamin, "Critique of Violence" in *Reflections* (New York: Schocken Books, 1978).

7   Ibid., 282.

8   Gayatri Chakravorty Spivak, "General Strike!" in *Tidal: Occupy Theory, Occupy Strategy*, December 2011, Issue 1, 8–9.

9   Georges Sorel, *Reflections on Violence* (Mineola, NY: Dover Publications, 2004).

10 Gayatri Chakravorty Spivak, "General Strike!," 9.

11 LeRoi Jones (Amiri Baraka), "What Does Nonviolence Mean?" in *Home: Social Essays* (New York: Akashic Books 2009), 169.

12 Karl Marx and Friedrich Engels, *The Communist Manifesto* (Baltimore: Penguin Books, 1967), 99.

13 Geoff Berner, "King of the Gangsters," *Klezmer Mongrels*, January 25, 2009, https://geoffberner.bandcamp.com/track/king-of-the-gangsters.

14 "Sept. 12 - Occupy Tactics Debate in NYC - Crimethinc. and Chris Hedges," *Anarchist News*, August 16, 2012, n.p., https://anarchistnews.org/content/sept-12- occupy-tactics-debate-nyc-crimethinc-and-chris-hedges.

15 Ibid.

16 Ibid.

17 CrimethInc., *Evasion* (Atlanta: CrimethInc., 2003).

18 Chris Hedges, "This is What Revolution Looks Like," *Truthdig*, November 15, 2011, n.p., https://www.truthdig.com/articles/this-is-what-revolution-looks-like/.

Did Someone Say Riot?

1 AK Thompson, *Black Bloc, White Riot: Anti-Globalization and the Genealogy of Dissent* (Oakland: AK Press, 2010).

2 Geoff Bylinkin, "Writing Resistance: Team Colors Collective's *Uses of a Whirlwind* and AK Thompson's *Black Bloc, White Riot*," in Institute for Anarchist Studies, *Perspectives 2011.* http://anarchiststudies.mayfirst.org/node/514.

3 Karl Marx, *The Economic and Philosophic Manuscripts of 1844* (New York: International Publishers, 1964), 107.

4 AK Thompson, *Black Bloc, White Riot*, 23.

5 Sigmund Freud, *Introductory Lectures on Psycho-Analysis* (New York: W.W. Norton & Company, 1966), 449–450.

6 Michel Foucault, *Discipline and Punish: The Birth of the Prison* (New York: Vintage Books, 1995), 19.

7 Sigmund Freud, *Civilization and its Discontents* (London: The Hogarth Press and the Institute of Psycho-Analysis, 1975), 52.

8 E.J. Hobsbawm, *Primitive Rebels: Studies in Archaic Forms of Social Movements in the 19th and 20th Centuries* (New York: W.W. Norton & Company, 1959).

9 Charles Tilly, *Social Movements, 1768–2004* (Boulder and London: Paradigm Publishers, 2004), 4.

10 James M. Jasper, *The Art of Moral Protest: Culture, Biography, and Creativity in Social Movements* (Chicago: The University of Chicago Press, 1997).

11 Lesley Wood, *Direct Action, Deliberation, and Diffusion: Collective Action After the WTO Protests in Seattle* (Cambridge: Cambridge University Press, 2012), 31.

12 Kris Hermes, *Crashing the Party: Legacies and Lessons from the RNC 2000* (Oakland: PM Press, 2015), 2.

13 Lesley Wood, "G20 Policing in Toronto—Something Old, Something New, Something Borrowed, Something Blue," *Toronto Media Co-op*, July 12, 2010, n.p., http://toronto.mediacoop.ca/story/20-policing-toronto-—-something-old-something-new-something-borrowed-something-blue…/4151.

14 AK Thompson, *Black Bloc, White Riot*, 35.

15 Georges Sorel, *Reflections on Violence* (Mineola, NY: Dover Publications, 2004), 216–249.

16 Quoted in Alex P. Schmid and Jenny de Graaf, *Violence as Communication: Insurgent Terrorism and the Western News Media* (London: SAGE Publications, 1982), 11.

17 Judy Rebick, "Toronto Is Burning! Or Is It?," *Rabble*, June 27, 2010, n.p., http://rabble.ca/blogs/bloggers/judes/2010/06/toronto-burning-or-it, and Neil Smith and Deborah Cowan, "Martial Law in the Streets of Toronto: G20 Security and State Violence" in Tomas Malleson and David Wachsmuth (eds.), *Whose Streets? The Toronto G20 and the Challenges of Summit Protest* (Toronto: Between The Lines, 2011), 139.

18 Many people pointed to a police car apparently abandoned on Queen Street—immediately North of the heavily fortified police line—as evidence that the police lured unthinking activists into illicit behavior. Be this as it may, it's clear that the police car trashed on Bay Street south of Queen in the heart of the financial district was clearly not intended to be a sitting duck. Protestors report hearing live ordinance going off inside its trunk as they ran past the burning husk.

19 Judy Rebick, "Toronto Is Burning! Or Is It?"

20 Stokely Carmichael and Charles Hamilton, *Black Power: The Politics of Liberation in America* (New York: Vintage Books, 1967), 83.

21 See, for instance, David Harvey, *The Condition of Postmodernity* (Cambridge, MA: Blackwell, 1990), 301–302.

22 Miranda Joseph, *Against the Romance of Community* (Minneapolis: University of Minnesota Press, 2002).

23 Himani Bannerji, "A Question of Silence: Reflections on Violence Against Women in Communities of Colour" in *The Dark Side of the Nation: Essays on Multiculturalism, Nationalism and Gender* (Toronto: Canadian Scholars Press, 2000), 154–62.

24 Amory Starr, "How Can Anti-Imperialism Not Be Anti-Racist? The North American Anti-Globalization Movement," *Journal of World-Systems Research*, Volume X, Number 1, Winter 2004, 119-151.

25 AK Thompson, *Black Bloc, White Riot*, 132.

26 C. Wright Mills, *White Collar: The American Middle Class* (New York: Oxford University Press, 1956), xvi.

27 Georges Sorel, *Reflections on Violence*, 89.

Making Friends With Failure

1 CrimethInc., "We Have Worked Hard to Improve Activism—Now It Must Be Destroyed," *Inside Front: International Journal of Hardcore Punk and Anarchist Action*, Postscript Issue #∞, n.d., 9.

2 Ibid., 10.

3 This motif has been borrowed and repurposed from Aldous Huxley's poem "Carpe Noctem."

4 Richard Day, *Gramsci is Dead: Anarchist Currents in the Newest Social Movements* (Toronto: Between the Lines, 2006).

5 Ibid., 18.

6 Ibid., 2.

7 Ibid., 3.

8 Ibid., 4.

9   Ibid., 3.

10 Ibid. 164.

11 Ibid., 214.

12 With respect to distortion, it should be noted that the genealogical method invariably produces the temptation to make things too clean. It is, after all, very difficult to effectively traverse the gulf between Ancient Greece and poststructuralist theory in a single text. These difficulties, significant in and of themselves, are exacerbated when one's goal is to make a text accessible to nonacademic audiences who might be turned off by the perceived belaboring of simple points. However, since Day's text is advanced as a strategic proposition, activists (whether or not they have academic training) should approach these historical glosses with great caution. At the end of each section of his genealogy, Day is the first to admit that his treatment of the issues is partial and that, in the space allotted by the tempo of his progression, it would not have been possible to provide a more detailed account. Each selected detail is therefore subordinated to the necessities of a predetermined prescriptive frame. And while history can always be submitted as evidence, the partiality of the accounts necessitated by Day's genealogy makes the veracity of some of this evidence doubtful.

13 Richard Day, *Gramsci is Dead*, 84.

14 Colin Raja, "Globalism and Race at A16 in D.C." *ColorLines*, October 10, 2000, n.p., https://www.colorlines.com/articles/globalism-and-race-a16-dc.

15 John Sanbonmatsu, *The Postmodern Prince: Critical Theory, Left Strategy, and the Making of A New Political Subject.* (New York: Monthly Review Press, 2004), 193.

16 Ibid.

17 Ward Churchill, *Pacifism as Pathology: Reflections on the Role of Armed Struggle in North America.* (Winnipeg: Arbeiter Ring, 1998). 63–64.

18 Ibid., 64.

19 Richard Day, *Gramsci is Dead*, 45.

20 Ibid., 80.

21 Ibid., 89.

22 Marcela Valente, "ARGENTINA: The Unemployed Movement—Fragmented But Active," *Inter Press Service News Agency*, June 28, 2004, n.p., http://www.ipsnews.net/2004/06/argentina-the-unemployed-movement-fragmented-but-active/.

23 Richard Day, *Gramsci is Dead*, 42.

24 Food Not Bombs, "Thirty Years of Cooking for Peace: A Short History of the Food Not Bombs Movement," Food Not Bombs, n.d., n.p., http://www.foodnotbombs.net/story.html. The point of this exercise, as I hope is clear, is not to dismiss the contributions of FNB activists. Rather, it is to highlight the conceptual dangers that arise when trying to compare apples with oranges.

25 Gerrard Winstanley, "A Declaration to the Powers of England, and to All the Powers of the World, shewing the Cause why the Common People of England have begun, and gives Consent to Digge up, Manure, and Sow Corn upon George-Hill in Surrey; by those that have Subscribed, and thousands more that gives Consent," *Gerrard Winstanley: Selected Writings*, Andrew Hopton, (ed.), (London: Aporia Press (1989), 10.

26 Ibid., 20.

27 Ibid., 19.

28 Richard Day, *Gramsci is Dead*, 123.

29 Ibid.

30 ibid., 215

31 Karl Marx, "The Eighteenth Brumaire of Louis Bonaparte" in *Karl Marx and Frederick Engels: Selected Works, Volume 1*. (Moscow: Progress Publishers, 1969), 401.

"Daily Life" Not a "Moment" Like the Rest

1   David Harvey, "Organizing for the Anti-Capitalist Transition," December 16, 2009, n.p., http://davidharvey.org/2009/12/organizing-for-the-anti-capitalist -transition/.

2   Greater Toronto Workers Assembly, "About This Group," n.d., n.p., https://www .facebook.com/groups/workersassembly/about/.

3   Mari Yamaguchi, "Japan Goes Manga Over Karl Marx Comics," *Seattle Times*, December 23, 2008, n.p., https://www.seattletimes.com/nation-world/ japan-goes-manga-over-karl-marx-comics/.

4   Jeff Free Luers, "Time's Up," *Heartcheck* (Independently produced zine, 2005), 8.

5   Ibid., 16.

6   Monsieur Dupont, *Nihilist Communism* (Ardent Press, 2009), 198–199.

7   According to Harvey, the following forces are among the potential contributors to contemporary anti-capitalist struggle: left sectarian micro-parties, NGOs, anarchists and autonomists gathered in grassroots organizations (GROs), traditional labor organizations, and left political parties. David Harvey, "Organizing for the Anti-Capitalist Transition."

8   Ibid.

9   Ibid.

10 Ibid.

11 And here we are simply proceeding in accordance with Marx's own premises. For instance, in his analysis of estranged labor in the *1844 Manuscripts*, Marx outlines how "the premises of political economy" allowed him to demonstrate how

political economy itself envisions the laborer reduced to the level of the commodity. Nevertheless, "political economy starts with the fact of private property but does not explain it to us. It expresses in general, abstract formulas the material process through which private property actually passes, and these formulas it then takes for laws. It does not comprehend these laws…" For this reason, Marx urges us to avoid returning to the "fictitious primordial condition" presupposed by political economy when it tries to explain the dynamic process it contemplates. "Such a primordial condition explains nothing; it merely pushes the question away into a gray nebulous distance" (1964:106–107). It goes without saying that our objective in this instance is to do the opposite.

12 David Harvey, "Organizing for the Anti-Capitalist Transition."

13 Ibid.

14 Ibid.

15 Ibid.

16 Ibid.

17 Ibid.

18 In the new "Political Preface" to *Eros and Civilization* penned in 1966, Marcuse recounts how, in the anti-colonial resistance movements, colonizing countries encountered "not only a social revolt in the traditional sense, but also an instinctual revolt—a biological hatred. The spread of guerilla warfare at the height of the technological century is a symbolic event: the energy of the human body rebels against intolerable repression and throws itself against the engines of repression." Herbert Marcuse, *Eros and Civilization* (Boston: Beacon Press,1974), xix. Although readers may have misgivings about Marcuse's Romanticism, it's hard to deny the similarity between the impulse to rebellion he describes and the one currently felt by many contemporary radicals. It is in this light that we can make sense of John Holloway's decision to begin his assessment of the possibility of "changing the world without taking power" with an account of "the scream," that seemingly universal feeling of revolt against the present. John Holloway, *Change the World Without Taking Power: The Meaning of Revolution Today* (London: Pluto Press, 2010).

19 Valia Kaimaki "Mass Uprising of Greece's Youth." *Le Monde Diplomatique, English Edition.* January, 2009. http://mondediplo.com/2009/01/06greece.

20 Ibid.

21 "No Conclusions When Another World Is Unpopular," *After the Fall: Communiqués from Occupied Oakland*, n.p., 2009, http://libcom.org/library/no-conclusions-when-another-world-unpopular.

22 Raoul Vaneigem, *The Revolution of Everyday Life* (Oakland: PM Press, 2003), 26

23 As George Katsiaficas recounts in *The Imagination of the New Left*, "as the popular

base of the New Left became increasingly dissolved in avenues of purely personal advancement and in the openings provided for the expression of professional dissent, tendencies within the movement developed which, if anything, only served to deepen the popular disillusionment with politics. George Katsiaficas, *The Imagination of the New Left: A Global Analysis of 1968* (Cambridge, MA: South End Press, 1987), 198.

24 See AK Thompson, "The Resonance of Romanticism: Activist Art and the Bourgeois Horizon," in *Cultural Activism: Practices, Dilemmas, and Potentialities.* (New York: Brill, 2010, and this volume).

25 David Harvey, "Organizing for the Anti-Capitalist Transition."

26 Camille de Toledo, *Coming of Age at the End of History* (Brooklyn: Soft Skull Press, 2008), 9.

27 For an account of this dynamic in the New Left, consult Martin Duberman, "Black Power and the American Radical Tradition" in *Left Out: The Politics of Exclusion: Essays 1964–2002.* (Cambridge, MA: South End Press, 2002),182.

28 David Harvey, "Organizing for the Anti-Capitalist Transition."

29 Ibid.

30 Ibid.

31 Slavoj Žižek, *Welcome to the Desert of the Real* (New York: Verso, 2002), 78–79.

32 Simon Critchley, *Infinitely Demanding: Ethics of Commitment, Politics of Resistance* (New York: Verso, 2007), 4.

33 And here it suffices to recall Marx's assessment from *The Communist Manifesto*: "Constant revolutionizing of production, uninterrupted disturbance of all social conditions, everlasting uncertainty and agitation distinguish the bourgeois epoch from all earlier ones." Karl Marx and Friedrich Engels, *The Communist Manifesto* (Baltimore: Penguin Books, 1967), 83.

34 Bertolt Brecht, "Parade of the Old New," *Poems: 1913–1956* (New York: Routledge, 1987), 323.

35 Walter Benjamin, *The Writer of Modern Life: Essays on Charles Baudelaire* (Cambridge, MA: Belknap Harvard, 2006), 161.

36 Noit Banait, "Sensorial Techniques of the Self: From the *Jouissance* of May '68 to the Economy of the Delay," in Daniel J. Sherman et al. (eds.), *The Long 1968: Revisions and Perspectives* (Bloomington: Indiana University Press, 2013), 303.

37 V.I. Lenin, *What Is To Be Done?* (Moscow: Progress Publishers,1983), 69.

38 Dorothy Smith, *The Everyday World as Problematic: A Feminist Sociology* (Toronto: University of Toronto Press, 1987).

39 David Harvey, "Organizing for the Anti-Capitalist Transition."

40 Karl Marx and Friedrich Engels, *The German Ideology* (New York: International Publishers, 1947), 47-48.

41 Karl Marx, *Capital, Volume I* (Moscow: Progress Publishers,1977), 293.

42 David Harvey, *The Condition of Postmodernity: An Inquiry Into the Origins of Cultural Change* (Cambridge, MA: Blackwell, 1990).

43 Karl Marx and Friedrich Engels, *The German Ideology*.

44 David Harvey, "Organizing for the Anti-Capitalist Transition."

45 Louis Althusser, "Preface to *Capital Volume 1.*" *Lenin and Philosophy and Other Essays* (New York: Monthly Review Press, 2001), 52.

46 Henri Lefebvre, *Critique of Everyday Life, Volume I* (New York: Verso, 2000), 57.

II • The Critical Moment

Waging War on Valentines Day

1 Karl Marx, *Grundrisse* (London: Penguin Book,1993), 162.

2 Sheila Sampath, "Made With Love: Shameless Presents The Love and Relationships Issue," *Shameless*, January 5, 2014, n.p., http://shamelessmag.com/blog/entry/made-with-love-shameless-presents-the-love-and-re/.

3 Ibid.

4 "Redefining Our Relationships: An Interview with Wendy-O Matik," *Revolution by the Book: The AK Press Blog*, February 19, 2010 n.p., http://www.revolutionbythebook.akpress.org/redefining-our-relationships-an-interview-with-wendy-o-matik/.

5 Che Guevera, "Socialism and Man in Cuba," *Marxists Internet Archive*, n.d., n.p., https://www.marxists.org/archive/guevara/1965/03/man-socialism.htm#body-31.

6 Ibid.

7 Martin Luther King Jr., "Martin Luther King Jr. Acceptance Speech," *Nobelprize.org*, n.d, n.p., https://www.nobelprize.org/nobel_prizes/peace/laureates/1964/king-acceptance_en.html.

8 Ibid.

9 Zaid Ali and Laura King, "U.S. Drone Strike on Yemen Wedding Party Kills 17," *Los Angeles Times*, December 13, 2013, n.p., http://articles.latimes.com/2013/dec/13/world/la-fg-wn-yemen-drone-strike-wedding-20131213.

10 "Wech Bagtu Wedding Party Airstrike," *Wikepedia*, n.d., n.p., https://en.wikipedia.org/wiki/Wech_Baghtu_wedding_party_airstrike.

11 "Haska Meyna Wedding Party Airstrike," *Wikepedia*, n.d., n.p., https://en.wikipedia.org/wiki/Haska_Meyna_wedding_party_airstrike.

12 Reuters Staff, "Air Strike Kills 15 Civilians in Yemen by Mistake: Officials," Reuters, December 12, 2013, n.p. https://www.reuters.com/article/us-yemen-strike/

air-strike-kills-15-civilians-in-yemen-by-mistake-officials-idUSBRE9B
B10O20131212.

13 Daniel Patrick Moynihan, *The Negro Family: The Case for National Action*. Office of
Policy Panning and Research, United States Department of Labor, March, 1965.

14 Oscar Romero, *The Violence of Love* (Maryknoll, NY: Orbis Books, 1988), 12.

15 Paulo Freire, *Pedagogy of the Oppressed* (New York: Continuum, 2005), 56.

16 Rita Mae Brown, "Sappho's Reply," *The Hand That Cradles The Rock* (Baltimore:
Diana Press, 1974), 77.

The Resonance of Romanticism

1 Walter Benjamin, "Paris, Capital of the Nineteenth Century," *Reflections* (New
York: Schocken Books, 1978), 157.

2 Ibid., 162.

3 Ibid., 148.

4 Isaiah Berlin, *The Roots of Romanticism* (Princeton, NJ: Princeton University
Press, 1999), 1.

5 I am indebted in this respect to M.H. Abrams's magisterial work *The Mirror
and the Lamp: Romantic Theory and the Critical Tradition* (New York: Oxford
University Press, 1953).

6 Carl Schmitt, *Political Romanticism* (Cambridge, MA: The MIT Press, 1986), 93.

7 René Girard, *Violence and the Sacred*, (Baltimore: The Johns Hopkins University
Press, 1977), 102.

8 Georg Lukács, *History and Class Consciousness: Studies in Marxist Dialectics*
(Cambridge, MA: The MIT Press, 1971), 113–114.

9 Isaiah Berlin, *The Roots of Romanticism* (Princeton, NJ: Princeton University
Press, 1999), 119–120.

10 Among these books are *Flood!* (1992, 2002), *Street Posters and Ballads* (1998),
Illuminated Poems (1996, 2006), and *Bloodsong: A Silent Ballad* (2002).

11 Eddie Yuen, George Katsiaficas, and Daniel Burton Rose (eds.), *The Battle of Seattle:
The New Challenge to Capitalist Globalization* (Brooklyn, Soft Skull Press, 2001).

12 Susan Buck-Morss, *The Dialectics of Seeing: Walter Benjamin and the Arcades
Project* (Cambridge, MA: The MIT Press, 1989), 114.

13 Luc Sante, "Introduction" in Eric Drooker, *Flood! A Novel in Pictures* (Milwaukie,
OR: Dark Horse Comics, 2002).

14 Patrick Barber, "Review of *Flood! A Novel in Pictures*," *The Rocket*, 1993.

15 Herbert Vigilla, "Review of *Flood! A Novel in Pictures*," *Graphic Novel Review*, 2004.

16 Rick Eymer, "Review of *Flood! A Novel in Pictures*," *The San Mateo Times*, 1992.

17 It is well known that many early twentieth-century radicals took Romanticism to

be a reactionary force that enabled fascism to proliferate. Eventually, these debates encapsulated turn-of-the-century German expressionism—a visual archive to which Drooker owes obvious debts. To get a sense of the divergent responses to this works' political ambivalence, it is useful to recall Ernst Bloch and Georg Lukács' deliberations on the matter. For Bloch, expressionism contained an energetic anti-capitalist sentiment that could be mobilized by the Left. In contrast, Lukács saw its willful embrace of irrationalism as an obvious precursor to fascism. Because the content of his images seems to disclose an unambiguously radical allegiance, this debate may seem far removed from Drooker's own work. However, when the question is transposed from the realm of "what is depicted" to the more difficult one of "how is change envisioned," ambivalence overtakes certainty. See Georg Lukács, "Realism in the Balance" in *Aesthetics and Politics: The Key Texts of the Classic Debate within German Marxism* (New York: Verso, 2002), 9–59.

18 Walter Benjamin, *The Arcades Project* (Cambridge, MA: Harvard University Press, 2003), 479.

19 Banksy, *Wall and Piece* (London: Century, 2005), 100–1.

20 Ibid., 57.

21 Georg Lukács, "Realism in the Balance," 43.

22 Hans Magnus Enzensberger, "Constituents of a Theory of the Media" in *The Consciousness Industry: On Literature, Politics and the Media* (New York: Continuum, 1974), 102.

23 Giorgio Agamben, *The Man Without Content* (Stanford, CA: Stanford University Press, 1999), 63.

24 Robert Hughes, *The Shock of the New: Art and the Century of Change* (London: Thames and Hudson, 1991).

25 Banksy, *Wall and Piece*, 116.

26 Swoon, "New York Street Art: Layers of Meaning," *New York Times*, July 9, 2004, n.p., http://www.nytimes.com/packages/khtml/2004/07/09/nyregion/20040708_STREET_AUDIOSS.html?ex=1247112000&en=58aea13330d86c89&ei=5090.

27 Ibid.

28 Walter Benjamin, "The Author as Producer," *Reflections* (New York: Schocken Books, 1978), 235.

29 Swoon, "New York Street Art: Layers of Meaning."

30 Banksy, *Wall and Piece*, 100–101.

31 Max Raphael, *Proudhon, Marx, Picasso: Three Studies in the Sociology of Art* (London: Lawrence and Wishart, 1980), 89–90.

32 Ibid., 123.

33 In "The Author as Producer," Benjamin recounts how the "matter of fact" style of depiction that gained ground with photography at the beginning of the

twentieth century had the effect of aestheticizing that which it desired to illuminate: According to Benjamin, matter-of factness "succeeded in transforming even
abject poverty, by recording it in a fashionably perfected manner, into an object
of enjoyment." Although working in a different medium, it is clear that Picasso (in
his sentimental phase) shares in the epistemic conceits of early twentieth-century
matter-of factness. See Walter Benjamin, "The Author as Producer," 230.

34 Banksy, *Wall and Piece*, 20.

35 CrimethInc. gave this Romantic sentiment a concrete form when they wrote:
"Whatever medical science may profess, there is a difference between Life and
survival… Their instruments measure blood pressure and temperature, but overlook joy, wonder, love, all the things that make life really matter . . . Many of us
live as though everything has already been decided without us, as if living is not
a creative activity but rather something that happens to us. That's not being alive,
that's just surviving; being undead." *Days of War, Nights of Love* (2001), 275.

Avatar and the Thing Itself

1 Larry and Andy Wachowski, *The Matrix: Numbered Shooting Script*, March 29,
1998, http://www.dailyscript.com/scripts/the_matrix.pdf, 53.

2 It's on this basis that we can understand the addictive nature of commodities
lacking entirely in substance. In *The Fragile Absolute*, Slavoj Žižek makes this
point in relation to caffeine free Diet Coke. See *The Fragile Absolute: Or Why Is
the Christian Legacy Worth Defending?* (New York: Verso, 2008), 28.

3 As I write this, Toronto's media-ecology is saturated with ads that draw upon
revolutionary desires in order to fuel consumption. A radio station enjoins me to
"join the movement." A financial house reminds me: "free your assets and the rest
will follow."

4 Characterizing Christ as a revolutionary figure is, of course, not the invention of the
Churches Advertising Network. From the seventeenth-century radical Protestant
sects that actively sought to undo ecclesiastical power to twentieth-century anti-
clerical liberation theology, the revolutionary dynamic within Christianity has been
omnipresent. For his part, James Baldwin argued that liberation from the duplicity
of American life required that the spirit of Christ be exhumed from beneath the
church that St. Paul had built on his back. Missing from this account, however,
is recognition of the degree to which the "fanatical and self-righteous" church has
always drawn upon images of the spirit of rebellion it squashed in order to gain
legitimacy. In this sense, Christ's *chutzpah* has always been an ad for the church. See
James Baldwin, *The Fire Next Time* (New York: A Delta Book,1964), 58.

5 Slavoj Žižek has advanced a similar argument in relation to the film *Shrek*. After

noting the various "subversions" of the traditional fairytale at work in the film, Žižek raises the following caution: "Instead of praising these displacements and reinscriptions too readily as potentially 'subversive' and elevating *Shrek* into yet another 'site of resistance', we should focus on the obvious fact that, through all these displacements, the same story is being told…. This is how we are believers today—we make fun of our beliefs, while continuing to practice them." *Welcome to the Desert of the Real*, (New York: Verso, 2002), 70–71.

6 Max Horkheimer *Critical Theory: Selected Essays* (New York: Continuum, 1995), 208.

7 Walter Benjamin, *The Arcades Project* (Cambridge, MA: Harvard University Press, 2003), 463.

8 To get a sense of this oscillation, one could do no better than to consider the profound differences between Danny Boyle's *28 Days Later* and Juan Carlos Fresnadillo's sequel, *28 Weeks Later*. Both are excellent zombie films. Both explore the intersection between life, biopolitics, and militarization. Both will scare the shit out of you. However, in the first film, the principal characters flee the "security" promised by the army once they recognize that, while zombies—as a species of bare life—may be terrifying, the biopolitical project of the military is unquestionably worse. The resolution finds the characters distancing themselves from the military and intensifying their identification with bare life (at one point seeming to channel the zombies' energy). In the second film, it is precisely this identification with life, this ethical commitment to that which makes us—or keeps us—human, that leads to the catastrophic spread of infection. Once the identification with life permeates the military, the infection is given free reign to spread beyond England and into continental Europe. Although dealing with the same political content in a manifestly similar fashion, the political implications are extremely different. If *28 Days Later* was channeling Giorgio Agamben, *28 Weeks Later* was channeling an unreconstructed Carl Schmitt.

9 Robert Jensen, "What Michael Moore Misses About the Empire," *Counterpunch*, July 5, 2004, n.p., http://www.counterpunch.org/jensen07052004.html.

10 Ibid.

11 Ibid.

12 Ibid.

13 Ibid.

14 "Avatar-Induced Depression: Coping With The Intangibility Of Pandora," *Huffington Post*, March 18, 2010, n.p., http://www.huffingtonpost.com/2010/01/12/avatarinduced-depression_n_420605.html.

15 Walter Benjamin, "Paris, Capital of the Nineteenth Century." *Reflections* (New York: Schocken Books, 1978), 148.

16 The success of Quentin Tarantino's *Inglourious Basterds* (2009), however, should alert us to the fact that—at present—revisionism has indeed become an acceptable vector for "redemption." This development is troubling; however, it is beyond the scope of this commentary to consider it in any detail.

17 The end is, of course, never the end. Many commentators have noted that the film is practically begging for a sequel. "What happens when the earthlings come back?" This question has often been posed cynically, as if the fact that the glorious resolution was, in fact, no resolution at all arose primarily from bad scripting. But despite this cynicism, it's impossible to ignore the explicitly *political* character of the question the film has compelled people to ask: what *will* people do when their livelihoods are threatened?

18 Although the Na'vi are modeled after several different earthly tribal peoples, they remain mythic expressions of these people. This is so not only because of their fantastical sci-fi attributes but also because, through their depiction, the history of earthly tribal people's domination of nature is effectively erased. Like many contemporary radicals who celebrate tribal cultures, Cameron does not sully his Na'vi with less noble traits like inter-tribal war and the widespread destruction of natural habitats to facilitate hunting and agriculture. For more on these aspects of earthly tribal life and on the tendency among contemporary radicals to mythologize this existence, see Murray Bookchin, *Social Anarchism or Lifestyle Anarchism: An Unbridgeable Chasm* (Oakland: AK Press, 1995), 36–49.

19 "'Avatar is real' say tribal people," *Survival International*, January 25, 2010, n.p., http://www.survivalinternational.org/news/5466.

20 Ibid.

21 Ibid.

22 Ibid.

23 Friends of Freedom and Justice, "Bil'in weekly demonstration reenacts the Avatar film," *International Solidarity Movement*, February 12, 2010, n.p., https://palsolidarity.org/2010/02/bilin-weekly-demonstration-reenacts-the-avatar-film/.

24 It was bound to happen eventually. Even the film's most hardened radical detractors seem to have appreciated the visual analogy between the forest clearing bulldozers deployed on Pandora and those used by the IDF to demolish Palestinian homes.

25 Dan Farber, "The Politics of Avatar," *CBS News*, January 12, 2010, n.p., https://www.cbsnews.com/news/the-politics-of-avatar/.

26 Nagesh Rao, "Anti-Imperialism in 3-D." *Socialistworker.org*, January 7, 2010, n.p., http://socialistworker.org/2010/01/07/anti-imperialism-in-3D.

27 Annalee Newitz, "When Will White People Stop Making Films Like Avatar?" *io9: We Come From the Future*, December 18, 2009, n.p., http://io9.com/5422666/when-will-white-people-stop-making-movies-likeavatar.

28 Ibid.

29 Ibid.

30 Ibid.

31 It's significant that Newitz's conclusion is not a logical aberration; the multicultural twist arises directly and consistently from the very manner in which the problem is posed. Pushed to their logical conclusion, this may well be the fate of all representational critiques.

32 David McNally, *Bodies of Meaning: Studies on Language, Labor, and Liberation.* (Albany: SUNY Press, 2001), 4–5.

33 Richard Dyer, *White* (New York: Routledge,1997).

34 This situation was undoubtedly more frequently the case for bourgeois whites than it was for their proletarian counterparts (who—especially in the nineteenth-century—were themselves often racialized, sexualized, and animalized). However, we should be careful not to forget the degree to which bourgeois habits have a way of finding more general expression. It's not for nothing that, for Marx, "the ideas of the ruling class are in every epoch the ruling ideas." Karl Marx and Friedrich Engels, *The German Ideology* (New York: International Publishers, 1947), 64.

35 Karl Marx, "Letter to Arnold Ruge," quoted in Walter Benjamin, *The Arcades Project* (Cambridge, MA: Harvard University Press, 2003), 467.

Matter's Most Modern Configurations

1 The term "dialectical image" does not appear in "Theses on the Philosophy of History." However, terms like "monad," "true image of the past," and "constellation" are used to denote the same thing. In line with Michael Löwy's reading of the "Theses"—where he points out that "in a first version of [Thesis XVII] to be found in the *Arcades Project*, in place of the concept of the monad there appears that of the 'dialectical image'" [Michael Löwy, *Fire Alarm: Reading Walter Benjamin's 'On The Concept of History'*, (London: Verso, 2005), 132.]—I treat these terms as synonyms; see Walter Benjamin, *The Arcades Project* (Cambridge, MA: Harvard University Press, 2003), 462. For the sake of clarity and convenience, I restrict myself here primarily to the term "dialectical image," which I feel most closely captures what Benjamin was aiming at.

2 Walter Benjamin, "Theses On the Philosophy of History," *Illuminations* (New York: Schocken, 1968), 263.

3 Susan Buck-Morss, *The Dialectics of Seeing: Walter Benjamin and the Arcades Project* (Cambridge, MA: The MIT Press, 1991), 46.

4 Ibid.

5 Ibid.

6   There's little evidence to suggest that either Rivera or Picasso were directly familiar with Benjamin's work. However, given the intellectual terrain within which they operated, and given the indirect connections they shared through mediating figures like Georges Bataille and Leon Trotsky, it's likely that Benjamin's *ideas* were at least partially available to Rivera and Picasso through the informal structure of feeling that pervaded the early-twentieth century radical scene. Presenting artworks—actual painted images—as dialectical images is somewhat out of keeping with Benjamin's own eclectic use of the concept. However, while I acknowledge that dialectical images do not have to be images in the artistic sense, I have chosen to focus on artworks because they help to pose the question of operationalization most acutely.

7   Fredric Jameson, "Future City," *New Left Review* 21 (May–June 2003): http://www.newleftreview.org/?view=2449.

8   These images were based on sketches that Rivera produced while attending the 1928 May Day Parade in Moscow. Abby Aldrich Rockefeller found these images so compelling that, while Rivera was working on *Man at the Crossroads*, she bought his sketchbook. See Andrea Kettenmann, *Diego Rivera: A Revolutionary Spirit in Modern Art* (New York: Taschen, 2000), 52.

9   Ezekiel 1:19–21 *New International Version*.

10 Susan Buck-Morss, *Dialectics of Seeing*, 70.

11 Viewing dialectical images in this way is justified on the grounds of a note Buck-Morss found in the Bataille Archive, in which Benjamin recounts his own thinking in the schematic terms of intersecting axes. See Buck-Morss, *Dialectics of Seeing*, 215.

12 It's significant that Rivera did not land upon this composition immediately. In early sketches for the mural, the cast of assembled characters have yet to be arrayed in the fashion that would yield the tension so central to the final work. Although they are all present in the earlier sketches, their explosive *configuration* had yet to be discovered. For a reproduction of an earlier sketch, see Leah Dickerman and Anna Indych-López (eds.), *Diego Rivera: Murals for the Museum of Modern Art* (New York: The Museum of Modern Art, New York, 2011), 37.

13 Pete Hamill, *Diego Rivera* (New York: Harry N. Abrams, 1999), 166.

14 Ibid.

15 Ibid.

16 The only one known to exist, clandestinely shot by assistant Lucienne Bloch after Rivera's dismissal (Frida Kahlo ran interception). The image presented above is a reproduction of *Man, Controller of the Universe* (1934). See also Benjamin, "Theses on the Philosophy of History," 255.

17 Irene Herner De Larrea et al., eds. *Diego Rivera: Paradise Lost at Rockefeller Center*

(Mexico City: Edicupes, 1987), 42.

18 Ibid.

19 Ibid.

20 V.I. Lenin, "Report on the Work of the Council of People's Commissars," December 29, 1920, *Marxists Internet Acrhive*, n.p., n.d., https://www.marxists.org /archive/lenin/works/1920/8thcong/ch02.htm

21 Robert Hughes, *The Shock of the New: Art and the Century of Change* (London: Thames and Hudson, 1991), 29.

22 Frank D. Russell, *Picasso's Guernica: The Labyrinth of Narrative and Vision* (London: Thames and Hudson, 1980), 3.

23 Fredric Jameson, *Postmodernism or, The Cultural Logic of Late Capitalism* (Durham: Duke University Press, 1991), 4.

24 Quoted in Ellen Oppler, *Picasso's Guernica* (New York: W.W. Norton & Co., 1988), 199-200.

25 John Berger, *The Success and Failure of Picasso* (New York: Pantheon, 1980), 169.

26 Ibid.

27 Ibid.

28 Ibid., 166.

29 Susan Buck-Morss, *Dialectics of Seeing*, 161.

30 Retort, *Afflicted Powers: Capital and Spectacle in a New Age of War* (New York: Verso, 2005), 191.

31 Ibid.

32 William S. Lieberman, *The Nelson A. Rockefeller Collection: Masterpieces of Modern Art* (New York: Hudson Mills Press, 1981), 17.

33 Jerry Cheslow, "If You're Thinking of Living In: Turtle Bay," *The New York Times*, April 26, 1992, 7.

34 Benjamin, "Theses on the Philosophy of History," 265.

35 Maureen Dowd, "Powell Without Picasso," *The New York Times*, February 5, 2003, 27.

36 Retort, *Afflicted Powers*, 16.

37 Berger, *The Success and Failure of Picasso*, 70.

38 Benjamin, *The Arcades Project*, 471.

39 Frank D. Russell, *Picasso's Guernica*, 92.

40 Patrick Marnham, *Dreaming With His Eyes Open: A Life of Diego Rivera* (Berkeley: University of California Press, 2000), 192.

41 Ibid.

42 Karl Marx, "Introduction," *A Contribution to the Critique of Hegel's Philosophy of Right, Marxists Internet Archive*, n.p., n.d., https://www.marxists.org/archive/ marx/works/1843/critique-hpr/intro.htm

43 Benjamin, "Theses on the Philosophy of History," 254; Benjamin's "*weak* Messianic power" has been the subject of considerable debate and commentary—and for good reason. As with many of Benjamin's concepts, *weak* Messianic power is an allegorical profanation in which a category of religious thought finds its point of actualization in matter's most modern configurations. In both Judaism and Christianity, the Messiah was conceived as a redeemer who would make the shattered world whole. Extended to apply to materialist concerns, Messianic power takes our accumulated historic failures to attain happiness as its object. For this reason, rather than lulling us with visions of a utopian future (where all men are angels), Benjamin enjoins us to consider what must be done to save *the dead* from the ongoing deferral of their dreams or—worse—from their induction into the triumphant processions of oppressive victors. In Benjamin's formulation, Messianic power is qualified as "*weak*" to make clear that it pertains to a material and not a mythic-religious phenomenon. As with Michael Gold, who concluded his autobiographical gem *Jews Without Money* with the realization that—after endless searching and religious doubt—the Messiah was in fact none other than the "workers' Revolution" [Michael Gold, *Jews Without Money*, (New York, NY: Carroll & Graff Publishers, 1930), 309], Benjamin imagined that the claims of the past could only be settled through organized, decisive action.

44 Walter Benjamin, *The Arcades Project*, 461.

45 Such recourse can be seen in his regular deployment of figures like the Minotaur in works like 1935's *Minotauromachy*, an obvious visual precursor to *Guernica*.

46 Frank D. Russell, *Picasso's Guernica*, 10.

47 Ibid., 5.

48 Ibid., 9.

49 Ibid., 10.

50 Georg Lukács, "Realism in the Balance," in Adorno et al. *Aesthetics and Politics* (London: Verso, 2002), 43.

51 Ibid., 33.

52 Oppler, *Picasso's Guernica*, 47.

53 It's solely on this basis that we can understand how—despite its cubist inflections and claustrophobically topographical character—some early commentators went so far as to conceive *Guernica* as a work of "social realism." See Roland Penrose, *Picasso: His Life and Work* (London: Gollanez, 1962), 277.

54 Ibid., 277–278.

55 Benjamin, "Theses on the Philosophy of History," 261.

56 Ibid.

57 Ibid., 255.

III • Progress

Obituary in Absentia

1 T.S. Eliot, "The Hollow Men," *Selected Poems* (London: Faber and Faber, 1961), 80.

2 Shankar Chaudhuri, "Mayan Apocalypse: Are There Any Facts Behind This Doomsday Scenario? (No)," *The Guardian*, December 21, 2012, n.p., https://www.theguardian.com/world/us-news-blog/2012/dec/20/mayan-apocalypse-facts-doomsday-scenario.

3 Ibid.

4 Ibid.

5 Fredric Jameson, *Postmodernism or, The Cultural Logic of Late Capitalism* (Durham: Duke University Press, 1991), 54.

6 "Neil Armstrong: 1930–2012," NASA, August 25, 2012, n.p., https://www.nasa.gov/topics/people/features/armstrong_obit.html.

7 Ibid.

8 Mike Davis, "Burning All Illusions," *Dead Cities* (New York: The New Press, 2002), 229.

9 Ibid.

10 Ibid.

11 Jennifer Medina, "Rodney King Dies at 47: Police Beating Victim Who Asked 'Can We All Get Along?'" *The New York Times*, June 17, 2012, n.p., http://www.nytimes.com/2012/06/18/us/rodney-king-whose-beating-led-to-la-riots-dead-at-47.html.

12 Margalit Fox, "Shulamith Firestone, Feminist Writer, Dies at 67," *The New York Times*, August 30, 2012, n.p., http://www.nytimes.com/2012/08/31/nyregion/shulamith-firestone-feminist-writer-dies-at-67.html.

13 Shulamith Firestone, *The Dialectic of Sex: The Case for Feminist Revolution* (New York: Farrar, Strauss and Giroux, 1970).

14 Quoted in Margalit Fox, "Shulamith Firestone, Feminist Writer, Dies at 67."

15 Jeffrey Eugenides, "Posthumous," *The New Yorker*, December 21, 2012, n.p. https://www.newyorker.com/books/page-turner/posthumous.

16 Albert Camus, "The Wager of Our Generation," *Resistance, Rebellion, and Death* (New York: Vintage Books, 1988), 247.

Occupation, Decolonization, and Reciprocal Violence

1 Walter Benjamin, "Surrealism: The Last Snapshot of the European Intelligentsia," *Reflections* (New York: Schocken Books, 1978), 177.

2 Written in 1962 by Tom Hayden and other contributors at an SDS retreat in Port

Huron, Michigan, *The Port Huron Statement* became a defining document of the American New Left. Throughout its pages, one notes a refusal both of America's stale bureaucratized democracy and of the horrors of Soviet-style authoritarian socialism. In their place, the SDS authors advanced a vision of participatory democracy that quickly became the movement's common sense. See Tom Hayden, *The Port Huron Statement: The Visionary Call of the 1960s Revolution* (New York: Thunder's Mouth Press, 2005).

3 Alexis de Tocqueville, *Democracy in America* (New York: Bantam Classic, 2002).

4 Walter Benjamin, "Paris, Capital of the Nineteenth Century," *Reflections* (New York: Schocken Books, 1978), 148.

5 The Imperative Committee, *Preoccupied: The Logic of Occupation* (self-published activist pamphlet circulated following the December 2008 occupation of The New School for Social Research), January 2009, https://libcom.org/files/preoccupied -reading-final.pdf.

6 Ibid. Grad students will be grad students. Both the name "the Imperative Committee" and the formulation "the coming occupations" reveal the authors' debts to a particular strand of Romantic insurrectionary thought associated with the work of Giorgio Agamben (author of, among other books, *The Coming Community*) and elaborated by groups like the anonymous Frenchmen who penned *The Coming Insurrection* under the name The Invisible Committee.

7 George Katsiaficas, *The Imagination of the New Left: A Global Analysis of 1968* (Cambridge, MA: South End Press, 1987).

8 Conor Tomás Reed, "Step 1: Occupy Universities. Step 2: Transform Them," *Tidal: Occupy Theory, Occupy Strategy*, Volume 1, 4.

9 Ibid.

10 Mikhail Bakhtin, *Rabelais and His World* (Bloomington IN: Indiana University Press, 1984).

11 Naomi Klein, "Does Protest Need a Vision?" *New Statesman*, July 3, 2000, n.p. https://www.newstatesman.com/radical-century/2013/05/3-july-2000-does -protest-need-vision.

12 King James Version, Book of Acts 17:6–7, *The Bible*, https://www.biblegateway .com/passage/?search=Acts+17%3A5-7&version=KJV.

13 Jessica Yee, "Occupy Wall Street: The Game of Colonialism and Further Nationalism to be Decolonized from the 'Left,'" *Rabble.ca*, October 1, 2011, n.p., http://rabble .ca/columnists/2011/10/occupy-wall-street-game-colonialism-and-left.

14 Ibid.

15 Decolonize Oakland, "Decolonize Oakland: Creating a More Radical Movement," *Occupy Oakland*, December 3, 2011, n.p., http://occupyoakland.org/2011/12/ decolonize-oakland/.

16 Some commentators have observed that opposition to the resolution came primarily from white participants and, as such, should be read as further indication of the movement's insensitivity to questions of racism and colonialism; however, to the dismay of many activists, revolutionary hip-hop act The Coup's frontman Boots Riley also spoke in opposition to the proposal. This led to an interesting exchange, which can be found here: http://disoccupy.wordpress.com/page/2/.

17 Decolonize Oakland, "Decolonize Oakland: Creating a More Radical Movement," *Occupy Oakland*, December 3, 2011, n.p., http://occupyoakland.org/2011/12/decolonize-oakland/.

18 This quote is taken from an unpublished statement made by Mueller at the event, recorded by the author.

19 POC National Statement, "For People Who Have Considered Occupation But Found It Is Not Enuf," *DisOccupy*, April 24, 2012, n.p., disoccupy.wordpress.com.

20 Lester Spence and Mike McGuire, "Occupy and the 99%," *We Are Many: Reflections on Movement Strategy from Occupation to Liberation* (Oakland: AK Press, 2012), 56–57

21 Ibid., 63

22 Carl von Clausewitz, *On War* (Princeton: Princeton University Press, 1989).

23 Melanie Kaye/Kantrowitz, *The Issue is Power: Essays on Women, Jews, Violence and Resistance* (Aunt Lutte Books, 1992), 24.

24 Frantz Fanon, *The Wretched of the Earth* (New York: Grove Press, 1963), 37

25 Ibid., 39

26 See Sophie Lewis, "As Odious as the Word Occupy," *Journal of Occupied Studies*, February, 2012, n.p., http://occupiedstudies.org/articles/as-odious-as-the-word-occupy.html.

27 Quoted in Stephen Bradley, *Harlem Vs. Columbia University: Black Student Power in the Late 1960s* (Urbana, Chicago, and Springfield: University of Illinois Press, 2009), 57.

28 Ibid., 99.

29 Michael Stern, "1 Arrested in Park in Violent Protest," *Columbia Daily Spectator*, Vol. CXII, No. 101, April 24, 1968, 1.

30 Ibid., 2.

31 "Protestors Crowd Into Hamilton Hall for All-Night Vigil," *Columbia Daily Spectator*, Vol. CVII, No. 101, April 24, 1968, 1.

32 Ibid.

33 Ibid.

34 Robert Stulberg, "Protesters Say They Will Not Negotiate Until CU Grants Disciplinary Amnesty," *Columbia Daily Spectator*, Vol. CXII, No. 101, April 24, 1968, 1–3

35 Ibid.

36 "A Day of Warning," *Columbia Daily Spectator*, Vol CXII, No. 101, April 24, 1968, 4.

37 Ibid., 3.

38 Robert Stulberg, "Protesters Occupy 2 New Buildings," *Columbia Daily Spectator*, Vol. CXII, No. 102, April 25, 1968, 1–2.

39 Ibid.

40 Ibid.

41 Ibid.

42 Arthur Krokot, "Two Black Leaders Support Strikers," Columbia Daily Spectator, Vol. CXII, No. 104, April 27, 1968, 1–4.

43 Ibid.

44 "University Calls in 1,000 Police to End Demonstration as Nearly 700 are Arrested and 100 Injured; Violent Solution Follows Failure of Negotiations," *Columbia Daily Spectator*, Vol. CXII, No.107, April 30, 1969, 1.

45 Adam Fortunate Eagle, *Alcatraz! Alcatraz!* (Berkeley: Heyday Books, 1992), 39.

46 Ibid.

47 Ibid.

48 Ibid., 54.

49 Conor Tomás Reed, "Step 1: Occupy Universities. Step 2: Transform Them."

50 Hannah Dobbs, *Nine-Tenths of the Law: Property and Resistance in the United States* (Oakland: AK Press, 2012), 24. Similarly, as Feigenbaum, Frenzel, and McCurdy point out in *Protest Camps*, protestors in Tahrir Square erected barricades "to protect the encampment" and preserve it as a "space for democracy building." Anna Feigenbaum, Fabian Frenzel, and Patrick McCurdy, *Protest Camps: Imagining Alternative Worlds* (London: Zed, 2013), 37.

51 Carl Schmitt, *The Concept of the Political* (Chicago: University of Chicago Press, 1996), 26–27.

52 Ibid., 27.

53 Adam Fortunate Eagle, *Alcatraz! Alcatraz!*, 43.

54 Ibid., 44.

55 Although Indians of All Tribes briefly cited nineteenth century American treaty law to legitimate their claim, this action is best understood as an example of what, in his "Critique of Violence," Walter Benjamin described as an act of violence that arises from the intent to exercise a right "in order to overthrow the legal system that has conferred it." Walter Benjamin, "Critique of Violence," *Reflections* (New York: Schocken Books, 1978), 282.

56 Adam Fortunate Eagle, *Alcatraz! Alcatraz!*, 56.

57 Troy R. Johnson, *The Occupation of Alcatraz Island* (Chicago: University of Illinois

Press, 1996), 223.

58 Ibid., 224.

59 Ibid., 225.

60 Ibid., 225–226.

61 Ibid., 226.

62 Ward Churchill, *From a Native Son: Selected Essays on Indigenism, 1985–1995* (Cambridge, MA: South End Press, 1999), 64.

The Work of Violence in the Age of Repressive Desublimation

1 The arguments rehearsed here coincide with those advanced in AK Thompson, "The Resonance of Romanticism: Activist Art and the Bourgeois Horizon," in *Cultural Activism: Practices, Dilemmas, and Possibilities,* ed. Begüm Özden Firat and Aylin Kuryel (Amsterdam: Rodopi, 2011) and in this volume.

2 Herbert Marcuse, *One-Dimensional Man: Studies in the Ideology of Advanced Industrial Society* (Boston: Beacon Press, 1964), 59.

3 Walt Whitman, "I Sing the Body Electric," in *The Portable Walt Whitman*, ed. Mark van Doren (New York: Viking, 1972), 158.

4 Ibid., 70.

5 For a discussion of the relationship between political violence and what it means to be human, please consult AK Thompson, *Black Bloc, White Riot: Anti-Globalization and the Genealogy of Dissent* (Oakland, CA: AK Press, 2010), esp. 7–9 and 22–25.

6 John Cameron Mitchell (director), *Shortbus* (New York: THINKFilm, 2006).

7 Fredric Jameson, *Postmodernism, or, The Cultural Logic of Late Capitalism* (Durham, NC: Duke University Press, 1991), 16–20.

8 Walter Benjamin, "Paris, Capital of the Nineteenth Century," *Reflections: Essays, Aphorisms, Autobiographical Writings* (New York: Schocken, 1978), 148.

9 Marveling at the counterculture, for instance, Marcuse could not help but note how music could "move the body, thereby drawing nature into rebellion." Furthermore, he thought that such "Life music" found its authentic basis in "black music," which he took to be "the cry and song of the slaves and the ghettos." Succumbing to what now strikes us as an unnerving Romanticism, Marcuse noted how, "in this music, the very life and death of black men and women are lived again. The music is body; the aesthetic form is the 'gesture' of pain, sorrow, indictment." As a result of this powerful assault on mediation, Marcuse found it self-evident that such music would also appeal to white radicals entrapped by one-dimensionality's "pleasant unfreedom." Nevertheless, even here, and "with

the takeover by the whites, a significant change occurs: white 'rock' is what its black paradigm is *not*, namely, *performance*." Herbert Marcuse, *Counterrevolution and Revolt* (Boston: Beacon Press, 1972), 114.

10 Jean-Paul Sartre, *Baudelaire* (New York: New Directions Publishing, 1950), 51–52.

11 This dynamic has been recounted extensively by commentators reviewing the legacy of the New Left and, in particular, the tragic *denouement* of May '68. To get a sense of the degree to which this dynamic now saturates our culture (and even our counterculture), it suffices to consider how, in *Shortbus*, the protagonist's experience of lack—i.e., sexual frustration—is depicted as being enough to knock the power out in Manhattan (presented in maquette, a cardboard stand-in for itself). By finally attaining sexual ecstasy, however, the scene is once again illuminated. For those prone to historical recollection, lights going out in Manhattan cannot help but evoke the 1987 blackout; however, in this case, the pursuit of a purely personal libidinal resolution is enough to dissuade mass violence and looting. In this way, erotic stimulation becomes social regulation. Correspondingly (though it was probably not the director's intention), the city is correctly presented as running on sexual energy (Eros), which, in vampiric fashion, is channeled directly into its rational and calculating infrastructure.

12 As Horkheimer noted, such theory was grounded in "a concept of man as in conflict with himself" until all social contradictions were resolved. Max Horkheimer, "Traditional and Critical Theory," *Critical Theory: Selected Essays* (New York: Continuum Publishing, 1968), 210.

13 Herbert Marcuse, *An Essay on Liberation* (Boston: Beacon Press, 1969).

14 Fredric Jameson, *Postmodernism, or, The Cultural Logic of Late Capitalism* (Durham, NC: Duke University Press, 1991).

15 Marcuse, *One-Dimensional Man*, 50.

16 Ibid., 77.

17 Fredric Jameson, *Postmodernism*, 4.

18 Herbert Marcuse, *Counterrevolution and Revolt* (Boston: Beacon Press, 1972), 116.

19 Marcuse, *One-Dimensional Man*, 76–78.

20 Karl Marx, *The Eighteenth Brumaire of Louis Bonaparte* (New York: Mondial, 2005), 3.

21 For more on the relationship between social movements and the advent of the public sphere, see Charles Tilly, *Social Movements, 1768–2004* (Boulder, CO: Paradigm Publishers, 2004), especially 35–37; and Sidney Tarrow, *Power in Movement: Social Movements and Contentious Politics*, 2nd ed. (Cambridge: Cambridge University Press, 1998), especially 54–56.

22 This is one of the guiding contentions of "the social movement society" thesis. See

David S. Meyer and Sidney Tarrow, eds., *The Social Movement Society: Contentious Politics for a New Century* (Lanham, MD: Rowman and Littlefield, 1998).

23 Jürgen Habermas, *The Structural Transformation of the Public Sphere: An Inquiry into a Category of Bourgeois Society* (Cambridge, MA: MIT Press, 1981).

24 Tiqqun (Collective), *Introduction to Civil War* (Los Angeles: Semiotext(e), 2010), 34.

25 Tiqqun have been associated with The Invisible Committee and, in turn, "the Tarnac Nine," a group—classified by the state as a "terrorist enterprise"—predominantly comprised of graduate students charged in 2008 with using sabotage to disrupt train traffic throughout France.

26 CrimethInc., "Crowd Dynamics and the Mass Psychology of Possibility: An Account of Spatial Movement, An Allegory of Social Movement," *Harbinger, Fifth Communiqué,* 2002, http://www.crimethinc.com/tools/downloads/zines.html#harbinger3.

27 Herbert Marcuse, *One-Dimensional Man*, xv.

28 The advent of Black Lives Matter and the riots that have erupted in the wake of recent police shootings of unarmed Blacks have yielded more indictments of police and transformations of the state's violent practices than have years of petitions and peaceful protests. See Ret Marut, "Next Time it Explodes," *CrimethInc. Ex-Workers' Collective* (blog), August 13, 2015, http://www.crimethinc.com/blog/2015/08/13/since-the-ferguson-uprising/.

29 Herbert Marcuse, *One-Dimensional Man*, 1.

30 AK Thompson, *Black Bloc, White Riot: Anti-Globalization and the Genealogy of Dissent* (Oakland, CA: AK Press, 2010).

31 The "Miami Model" is a repressive police strategy involving preemptive arrest, strategic incapacitation, and overwhelming force first devised by John Timoney to deal with protests against summit meetings of the Free Trade Area of the Americas (FTAA) in Miami in 2003. See Kris Hermes, *Crashing the Party: Legacies and Lessons from the RNC 2000* (Oakland, CA: PM Press, 2015), 308n89.

32 For more information about the "main conspiracy group" and the context in which they were charged, see "Toronto G20 Main Conspiracy Group: The Charges and How They Came to Be," *Infoshop* (blog), October 19, 2014, http://www.infoshop.org/toronto-g20-conspiracy.

33 For a full account of the action on that afternoon, see "Behind the Mask: Violence and Representational Politics," *Upping the Anti: A Journal of Theory and Action,* no. 11, November 2010.

34 Adam Davidson-Harden, "How the 'Black Bloc' Protected the G20," *Canadian Dimension,* June 29, 2010, https://canadiandimension.com/articles/view/web-exclusive-how-the-black-bloc-protected-the-g20).

35 Sid Ryan, "Thousands Stood Up for Humanity: Anti-Summit Marchers Braved Hooligans, Police and Even the Weather to Push a People's Agenda," op-ed, *Toronto Star*, June 29, 2010, http://www.thestar.com/opinion/editorialopinion/2010/06/29/thousands_stood_up_for_humanity.html.

36 Canadian Labour Congress, "Statement by Ken Georgetti, President of the Canadian Labour Congress on Vandalism Surrounding Toronto G20 Meeting," CLC Communications, press release, Marketwire, June 26, 2010, http://www.marketwired.com/press-release/statement-ken-georgetti-president-canadian-labour-congress-on-vandalism-surrounding-1282103.htm.

37 Fred Hahn and Candace Rennick, "Statement on G20 Protests and Aftermath by CUPE Ontario," CUPE Communications, CUPE/SCFP Ontario Archives, June 30, 2010, http://cupe.on.ca/archivedoc1168/; also quoted in Krystalline Kraus, "G8/G20 Communique: Is the Left Abandoning the Movement when Solidarity is Needed Most?," *Rabble.ca* (blog), July 20, 2010, http://rabble.ca/blogs/bloggers/statica/2010/07/g8g20-communiqué-left-abandoning-movement-when-solidarity-needed-most.

38 Milan Ilnyckyj, "Black Blocheads," *Sindark.com* (blog), June 28, 2010, https://www.sindark.com/2010/06/28/black-blocheads/.

39 Chris Hedges, "The Cancer in Occupy," *Truthdig.com* (blog), February 6, 2012, http://www.truthdig.com/report/item/the_cancer_of_occupy_20120206.

40 John Blackstone, "Is 'Black Bloc' Hijacking Occupy Oakland?," *CBS News*, November 4, 2011, http://www.cbsnews.com/news/is-black-bloc-hijacking-occupy-oakland/.

41 Sheila Musaji, "The 'Black Bloc's' Tactics are Hurting the Occupy Movement," *The American Muslim* (blog), November 5, 2011, http://theamericanmuslim.org/tam.php/features/articles/the-black-bloc/0018863.

42 Rashid Patch, quoted in Musaji, "The 'Black Bloc's' Tactics are Hurting the Occupy Movement."

43 See, for instance, *Zig Zag. Fires and Flames!: A Militant Report on Toronto Anti-G20 Resistance* (July 2010), http://www.kersplebedeb.com/blog/torontog20_firesandflames.pdf.

44 Herbert Marcuse, *One-Dimensional Man*, 57.

45 Although it is not universally accepted as an accurate description of the defining features of political life, Carl Schmitt's friend-enemy distinction has regained currency in the neoliberal era. Although critical of his account in some respects (especially concerning the mythological basis of his purely national conception of discrete "modes of existence"), I have found it to be a useful reference point for the discussion at hand. See Carl Schmitt, *The Concept of the Political* (Chicago: University of Chicago Press, 1996).

46 Herbert Marcuse, "Repressive Tolerance," Robert Paul Wolff, Barrington Moore,

Jr., and Herbert Marcuse, *A Critique of Pure Tolerance* (Boston: Beacon Press, 1965), 84.

47 Ibid., 92.

48 Herbert Marcuse, *One-Dimensional Man*, 63.

49 Ibid.

50 Karl Marx, *Capital: Critique of Political Economy*, vol. 1 (1867; Moscow: Progress Publishers, 1977).

51 Herbert Marcuse, *Counterrevolution and Revolt*, 130.

52 Herbert Marcuse, *Eros and Civilization: A Philosophical Inquiry into Freud* (Boston: Beacon Press, 1966), xix.

53 Marcuse, *Counterrevolution and Revolt*, 130.

54 Marcuse, "Repressive Tolerance," 102.

55 Ibid., 108.

The Battle for Necropolis

1 David Harvey, *Rebel Cities: From The Right to the City to the Urban Revolution* (New York: Verso, 2012), 22, 18.

2 And here we must include both the machinery and infrastructure required by capital-intensive production as well as the concentrated labor power made available through the process of urbanization itself.

3 David Harvey, "The Right to the City," *New Left Review 53* (Sept–Oct 2008): 24.

4 Karl Marx, *Capital, Volume 1* (Moscow: Progress Publishers, 1977), 224 (emphasis added).

5 Ibid.

6 As fixed or constant capital, the "means of production" most obviously include machines; however, it is important to remember that they also include buildings and other "externalities" like roads, sewers, and electricity grids that are not necessarily factored directly into the production costs of individual capitalists but nevertheless play a fundamental role in the generation of surplus value. This dynamic is emphasized in the work of Autonomous Marxists who have foregrounded the importance of the "social factory."

7 As Marx explains in Chapter IX of *Capital Volume 1*, the extraction of surplus value is possible to present as a consensual arrangement on account of the specific attributes of the commodity labor power. In particular, he notes how payment for the working day, which is indexed to the cost of the daily reproduction of the commodity labor power, is less than the value of the product produced through the consumption of the commodity labor power itself.

8 To get a sense of this sublime alienation, one could do no better than to consider Spike Jonze's recent film *Her* (2013), in which a lonely guy falls in love with his

computer's operating system while perched in a glass tower overlooking a near-future Los Angeles played by a present-day Shanghai (currently the largest city in the world). For Benjamin's discussion of the steel girder, see "Paris, Capital of the Nineteenth Century," *Reflections* (New York: Schocken Books, 1978).

9   John Berger, "Twelve Theses on the Economy of the Dead," in *Hold Everything Dear: Dispatches on Survival and Resistance* (New York: Pantheon Books, 2007), 3–4

10 Walter Benjamin, "Theses on the Philosophy of History," in *Illuminations* (New York: Schocken Books, 1968), 254.

11 Jared Davidson, *Remains to be Seen: Tracing Joe Hill's Ashes in New Zealand,* (Wellington: Rebel Press, 2011).

12 From an interview with Pierre van Paassen published in *The Toronto Daily Star*, August 5, 1936. Durruti died three months later on November 20, 1936 after being shot while trying to defend Madrid from Fascist incursion.

13 Then again, maybe not—after all, Walter Benjamin himself noted that one eye-witness to the July revolution "may have owed his insight to the rhyme" when he recounted in verse how, in the moment of insurrection, street fighters fired upon clock towers to stop time itself (1968: 262).

14 ibid., 261.

15 Ibid., 254.

16 Ibid., 255

17 Ibid., 256.

18 Ibid., 261.

19 Ibid., 257.

20 Ibid., 254.

21 Although it is difficult to know whether any of the workers who died building the dam felt a strong mythological bond to the national project (as soldiers sometimes do in their final moments), the objective conditions of depression-era America suggest that they were probably motivated by more pedestrian concerns. As soon as the project began in 1931, both the dam site and the nearby town of Las Vegas became overrun with unemployed workers looking for relief. By some estimates, their numbers reached 20,000. See Andrew J. Dunar and Dennis McBride, *Building Hoover Dam: An Oral History of the Great Depression* (Reno: University of Nevada Press, 2001). The timing of the project suggests that at least some of these workers may have had Robinson's "Ballad of Joe Hill" on their lips as they trudged from camp to work site. Meanwhile, to get a sense of the properly mythological dimension of the Hoover Dam commemoration plaque's claim, it's useful to recall the oblique Biblical reference (Isaiah 35) upon which it relies. This same reference can be found underwriting the historic conquest of

Palestine, as Zionists following Herzl's proclamations in *The Jewish State* (1896) sought to make a supposedly uninhabited desert bloom: "The word 'impossible' has ceased to exist in the vocabulary of technical science. Were a man who lived in the last century to return to the earth, he would find the life of today full of incomprehensible magic. Wherever the moderns appear with our inventions, we transform the desert into a garden. To build a city takes in our time as many years as it formerly required centuries; America offers endless examples of this…" (Rockville, MD: Wildside Press, 2008),115.

22 "Modern History: Revolution and Innovation Intersect at The Boston Tea Party Museum" (*The Voice of Downtown Boston.* December 10, 2013). Retrieved November 19, 2014. http://www.thevoiceofdowntownboston.com/modern-history -revolution-and-innovation-intersect-at-the-boston-tea-party-museum/.

23 Ruth Richardson, *Death, Dissection, and the Destitute* (Chicago: University of Chicago Press, 2000), 90.

24 Ibid.

25 Ibid., 91.

26 Walter Benjamin, *Reflections* (New York: Schocken Books, 1978), 148.

27 Ray Oldenburg, *The Great Good Place: Cafés, Coffee Shops, Community Centers, Beauty Parlors, General Stores, Bars, Hangouts and How The Get You Through The Day* (New York: Paragon House, 1989), 23.

28 Ibid., 186.

29 Ibid., 24.

30 Ibid., 41.

31 Ibid., 192.

32 Ibid., 32.

33 Ibid., 34.

34 Silvia Federici, *Caliban and The Witch: Women, The Body and Primitive Accumulation* (New York: Autonomedia, 2004), 24.

35 Ibid., 71.

36 Ibid.

37 Andrew Hopton (ed), *Gerrard Winstanley: Selected Writings.* (London: Aporia Press, 1989), 19.

38 Acts of the Apostles, 4:32, *King James Bible*, http://biblehub.com/acts/4-32.htm.

39 Karl Kautsky, *Foundations of Christianity* (New York: Monthly Review Press, 1972), 345–354.

40 Ibid., 329.

41 Ibid., 330.

42 Ibid., 331.

43 Anonymous, *Martyr of the Catacombs: A Tale of Ancient Rome* (Grand Rapids, MI:

Kregel Classics, 1990), 79.

44 Ibid., 84.

45 Ibid., 87–88.

46 Ibid., 90.

47 Jean-Victor Schnetz, *Combat devant l'hôtel de ville (1830)*.

48 Victor Hugo, *Notre Dame de Paris* (New York: The Riverdale Press, 1903), 88.

49 CrimethInc., *Expect Resistance: A Field Manual* (CrimethInc. Collective, 2008), 71.

50 Cited in Jonathan Sachs, *Romantic Antiquity: Rome in the British Imagination, 1789–1832* (Oxford: Oxford University Press, 2010), 153.

51 Karl Marx and Friedrich Engels, *Selected Works, Volume 1*. "The Eighteenth Brumaire of Louis Bonaparte" (Moscow: Progress Publishers, 1969), 398.

52 David Harvey, *Rebel Cities*, 73.

53 It's noteworthy that, while Schmitt's analysis presupposes the nation state as the primitive, mythological, unit for the elaboration of forms of existence, his category can be applied equally well—and perhaps more accurately—to contests *within* the nation state. Here, the most extreme form of friend-enemy antagonism is civil war. By dispensing with Schmitt's fascist mythology, it becomes clear that the most universal contest between different "forms of existence" concerns class war. Indeed, Schmitt refers to this possibility directly in *The Concept of the Political* when he notes how "a class in the Marxist sense ceases to be something purely economic and becomes a political factor when it reaches this decisive point, for example, when Marxists approach the class struggle seriously and treat the class adversary as a real enemy and fight him … in a civil war within a state." (Chicago, University of Chicago Press, 1996), 37. This position holds regardless of the qualification Schmitt tries to establish in Note 9 where, following a distinction advanced by Plato in the *Republic*, he proposes that "a people cannot wage war against itself and a civil war is only a self-laceration and it does not signify that … a new people is being created" (Ibid., 29).

54 Carl Schmitt, *The Concept of the Political*, 26–27.

55 Ibid., 27.

56 David Harvey, *Rebel Cities*, 71.

57 Ibid., 70.

58 Ibid., 140.

INDEX